D1478835

Doctor Quintard, Chaplain C.S.A.
and Second Bishop of Tennessee

Doctor Quintard, Chaplain C.S.A. and Second Bishop of Tennessee

The Memoir and Civil War Diary of
Charles Todd Quintard

EDITED BY

Sam Davis Elliott

LOUISIANA STATE UNIVERSITY PRESS
Baton Rouge

Copyright © 2003 by Louisiana State University Press
Bishop Charles Todd Quintard Diary © 2003 by the University of the South
Manufactured in the United States of America
First printing

12 11 10 09 08 07 06 05 04 03
5 4 3 2 1

Designer: Amanda McDonald Scallan
Typeface: Electra
Typesetter: Coghill Composition Co., Inc.
Printer and binder: Thomson-Shore, Inc.

Library of Congress Cataloging-in-Publication Data

Quintard, C. T. (Charles Todd), 1824–1898.
    Doctor Quintard, Chaplain C.S.A. and second Bishop of Tennessee : the
memoir and Civil War diary of Charles Todd Quintard / edited, with an
introduction, by Sam Davis Elliott.
        p.   cm.
Includes bibliographical references and index.
    ISBN 0-8071-2846-5 (cloth : alk. paper)
    1. Quintard, C. T. (Charles Todd), 1824–1898.   2. Confederate States
of America. Army—Chaplains—Biography.   3. Confederate States of
America. Army. Tennessee Infantry Regiment, 1st.   4. Chaplains,
Military—Confederate States of America—Biography.   5. United
States—History—Civil War, 1861–1865—Chaplains.   6. United
States—History—Civil War, 1861–1865—Religious aspects.
7. Tennessee—History—Civil War, 1861–1865—Personal narratives.
8. United States—History—Civil War, 1861–1865—Personal narratives.
9. Episcopal Church—Tennessee—Bishops—Biography.   I. Elliott, Sam Davis,
1956– II. Title.
    E635 .Q56 2003
    973.7′78′092—dc21   2002015761

For my parents, Ruth Davis Elliott and Charles Eugene Elliott
and my brother, Jefferson Lee Elliott

CONTENTS

ILLUSTRATIONS

PREFACE

In the cold daylight of November 23, 1864, the Reverend Dr. Charles Todd Quintard had breakfast and set off to join his flock, the Confederate Army of Tennessee. Energized now that he had returned to his adopted home state of Tennessee, by 10:30 that morning Quintard overtook along its line of march the Tennessee brigade of Brigadier General Otho French Strahl. Encountering Strahl and then Strahl's aide, Lt. John Marsh, Quintard was reunited with men he had joyfully baptized the previous spring. With his friends, he marched northward with the gray and butternut column, ultimately toward the Tennessee capital of Nashville. Like the soldiers he served as a priest and a physician, Quintard looked for great results for the Confederacy in this daring campaign into the heart of Federally occupied Tennessee.

Just one week later, Strahl and Marsh would lie dead on the field of Franklin, victims of one of the most appalling mistakes in American military history. Quintard would undertake the sad duty of burying his two friends with other comrades killed on that sad and bloody field. By the week of Christmas, 1864, the Army of Tennessee's triumphant march gave way to the most dismal of its many retreats, its defeated men streaming southward in the cold rain and snow. As Quintard left the state, he recalled the march into Tennessee, "so full of delightful intercourse with Strahl and Marsh and other friends and I still remember them now silent in the tomb and I turn away from the place of their burial with a very bitter spirit."

At the time of these events, Quintard was both physically and spiritually a long way from his father's home in Stamford, Connecticut, where he was born on December 22, 1824. Educated in New York City, Quintard was trained as a physician and graduated from the University of New York in 1846. After spending a year practicing medicine in the New York City, he moved to Georgia in 1848. There Quintard married Eliza Catherine Hand, a granddaughter of the early Georgia industrialist Roswell King. In

1851, they moved to Memphis, Tennessee, where Quintard occupied the chair of Physiology and Pathological Anatomy at the Medical College of Memphis. In Memphis, Quintard was inspired by the Episcopal bishop of Tennessee, James Hervey Otey, and was eventually ordained a priest. At the time Tennessee seceded, in May 1861, Quintard had charge of two parishes in Nashville.

Caught up in the maelstrom of civil war, Quintard joined the Confederate First Tennessee Infantry Regiment as its chaplain. Quintard's remarkable energy and intelligence, as well as the fortunes of war, placed him in a position to observe events and interact with men that had a substantial influence on the progress of the internecine struggle. In the course of events, Quintard met Jefferson Davis, Robert E. Lee, Braxton Bragg, Joseph E. Johnston, Leonidas Polk, John Bell Hood, and a host of lesser luminaries. Quintard was present during the early fighting in Virginia, observed the *Monitor* and the *Virginia*, and tended the wounded at Perryville, Murfreesboro, and Chickamauga before accompanying the Army of Tennessee on its desperate advance to and tragic retreat from the outskirts of Nashville in 1864. He then made his way back to his family, traveling across the tottering Confederacy in the winter of 1865. The physician and priest rejoined his loved ones in Columbus, Georgia, only a few weeks before Union troops swept through the town on Easter Sunday, 1865. During the course of his travels, Quintard preached at hospitals, treated the sick and wounded, organized soldiers' relief efforts, compiled prayer books for the army, served two churches, and sadly conducted the funerals of friends and mentors.

Upon first becoming acquainted with Quintard during the war, Confederate nurse Kate Cumming noted that he was "a man of great energy." Observers often noted that Quintard admirably combined his knowledge as a physician with his role as a minister of the Gospel. Sam Watkins, a member of Company "Aytch" of the 1st Tennessee Regiment, wrote of Quintard's dual role in service of the regiment, and concluded that Quintard was "one of the purest and best men I ever knew." During the course of the war, Bishop Henry Champlin Lay of Arkansas stated that "[t]here is no Chaplain comparable to him in point of usefulness, and he cannot possibly be spared."[1]

1. Kate Cumming, *Kate: The Journal of a Confederate Nurse*, ed. Richard Harwell (1957; reprint, Baton Rouge: Louisiana State University Press, 1998), 116; Sam R. Watkins, "Co. Aytch": A Side Show of the Big Show (New York: Collier Books, 1962), 132; Joseph Blount Cheshire, *The Church in the Confederate States: A History of the Protestant Episcopal Church in the Confederate States* (New York: Longmans, Green & Co., 1912), 82.

A fellow churchman described the unique nature of Quintard's personality:

> He was a man of striking personality, of immense force, whom to
> see and talk with once was to remember forever. This clean-carved,
> positive individuality gave him great power as a preacher, but even
> more power in private conversation. . . . His heart was so tender and
> sympathetic, and his faith was so strong and entire, that his consola-
> tions were to the suffering and sorrowful a message from God. And
> his culture was so wide and varied, his humor so buoyant, his physi-
> cal nature so alert, that he was a very prince of hospitality. Few men
> have combined such gifts of mind and heart.[2]

Thirty years after his wartime experiences, Quintard, then the Episcopal bishop of Tennessee, recalled his role in the tumultuous time of the
Civil War and undertook to tell that story in a small book. Consulting his
diary from those times and calling upon his memories and those of his
fellow veterans, Quintard began a work that was cut short by his death in
February 1898, at the age of 73. Completed by his friend, Episcopal
Church historian Rev. Arthur Howard Noll, the book was published by
the University Press at Sewanee seven years after Quintard's death as *Doctor Quintard, Chaplain C.S.A. and Second Bishop of Tennessee, Being His
Story of the War (1861–1865)*.

Although it was out of print for almost all of the twentieth century,
Doctor Quintard remains an interesting record of the memories and observations of a well-connected and intelligent man who had a unique opportunity to witness the Civil War from several vantage points. But *Doctor
Quintard* is not all that the bishop left for future students of the war. A
fragment of Quintard's diary for 1864 and 1865 survives, as do portions of
his wartime correspondence and some of the replies to inquiries sent by
the bishop in the 1890's seeking particulars from participants on certain
points. Archived at the University of the South, of which Quintard was
truly a second founder, the diary fragment has been underutilized by his-
torians. A typescript of the diary prepared in the 1950s by a university faculty member's wife recorded Quintard's activities from mid-October 1864
to the end of January 1865, when the Army of Tennessee moved out of

---

2. Thomas Frank Gailor, *Some Memories* (Kingsport, Tenn.: Southern Publishers,
1937), 81–82.

Georgia, across Alabama, and into and then out of Tennessee in Hood's Tennessee campaign. Most modern studies of this campaign make use of this portion of the diary. However, the diary extends (with some interruption) to the end of May 1865 and contains valuable insight into the collapse of the Confederacy in the lower South.

When I matriculated at the University of the South in the fall of 1974, I had more than a passing interest in the Civil War. That interest, however, was almost exclusively in the eastern theater of the war, where the Army of Northern Virginia and the Army of the Potomac contended on the famed battlefields of Antietam, Chancellorsville, and Gettysburg. My knowledge of the western theater was scant, even though I was raised only twenty-five miles from the Chickamauga battlefield. I gradually learned that the Confederate roots of the University of the South lay in the Army of Tennessee, which fought on fields equally as glorious, but with far less fame than its eastern counterparts. The most obvious reason for Sewanee's connection with the Army of Tennessee was the leading role taken in the founding of the university by Leonidas Polk, Episcopal bishop of Louisiana and the commanding general of one or another of the Army of Tennessee's army corps during most of the war. But in the course of my experience at Sewanee, I learned there were other Sewanee names connected to the Army of Tennessee: Kirby Smith, Sevier, Shoup, Fairbanks, and Quintard.

Years later, after I had reached a fuller appreciation for the war in the western theater, I would encounter Quintard's name on occasion in my readings, with references either to *Doctor Quintard* or to the first portion of the surviving diary. Except for a touch of pride relating to Quintard's connection to Sewanee, I took little note of these incidents. Even during the first phases of my work on Alexander P. Stewart, Quintard did not seem to be anything more than an interested observer of the 1864 Tennessee campaign, especially as Quintard and Stewart had little, if any, interaction during that time. Later, I found an 1895 letter from Stewart to Quintard in Quintard's papers at Duke University, which was one of several letters from that time responding to Quintard's efforts to gather information for *Doctor Quintard*.

Thus reacquainted with Quintard, my original intention was to reintroduce *Doctor Quintard* to the modern reader in an annotated form. It became apparent, however, that for *Doctor Quintard* to be complete for the purposes of modern readers, the surviving diary should be included. Untainted by Quintard's (or Noll's) subsequent editing, the diary reflects its writer's unvarnished viewpoints during the momentous final months of the Confederacy. In its pages, we see Quintard's brief upsurge of hope that accompanied his journey into Tennessee, his efforts to maintain his southern patriotism in the face of defeat, and the political and economic decline of the fragment of the Confederacy through which he traveled. In the diary, there is marvelous detail that *Doctor Quintard* omits or glosses over: the many and varied means of transportation necessary to travel the tottering Confederacy, the political views of prominent citizens as the Confederate cause sank, the difficulty of obtaining clothing, and the contrast between civilian life in areas contested by the armies and those left untouched by the struggle.

Both the diary and, to a lesser extent, *Doctor Quintard* are significant sources for any future study of the upper echelons of Confederate society during the final months of the war. Quintard's descriptions of his visits and dinners with prominent citizens in the areas in which he traveled, his encounters with editors James D. B. DeBow and Henry Watterson, and his travels with various officers and politicians, indicate many of their viewpoints and often portray their situations in a way not seen in other sources. Quintard's personal charm was such that even Federal officers were glad to lend him assistance.

As would be the case in any intimately kept diary, Quintard the man is revealed in depth. His deep devotion to his religion cannot be questioned. Previously designated a missionary to the army, he in fact acted as a missionary in every location he visited: comforting those who had lost loved ones, holding services in empty churches, raising funds for benevolent purposes, and sharing his religion with those in need of hope and encouragement. Quintard's racial viewpoints were paternalistic, so that he could express sadness at the treatment of African American prisoners and quiet disgust at the facilities provided by the local masters for the religious instruction of their slaves. Yet he could not understand why his slave Henry chose to run away when Federal troops occupied Columbus, and expressed satisfaction when he learned that his purported liberators mistreated Henry.

The combination of the diary fragment and *Doctor Quintard* presented a practical challenge. Since both were originally presented chronologically, I first planned to integrate relevant portions of the diary in the manner of an appendix to the chapter to which those portions corresponded chronologically. This proved unwieldy and disrupted the flow of the narrative in *Doctor Quintard*. In reality, the diary fragment and *Doctor*

Quintard are separate documents, requiring separate presentation. Therefore, with the exception noted below, *Doctor Quintard* is presented here
without interruption, followed by the diary fragment.

As explained by Rev. Noll, the first and the last two chapters of *Doctor
Quintard* tell the story of the bishop's life before and after the Civil War.
They are included here for the purpose of completeness and to give the
reader a full sense of who Quintard was. Since the final two chapters do
not relate to the Civil War, I have chosen to present them without annota-
tions. The postwar volumes of Bishop Quintard's diary await a historian
of the Episcopal Church, for whom they will doubtless prove a rich re-
source.

In the notes, I have sought to identify names unfamiliar to the general
reader. Where no identification could be made or identification is uncer-
tain, there will be a notation to that effect.

I have corrected only a very small number of typographical errors that
appeared in the 1905 edition of *Doctor Quintard*, and I have occasionally
transposed punctuation (such as commas and semicolons in relation to
parentheses and quotation marks) for conformity with modern expectations and to avoid confusion. By and large, however, I have retained the
oddities of the original *Doctor Quintard*'s now antiquated punctuation
style, as well as a number of minor stylistic inconsistencies and occasional
grammatical errors found in the original edition.

Probably not anticipating future public review of his handwritten
diary, Bishop Quintard utilized unique abbreviations, made abrupt tran-
sitions, ran his paragraphs together, and pasted newspaper clippings,
poetry, and bits of correspondence in its pages. I have attempted to
smooth out these irregularities for better reading, while retaining the fla-
vor of Quintard's style as much as possible. Therefore, I have eliminated
many of Quintard's shorthand devices, such as the use of a plus sign or
ampersand for the word *and* or the abbreviation "Ch" for *church*. I have
directly quoted materials pasted in the diary that do not disrupt the flow
of the text; otherwise, I have described them in a footnote.

As Bishop Quintard would doubtless have appreciated, this work owes
much to his beloved Sewanee. As is true of many of the good things in
life, my appreciation for this unique community of scholars, artists, and
Christians has grown in the years since I left the Mountain. The friends
that I made in my time there and those I have made subsequently through
that connection have enriched my life in incalculable ways. While they

are too numerous to mention here, I gratefully acknowledge the bond I have with them and our alma mater that gave me a deep appreciation for Bishop Quintard and his herculean efforts to preserve the University of the South in the postwar era.

Of my Sewanee contemporaries, I would particularly like to thank the university archivist, Anne Armor-Jones, for her help in providing access to the diary, most of the images of the bishop used in this book, and the remainder of his papers at Sewanee's du Pont Library. Annie went beyond the call of duty to make my task easier and my visits to the archives pleasant. Annie also placed me in contact with Michael Hammerson of London, England, who kindly granted permission to use a photograph of Quintard in his possession.

Thanks are also due to my friend and colleague in the Chattanooga bar, Donna Pierce, the university's general counsel, who worked with me to obtain the university's permission to publish the diary portion of this work.

I also extend my deep appreciation to the longtime university historiographer, Dr. Arthur Ben Chitty, and his wife, the late Dr. Elizabeth N. Chitty. Fixtures on the Mountain for many years, there is no one as steeped in the history of the University of the South or more knowledgeable of the lives of the remarkable men and women who founded the university and nurtured it in its early years. Both took time to patiently answer my many questions during visits to their home (itself worthy of a book) that doubtless caused them much inconvenience.

The other significant collection of Quintard's papers is located at the Perkins Library of Duke University in Durham, North Carolina, where I was assisted with the quiet and efficient professionalism that one would expect from that fine institution. Thanks are also due to the staffs at the Wilson Library of the University of North Carolina in Chapel Hill; the Tennessee State Library and Archives in Nashville; the Georgia Department of Archives and History in Atlanta; the Charleston County Library in Charleston, South Carolina; the Sara Hightower Regional Library in Rome, Georgia; and the Williamson County Library in Franklin, Tennessee. I would also like to extend my appreciation to Robert S. Davis, Jr., of Wallace State University in Hanceville, Alabama, who took pains to point out possible avenues of inquiry in connection with my research. Finally, I would be remiss if I failed to acknowledge Clara Swann and the fine staff of the Local History section of the Chattanooga–Hamilton County

Bicentennial Library, always the first and most convenient place to look for Civil War sources.

Within the Episcopal Church, it is appropriate to note the kindness of the Episcopal Diocese of Georgia, which granted time-saving permission for me to obtain a microfilm copy of Bishop Stephen Elliott's diary at the Georgia Archives. Since he is now formally a servant of the Church, this is also the place to acknowledge my good friend and Sewanee classmate, Rev. John R. Jacobs, who helped me define ecclesiastical terms that were simply unknown to my all too secular mind.

Others due thanks for their help in making this work possible are Rev. Larry Daniel, Murray, Kentucky; Tom Price, curator of collections at the James K. Polk home, Columbia, Tennessee; Dr. Pope Holliday, Signal Mountain, Tennessee; Rodney Hinds, Soddy Daisy, Tennessee; Charles R. West, Knoxville, Tennessee; and my in-laws, Arvid and Claire Honkanen, Isle of Palms, South Carolina.

I am fortunate to live in a community where acknowledged Civil War scholars are accessible as friends and colleagues. This book has benefitted from my discussions with James Ogden III, historian of the Chickamauga-Chattanooga National Military Park at Ft. Oglethorpe, Georgia, and Keith Bohannon, lately of Chattanooga, but recently removed to a faculty position at the State University of West Georgia in Carrollton.

As always, I am indebted to Dr. Nathaniel C. Hughes, Jr., also of Chattanooga, for his invaluable assistance in this work. Dr. Hughes suggested I consider Bishop Quintard as an avenue of endeavor, was kind enough to read and comment on the manuscript, and provided a necessary sounding board. Without his contributions, this undertaking would have been far more difficult and consequently far less enjoyable.

Insofar as I have a "real" job, I also would like to thank my law partners, Charlie Gearhiser, Wayne Peters, Bob Lockaby, Chuck Tallant, Terry Cavett, Lane Avery, Wade Cannon, Robin Miller, Chris Varner, and Lee Ann Adams for the time I spent more focused on my research for this book than I did on our business. Also, I would like to extend my appreciation to my secretary, Margie Tricoglou, who put up with me as she always has during the years we have worked together and made sure my numerous mailings in connection with this work got out on time.

I also appreciate the delightful working relationship that I have with Sylvia Frank Rodrigue, George Roupe, and the staff of the Louisiana State University Press. The magic that they are able to do with what I submit to them never ceases to amaze me.

Finally, I cannot overemphasize the importance of my family in my life. I am grateful for the many years of love and support that I have received from my parents, Ruth and Gene Elliott, and my brother, Jeff Elliott. It is with the deepest appreciation and love that I dedicate this book to them. It goes without saying that words cannot adequately express my feelings of love for my wife, Karen, and my daughters, Mary Claire and Sarah Anne. I hope that this book, as I do all my endeavors, does them honor, and, as did the life of Bishop Quintard, gives God the glory.

Abbreviations Used in Notes

CMH
Confederate Military History Extended Edition: A Library of Confederate States History in Seventeen Volumes, Written by Distinguished Men of the South, and Edited by Gen. Clement A. Evans of Georgia. Clement A. Evans, ed. 17 vols. Atlanta: Confederate Publishing, 1899. Reprint, Wilmington, N.C.: Broadfoot, 1987–1989.

CSR
Compiled Service Record

CTQ
Charles Todd Quintard

CV
Confederate Veteran

CWCCT
Civil War Centennial Commission of Tennessee

DU
Duke University, William R. Perkins Library, Durham, N.C.

GDAH
Georgia Department of Archives and History, Atlanta, Ga.

NA
National Archives, Washington, D.C.

OR
War of the Rebellion: A Compilation of the Official Records of the Union and Confederate Armies. 128 vols. Washington, D.C.: U.S. Government

xxii / abbreviations used in notes

Printing Office, 1880–1901. OR citations take the following form: volume number (part number, where applicable): page number(s).

ORN
Official Records of the Union and Confederate Navies in the War of the Rebellion. 31 vols. Washington, D.C.: U.S. Government Printing Office, 1895–1929. ORN citations take the following form: volume number: page number(s).

RG
Record Group

SHSP
Southern Historical Society Papers

U of S
University of the South, du Pont Library, Sewanee, Tenn.

DOCTOR QUINTARD

CHAPLAIN C.S.A.

AND

SECOND BISHOP OF TENNESSEE

BEING HIS STORY OF THE WAR

(1861–1865)

EDITED AND EXTENDED

BY THE

REV. ARTHUR HOWARD NOLL

Historiographer of the Diocese of Tennessee, Author of "History of the Church

in the Diocese of Tennessee," etc.

THE UNIVERSITY PRESS

OF SEWANEE TENNESSEE

MCMV

TO

THE FRIENDS AND COMRADES OF

DOCTOR QUINTARD

IN THE ARMY OF THE CONFEDERACY

AND IN THE CHURCH MILITANT

THESE MEMOIRS OF HIS LIFE IN WAR TIMES—

EXTENDED TO INCLUDE AN ACCOUNT OF HIS WORK

FOR THE UPBUILDING OF THE CHURCH IN TENNESSEE

AND FOR THE ADVANCEMENT OF CHRISTIAN EDUCATION IN

THE SOUTH—ARE MOST AFFECTIONATELY

DEDICATED

PREFACE

The chapters of this volume containing the Memoirs of the war were written by Bishop Quintard about the year 1896 and are to be read with that date in mind. The work of the editor thereon has been devoted to bringing them into conformity with a plan agreed upon in personal interviews with Bishop Quintard about that time.

In the first and in the last two chapters of the book the editor has drawn freely, even to the extent of transcribing entire sentences and paragraphs, upon the Bishop's own addresses in the Diocesan Journals of Tennessee; upon Memorial Addresses by his successor, the Rt. Rev. Dr. Gailor; upon material used in some of the chapters of the Editor's "History of the Church in the Diocese of Tennessee"; and upon documents preserved in the archives of The University of the South.

Thanks are due to the Rev. Bartow B. Ramage, the Rev. Rowland Hale and Mr. George E. Purvis, among others, for valuable assistance in the original preparation of the Memoirs.

A. H. N.

Sewanee, Tennessee,
May, 1905.

CHAPTER I

Introduction to the 1905 Edition,
by Rev. Arthur Howard Noll

Writers upon the late Civil War have never done full justice to the high religious character of the majority of those who composed the Confederate government and its army, and the high religious principles which inspired them. Not only was the conviction of conscience clear in the Southern soldiers, that they were right in waging war against the Federal government, but the people of the South looked upon their cause as a holy one, and their conduct of affairs, civil and military, was wholly in accord with such a view. The Confederacy, as it came into existence, committed its civil affairs, by deliberate choice, to men, not only of approved morality, but of approved religious character as well. It was not merely by accident, that, in the organization of its army, choice was made of such men as Robert E. Lee and Thomas J. Jackson,—not to mention a large number of Christian soldiers,—as leaders. And it seemed in no way incongruous in the conduct of a war of such a character, that commissions were offered to and accepted by the Rev. William Nelson Pendleton, Rector of Grace Church, Lexington, Virginia, and the Rt. Rev. Leonidas Polk, D.D., Bishop of Louisiana.

A religious tone pervades the state papers pertaining to the Confederacy,—its proclamations, and its legislation. The same religious tone is conspicuous in a majority of the military leaders. It is found upon investigation to have impressed itself upon the officers of regiments and companies and upon the private soldiers in the ranks throughout the whole army. So that there is more than an ordinary basis for the statement, surprising as such a statement may appear at first, that the armies of the Confederate States had in them a larger proportion than any other in history since those of Cromwell's nicknamed "Roundheads," of true and active Christian men.

The provision made for the spiritual needs of the men in the field was quite remarkable. In the great haste with which the Army of the Confederacy was organized, equipped and sent to the field, there might have been found abundant apology for the omission of chaplains from the official staffs. Yet there was no need for seeking such an apology, for the chaplains were not overlooked. Even imputing a love of excitement and adventure to the young men who composed in such large measure the fighting forces of the Confederacy at the first, they did not neglect to secure the services of a chaplain for each regiment which went to the seat of war. It was naturally thought that work might be found for chaplains in the hospitals, but it was early discovered that a chaplain had opportunities for efficient work at all times,—in the midst of active campaigns and when the army was in winter quarters.

Nor was their work in vain. Few religious services in times of peace equaled in attendance, in fervor or results, those held at, or in the immediate vicinity of, encampments of the Confederate army. The camps of regiments which had been sent forth with prayer and benediction, were often the seats of earnest religious life. It is estimated that 15,000 men in the Army of Virginia alone, made some open and public profession of their allegiance to Christ during the war, and were affected in their subsequent lives by religious experiences gained in the war. And the number is especially remarkable of men in the Southern army who after the close of the war entered the sacred ministry and won distinction in their holy calling.

A study of what might be called "the religious phases" of this war history should be approached through a consideration of the chaplains of the Confederacy. They were a regimental institution, and their number might be determined by the number of regiments engaged in the war. They were, for the most part, men of brains, of a keen sense of humor, and of fidelity to what they regarded as their duty; sticking to their posts; maintaining the most friendly and intimate relations with "the boys"; ever on the look-out for opportunities to do good in any way; ready to give up their horses to some poor fellows with bare and blistered feet and to march in the column as it hurried forward; going on picket duty with their men and bivouacking with them in the pelting storm; sharing with them at all times their hardships and their dangers, gaining a remarkably wide experience during four years of army life, and probably with it all acquiring the pleasing art of the *raconteur.*

If an individual were desired for a more particular illustration of the religious phases of Confederate war history, he might be found in the Rev. Charles Todd Quintard, M.D., of the First Tennessee Regiment, and after the war, Second Bishop of Tennessee. He not only fully conformed to the type above indicated but in some respects he surpassed it, for his knowledge of the healing art and his surgical skill were ever at the demands of his fellow soldiers. He was one of the earliest to enter the service of the Confederate army, and was probably the most widely known and best beloved of all the chaplains.

Dr. Quintard was born in Stamford, Connecticut, on the 22nd of December, 1824. His ancestors were Huguenots who left France after the revocation of the Edict of Nantes and settled the country north of Manhattan Island, between Long Island Sound and the Hudson River. Those who knew Dr. Quintard at any period of his life had no difficulty in detecting his French ancestry in his personal appearance, as well as in his manner,—his vivacity and demonstrativeness. Though not a few who failed to get well acquainted with him fell into the error of supposing that some of his mannerisms were an affectation acquired in some of his visits to England subsequent to the war.

His father was Isaac Quintard, a man of wealth and education, a prominent citizen of Stamford, having been born in the same house in which he gave his son a birthplace, and in which he died in 1883 in the ninetieth year of his age. The Doctor was a pupil at Trinity School, New York City, and took his Master's degree at Columbia College. He studied medicine with Dr. James R. Wood and Dr. Valentine Mott, and was graduated, with the degree of Doctor of Medicine, at the University of the City of New York, in 1847. After a year at Bellevue Hospital, he removed to Georgia, and began the practice of medicine at Athens in that state, where he was a parishioner of the Rev. William Bacon Stevens, afterwards Bishop of Pennsylvania.[1]

1. Omitted from Noll's narrative at this point is CTQ's marriage to Eliza Catherine Hand (1826–1905), daughter of Bayard E. Hand and Eliza Barrington King. Eliza King was the daughter of Roswell King, an early and quite wealthy Georgia industrialist and the namesake of Roswell, Georgia. Their children were Bayard (1849–1849), Clara (1851–1852),

In 1851 he accepted the chair of Physiology and Pathological Anatomy in the Medical College of Memphis, Tennessee, and became in that city co-editor with Dr. Ayres P. Merrill, of the "Memphis Medical Recorder." There also he formed a close friendship with Bishop Otey, and in January, 1854, he was admitted a candidate for Holy Orders.[2] That year he appeared in the Twenty-sixth Annual Convention of the Church in the Diocese of Tennessee, held in St. John's Church, Knoxville, as the lay representative of St. Paul's Church, Randolph. St. Paul's Church has since passed out of existence, and the town of Randolph no longer appears upon the map of the State of Tennessee.[3]

Studying theology under the direction of his Bishop, he was ordered deacon in Calvary Church, Memphis, in January, 1855, and a year later was advanced to the priesthood. His diaconate was spent in missionary work in Tipton County,—one of the Mississippi River counties of Tennessee. Upon his advancement to the priesthood he became rector of Calvary Church, Memphis.

In the latter part of 1856, he resigned the rectorship of his Memphis parish, and at the urgent request of Bishop Otey, accepted the rectorship of the Church of the Advent, Nashville. He had charge also of the Church of the Holy Trinity in that city, and extended his work to Edgefield, (now East Nashville), and to the parish of St. Ann. He served the Diocese as a member of the Standing Committee, and as a clerical deputy to the General Convention meeting in Richmond, Virginia, in the Fall of 1859.

He was a man of varied and deep learning—a preacher of power and attractiveness, and ranked among the clergymen of greatest prominence and popularity in Nashville. He was of ardent temperament, affectionate disposition, and possessed personal magnetism to a remarkable degree, especially with young men, who looked up to him with an affection

---

George William (1856–1908), Edward Augustus (1860–1903), and Clara Eliza (1861–1915). Quintard Genealogy File, Quintard Papers, U of S.

2. A native of Virginia, James Hervey Otey (1800–1863) was the first Episcopal bishop of Tennessee. Initially an educator, Otey was an advocate of church-sponsored education. Arthur Ben Chitty, Jr., *Reconstruction at Sewanee: The Founding of the University of the South and Its First Administration, 1857–1872* (1954; reprint, Sewanee, Tenn.: Proctor's Hall Press, 1993), 46–48. It was "largely through [Otey's] influence" that CTQ decided to study for the ministry. "Death of the Bishop," *Memphis Commercial Appeal*, February 16, 1898.

3. Randolph was in Tipton County, where the Hatchie River enters the Mississippi.

which is now rarely if ever shown by young men to the ministry. This, and the influence he had over young men, are illustrated by the organization in 1859 of the Rock City Guard, a militia company composed largely of the young men of Nashville. Dr. Quintard was at once elected Chaplain of that organization, and its first public parade was for the purpose of attending services in a body at the Church of the Advent at which he officiated.

His was a churchmanship of a type in those days considerably in advance of the average in the antebellum period in the South. He was clearly under the spell of the "Oxford Movement" and of the English "Tractarians," and occupied a position to which Churchmen generally in this country did not approach until ten or twenty years later. He was a "sacerdotalist,"—a pronounced "sacramentarian" at times when the highest "High" Churchmen of the country would have hesitated long before applying those terms to themselves.[4]

To him baptism was not "a theory and a notion," but "a gift and a power." And baptized children were to be educated, "not with a view to their becoming Christians, but because they were already Christians." Consequently he regarded Confirmation, not as "joining the Church," or as merely a ratifying and renewing of the vows and promises of Holy Baptism, and hence as something which man does for God;—but as something which God does for man,—the bestowal of the gifts of the Holy Spirit. To the preparation of candidates for Confirmation he therefore gave his most earnest attention, even to the extent of preparing "A Plain Tract on Confirmation," and (in 1861), "A Preparation for Confirmation," a manual of eighty-nine pages.

His veneration for the Church's liturgical inheritance was great, and

4. The Oxford Movement took place within the Church of England between 1833 and 1845. Its "chief object" was the defense of the Church as a divine institution, of the doctrine of apostolic succession, and of the Book of Common Prayer. Those ideas were often expressed in tracts, thus, the term "Tractarians." A "sacramentarian" believes that the elements of the Eucharist are the Body and Blood of Christ in only a "sacramental," or metaphorical sense. *Oxford Dictionary of the Christian Church*, 3rd ed., s.v. "Oxford Movement," "sacramentarian." "Sacerdotalism" is the belief that priests act as mediators between humanity and God. *American Heritage Dictionary of the English Language*, 3rd ed., s.v. "sacerdotalism." As a "high churchman," CTQ would have subscribed to the Oxford Movement's emphasis on ritual and its belief in certain Catholic doctrines. *Columbia Encyclopedia*, 6th ed., s.v. "England, Church of."

the books of devotion he compiled and had printed for the use of soldiers during the war were drawn from the ancient sources.[5] He attached the utmost importance to the Holy Communion as a means of spiritual life, and throughout the war he availed himself of every opportunity of administering it to the soldiers in camp, in the wayside churches as he passed them, and in towns where he temporarily rested with the army.

With a host of friends in Nashville and vicinity, who looked up to him with love and reverence, it is not strange that Doctor Quintard should have been the choice for chaplain of those who enlisted from that city for the defence of their homes and firesides in 1861. Many of the young men of his parish enlisted in the First Tennessee regiment, of which he was elected chaplain, and feeling as he did that these young men would need his spiritual care far more than those of his parishioners who were left behind, he felt it his duty to accept the office and go with his regiment to the seat of war. Both he and his parishioners supposed that his absence would not exceed six months. He did not return to Nashville until after the collapse of the Confederacy and the surrender of Lee's army in 1865.

During those four years he gathered up a rich fund of experiences, both grave and gay. Always an accomplished *raconteur* and brilliant conversationalist, it is but natural that a wide circle of friends in different parts of the world should have begged him to commit to writing the story of the war as he saw it and as none but he could tell it, and permit its publication. About the year 1896 he consented to do this and entered with considerable enthusiasm upon the literary task thus set for him.

It was quite characteristic of him, however, that the work as he projected it was likely to have been a laudation of the men with whom he was brought into contact during the civil strife, at the expense of the personal experiences of which his friends were more anxious to read. For Doctor Quintard was an enthusiast and an optimist. No man was ever more loyal to his friends than he. His estimate of human character was always based upon whatever good he could find in a man. Nothing was a greater delight to him in recalling the scenes of the war than to describe some deed of heroism, some noble trait of character, or some mark of friendship that was shown him by a soldier; to acknowledge some kindness shown him, or to correct some error of judgment that had been passed upon some

5. CTQ published two books of devotion geared to the Confederate soldier, *The Confederate Soldier's Pocket Manual of Devotions* (Charleston: Evans & Cogswell, 1863) and the better-known *Balm for the Weary and Wounded* (Columbia: Evans & Cogswell, 1864).

actor in the drama of the civil war. Some of the men whom he paused to eulogize were those to whom fame had otherwise done but scant justice, and his estimate of them is in more than one instance an addition of worth to the history of the people of the Southern States.

The death of Doctor Quintard on the 15th of February, 1898, prevented the completion of the work he had begun more than two years previously; but left it in such form that it has not been entirely impossible to gratify the wishes of his friends in regard thereto, and to make a valuable contribution to the pictures of life in the Southern States during the troubled days of the Civil War.

CHAPTER II

Personal Narrative—
The Beginning of the War and Valley Mountain

While rector of the Church of the Advent, Nashville, I was elected chaplain of a military company of somewhat more than local fame, known as the "Rock City Guard."[1] This election was only a compliment shown me by the men who composed the Guard. I was not a military man nor had I any fondness for military life. So I regarded myself as chaplain only by courtesy. But on Thanksgiving Day, 1860, the Rock City Guard and other military organizations of Nashville requested me to officiate at the Thanksgiving services to be held under their auspices.

The services were held in the Hall of Representatives in the State Capitol, and there was an immense congregation present. It was a time of great anxiety and the occasion was a memorable one. Rumors of approaching war were abundant, and the newspapers were filled with discussions as to the course the South would pursue in case Mr. Lincoln, then recently elected, should take his seat as President of the United States. The subject of my discourse was: "Obedience to Rulers,"—my text

1. The third Episcopal church established in Nashville, the Church of the Advent met in the Odd Fellows Hall while a building was being constructed on a lot on Vine Street. At the time CTQ was rector, the lot was purchased and a basement constructed. John Woolridge, *History of Nashville, Tenn.* (1890; reprint, Nashville: Charles Elder Bookseller, 1970), 491.

being: "Righteousness exalteth a nation; but sin is a reproach to any people" (Proverbs, xiv, 34). My sermon was what might be called "a strong
plea for the Union."[2]

In December, South Carolina seceded, and on the 18th of the following April,—after a bombardment of thirty-four hours,—Fort Sumter surrendered and the Civil War was fairly begun. President Lincoln at once
called for seventy-five thousand volunteers to serve for ninety days and put
down the insurrection in South Carolina. Tennessee being called upon
for her quota, responded through her Governor, Isham G. Harris:—
"Tennessee will not furnish a single man for coercion, but fifty thousand,
if necessary, for the defence of her rights or those of her Southern brethren." This undoubtedly expressed the sentiments of the vast majority of
Tennesseans, who did not favor secession and deplored war, but who were
nevertheless determined to stand with the people of the South.[3]

In the Spring of 1861, the States of Virginia, North Carolina and Arkansas, which had hitherto refused to secede, joined their fortunes to
those of the already seceded states; and in June, Tennessee decided to
unite with the Southern Confederacy. She was slow to draw the sword. In
April, the Rock City Guard, now enlarged into a battalion, was mustered
into the service of the State. Subsequently a regiment was formed, consisting of the following companies;—The Williamson Greys, of Williamson County; The Tennessee Riflemen, and the Railroad Boys of
Nashville; The Brown Guards, of Maury County; The Rutherford Rifles,
of Rutherford County; and the Martin Guards, of Giles County.[4]

This was known as the First Tennessee Regiment. The field officers
elected were: Colonel George Maney (afterwards made a Brigadier Gen-

2. While advertised as a "complete military festival," CTQ intended that the event
have a charitable purpose: "It is the desire of the Chaplain to make the Thanksgiving of
some practical benefit, by taking up a collection for the aid of the suffering poor of the
city; so that while rendering thanks ourselves we may give the widows and the fatherless
occasion to rejoice also." *Nashville Daily Gazette*, November 25, 1860.

3. After the war, the *Memphis Daily Appeal* quoted a letter of CTQ's that stated his
initial views on secession: "I never was a secessionist; I used all my influence, both public
and private, against the movement. * * * I never believed in secession; I never taught secession; I never voted secession. But the crisis came; my path of duty was plain before me.
The State, in her sovereign capacity, had dissolved her connection with the Government.
The Church . . . must, of necessity, recognize the *de facto* government everywhere, and
submit to it." "Bishop Quintard's Position," *Memphis Daily Appeal*, November 17, 1865.

4. Interestingly, CTQ omits "Co. Aytch" (H), the Maury Grays of Private Sam Watkins.

eral); Lieutenant-Colonel, T. F. Sevier; Major, A. M. Looney.[5] Lieutenant R. B. Snowden, of Company C, was appointed Adjutant; Dr. William Nichol, Surgeon, and Dr. J. R. Buist, Assistant Surgeon.[6]

On the 10th of July, 1861, orders were received by the regiment to repair to Virginia. Being very urgently pressed by members of the Rock City Guard and their friends in Nashville to accompany the regiment as chaplain, I resolved to do so.[7] This, of course, made it necessary for me to break up my household. I removed my family to Georgia, left my parish in the hands of Rev. George C. Harris, and prepared to join my regiment in Virginia.[8]

My friend, General Washington Barrow, who had formerly been Minister to Portugal, thinking that I would have need of a weapon for my defence, sent me his old courtsword, which had enjoyed a long and quiet rest,—so long, indeed, that it had become rusted in its scabbard.[9] I re-

5. Mexican War veteran George Earl Maney was later promoted to brigadier general and served with the Army of Tennessee through the Atlanta campaign. A. M. Looney and T. Frank Sevier lost their positions in the regiment when it was reorganized in April 1862. Resigning his commission at Staunton, Virginia, Looney later served as a volunteer aide on the staff of Brig. Gen. Preston Smith in the Kentucky campaign. Sevier, a distant connection of Tennessee's first governor, John Sevier, found a place on the staff of Lt. Gen. Leonidas Polk and, after Polk's death, with his successor, Lt. Gen. Alexander P. Stewart. Ezra Warner, *Generals in Gray* (Baton Rouge: Louisiana State University Press, 1957), 210; John Berrian Lindsley, ed., *Military Annals of Tennessee: Confederate* (1886; reprint, Wilmington, N.C.: Broadfoot Publishing, 1995), 156–59, 171; *OR* 16(1):948; Chitty, *Reconstruction*, 125–26.

6. Robert Bogardus Snowden became lieutenant colonel of the 25th Tennessee Infantry and commanded it at the Battle of Chickamauga. William L. Nichol was later transferred to hospital duty. John R. Buist served during most of the war as brigade surgeon in Maney's Brigade. Lindsley, *Military Annals*, 156–159, 171, 408; Joseph H. Crute, Jr., *Confederate Staff Officers, 1861–1865* (Powhatan, Va: Derwent Books, 1982), 155, 186; A. M. Looney to CTQ, January 15, 1895, Quintard Papers, DU; Cumming, *Journal*, 113; *CMH*, 10:389–90.

7. At the end of the original *Doctor Quintard* edited by Noll was an appendix setting forth a petition signed by one hundred men of the Rock City Guard which "respectfully" invited "Rev. C. T. Quintard to accompany us throughout the campaign as our friend and spiritual adviser, and we hereby pledge ourselves to sustain him and attend regularly whatever service he may institute, being willing to be guided by him."

8. George C. Harris was at that time rector of the Church of the Holy Trinity in Nashville, succeeding CTQ in 1858. Harris would himself join the Confederate army as a chaplain in 1862. Sara Sprott Morrow, "The Church of the Holy Trinity: English Countryside Tranquility in Downtown Nashville," *Tennessee Historical Quarterly* 34 (1975): 333, 341.

9. George Washington Barrow (1807–1866) was a Nashville lawyer and newspaperman who served as a member of the Tennessee General Assembly and the United States Con-

member well my first attempt to unsheath the sword. I seized the handle and pulled with might and main, but to no effect. A friend came to my assistance. I took the sword handle,—he the scabbard. We pulled and we pulled, but the sword refused to come forth. I am not aware that I ever succeeded in drawing that sword "in defence of my country." On my departure for Virginia I left it at home.

The first battle of Bull Run was fought July 21, 1861. My cousin, Captain Thomas Edward King, of Georgia, having been severely wounded, I went to Richmond to look after him, leaving Nashville on the 1st of August.[10] After he had sufficiently recovered to return to his home, I joined my regiment at Valley Mountain on the 23rd of August. Some of the entries made in my pocket diary while on this trip are not devoid of interest as illustrating the condition of the Southern army and of the Southern country at this early stage of the war.

My route was through Knoxville and Bristol. At the latter place, which is on the boundary line between Tennessee and Virginia, I missed the train for Lynchburg by an hour, found all the hotels crowded, and the railroad pressed to its utmost in conveying troops.

While waiting I visited two sick men from Nashville of whom I had heard, and then strolled out to the camp, a mile from the town. There I witnessed the execution of the sentence of a court-martial upon two private soldiers convicted of selling whiskey to other soldiers. The culprits were drummed around the camp, riding on rails, each with three empty bottles tired to his feet, and a label, "Ten Cents a Glass," pinned to his back.

At Lynchburg I missed connections for Richmond Saturday night and so spent a very pleasant Sunday in the former place. I found Lynchburg a very quaint old town, built on steep hills, from the foot of which the

---

gress and as chargé d'affaires for the United States in Lisbon. In 1861, Barrow was appointed by Tennessee Governor Isham G. Harris as one of three commissioners to negotiate a "military league" with the Confederate States. He was briefly imprisoned when Nashville fell to the Federals in 1862, then removed to St. Louis until his death. Robert M. McBride and Dan M. Robison, *Biographical Directory of the Tennessee General Assembly*, vol. 1, 1796–1861 (Nashville: Tennessee State Library and Archives and Tennessee Historical Commission, 1975), 30.

10. Actually CTQ's wife's cousin, Thomas E. King was captain of the "Roswell Guards" of Cobb County, Georgia (Company H, 7th Georgia Regiment). He was disabled by an ankle wound at Manassas. Lillian Henderson, ed., *Roster of the Confederate Soldiers of Georgia, 1861–1865*, 6 vols. (Hapeville, Ga.: Longins and Porter, 1960), 1:890; Isabel Pratt, "Captain Thomas E. King," *Southern Bivouac* 2 (July 1884): 511–14.

James River finds its way sluggishly to the sea. I preached at St. Paul's Church on "The Love of God."

Arriving at Richmond, I found the place so crowded that I began to think I would not be able to even get a lodging. The Spottswood and Exchange Hotels were crowded to overflowing, and I could not get the sign of a room, though I did succeed in getting some dinner at the latter house. But calling on the Rev. Mr. Peterkin,[11] I was asked to stay with him, and had for a co-guest the Rev. A. Toomer Porter, chaplain of the Hampton Legion,—after the war a prominent educator and founder of a famous school in Charleston, S.C.[12]

At the Rev. Mr. Peterkin's I had the pleasure of meeting the Rev. William Nelson Pendleton, then a Colonel in the Confederate Army, afterwards a Major-General in command of Lee's Artillery.[13] He had been in command of the artillery that did such execution at the battle of Manassas, and gave me a most interesting account of that fight. There was not a masked battery on the ground. His guns were within two hundred yards of the nearest of those of the enemy and within four hundred yards of those that were at the greatest difference. Yet he did not lose a man.

I learned from Mr. Peterkin where to find my wounded cousin, and with him found two other wounded soldiers. I made daily visits to the wounded during my stay in Richmond; met Bishop Atkinson; called, with the Rev. Mr. Porter, upon Mrs. Wade Hampton, who was a daughter of the Honorable George Duffie; and visited Mr. John Stewart in his princely establishment four miles out from Richmond, where I attended

11. Rev. Dr. Joshua Peterkin was rector of St. James Church of Richmond. Peterkin is perhaps best known as the clergyman who comforted J. E. B. Stuart on his deathbed. "List of Virginia Chaplains, Army of Northern Virginia," SHSP 34 (1906): 313, 315; Fitzhugh Lee, "Speech of General Fitz. Lee, at A.N.V. Banquet, October 28, 1875," SHSP 1 (February 1876): 99, 102.

12. Rev. Anthony Toomer Porter served in the army as a chaplain for two years, returning to Charleston, South Carolina, to become rector of the Church of the Holy Communion. He once more entered Confederate service as a chaplain in 1865 when he accompanied Lt. Gen. William J. Hardee in his march to join Gen. Joseph E. Johnston in North Carolina, thereby witnessing the final scenes of the war. In 1866, Porter established Charleston's first African American school and, in 1867, a school for the sons of impoverished Confederate veterans, which survives as a private preparatory school today. CMH, 6:800–802.

13. William Nelson Pendleton (1809–1883), rector of Grace Church in Lexington, Virginia. CTQ is mistaken as to Pendleton's grade; he never ranked higher than brigadier general. Warner, Generals in Gray, 234–35.

services at the church built by Mr. Stewart and his brother at the cost of fourteen thousand dollars.[14] It was at this time that I received and accepted my appointment as Chaplain in the Confederate Army.

On the Sunday I spent in the city that was shortly afterwards to become the capital of the Confederate States, I preached at St. James' Church in the morning, at the Monumental Church in the evening, and again at St. James' at night.

Another interesting incident of this visit to Richmond was in regard to the Rev. John Flavel Mines, a chaplain in the Federal army, who had been captured, released on parole, and had been for two days at the Rev. Mr. Peterkin's house, where I met him.[15] By order of General Winder he was rearrested, and the poor fellow was quite crushed by the idea of having to go to prison.[16] He was especially fearful of contracting consumption, of which some of his family had died. He wrote two piteous letters to me begging me to intercede on his behalf. After two efforts I succeeded in visiting him in the afterwards famous "Libby" prison, where I found him in company with the Hon. Alfred Ely, a member of Congress from Rochester, N.Y., who had been captured at Manassas. I did all I could to cheer the prisoners up. Mr. Mines subsequently renounced the ministry and accepted a colonel's commission in the Federal army. After the war

14. Rt. Rev. Thomas Atkinson (1897–1881) was Episcopal bishop of North Carolina. George McDuffie (1788–1851) had been governor and senator from South Carolina. His daughter, Mary Singleton McDuffie, married the widower Wade Hampton in 1858. Hampton (1818–1902) fought in the Army of Northern Virginia for most of the war, rising to the rank of lieutenant general in 1865. Manly Wade Wellman, *Giant in Gray: A Biography of Wade Hampton of South Carolina* (New York: Charles Scribner's Sons, 1949), 28, 33. John Stewart was apparently the owner of "Brook Hill" in Henrico County, Virginia. Daniel Grinnen, "David Crockett Richardson," *Virginia Historical Magazine* 38 (1930): 64, 66.

15. John Flavel Mines (1835–1891) was the chaplain of a Maine regiment who was captured on the Manassas battlefield when he remained behind to comfort wounded on the field. After being overheard expressing views contrary to his parole, such as the illegality of secession, he was rearrested. Seeking release, he invoked his relationship with CTQ, stating that he had undergone a "total change in my impressions and opinions since my stay here and my consequent desire to go back with words of peace." See *OR*, Series 2, 2:1508–15. Apparently, he recanted his desire for peaceful relations, as he gave up the cloth and mustered out as a lieutenant colonel in 1865. As CTQ relates, after the war, Mines spent time as a writer and journalist. *Allibone's Dictionary of Authors*, supplement, s.v. "Mines, John Flavel."

16. Brig. Gen. John Henry Winder (1800–1865) of Maryland was provost marshal of Richmond, giving him responsibility over the prison camps in Richmond and its environs. Warner, *Generals in Gray*, 340–41.

he entered upon a literary career, and wrote some charming books under the *nom de plume* of "Felix Oldboy."[17]

On my way to my regiment I found in Staunton, Virginia, that the Deaf and Dumb Asylum was used as a hospital, and I wrote to the Editor of the Nashville "Banner" asking contributions from the citizens of Tennessee for the sick and wounded and advising the establishing of a depository at Staunton under the supervision of the Rev. James A. Latané.[18] The citizens of Staunton made up two boxes of stores and comforts for the sick of my regiment. I preached in Staunton Sunday morning and night and left for Milboro. I went thence to Huntersville, which I reached on the 21st of August after a bit of just the toughest travel I had ever made. I found Jackson's River so swollen by rains that it was impossible to ford with the stage. The passengers mounted the horses,—two on each horse,—and forded the stream.

My traveling companion on the night of this occurrence and the following day was Colonel Wheeler, Ex-Minister to Nicaragua, Vestryman in Dr. Pinckney's Church in Washington, D.C., one of the most agreeable men to take a trip with I had ever met. His wife was a daughter of Sully the artist.[19]

We were again delayed at Back Creek, and while waiting for a chance to cross, I read "Master Humphrey's Clock," a volume found in a knapsack on Jackson's Mountain. The owner's name on the fly-leaf was "B. B. Ewing, Comp. I, 12th Miss. Reg't." The book was wet and mouldy. I finally mounted one of the stage horses and swam the creek and so reached Gatewoods,—a delightful place,—a valley shut in on all sides by most picturesque mountains. It was twelve miles from Huntersville.

17. Alfred Ely (1815–1892) was a New York lawyer elected as a Republican to the 36th and 37th Congresses (1859–1863). He was not renominated after his capture at the First Battle of Manassas (Bull Run), and he returned to New York to practice law. Joint Committee on Printing, *Biographical Directory of the United States Congress, 1774–1989* (Washington: U.S. Government Printing Office, 1989), 965.

18. James A. Latané was rector of Trinity Church in Staunton.

19. John Hill Wheeler (1806–1882) of North Carolina. *Dictionary of American Biography*, s.v. "Wheeler, John Hill." Rev. Dr. William Pickney was rector of the Church of the Ascension in Washington, D.C. The church was seized by the Federal provost marshal early in the war because Pickney refused to give a prayer of Thanksgiving for recent Federal victories. Committee on the History of the Diocese, *Historical Sketches of the Parishes and Missions in the Diocese of Washington* (Washington: n.p., 1928), 35–38. Thomas Sully (1783–1872) was a well known painter of portraits. *American National Biography*, s.v. "Sully, Thomas."

I finally reached Colonel Fulton's camp, over the worst road I ever traveled, and thence found Huntersville,—a most wretched and filthy town in those days, where there were many sick soldiers in a meeting-house, in public and private buildings and in tents.[20] Huntersville was twenty-seven miles from Valley Mountain where our troops were stationed. I was very anxious to get on for there was a battle daily expected.

Resuming the journey in an ambulance, I had to leave it within a mile in consequence of the wretched state of the roads, and walked all day over the most horrible roads, the rain at time coming down in torrents. I felt occasionally that I must give out, but finally reached Big Springs and received a warm welcome from General Anderson, General Donelson, Colonel Fulton, Major Duval and other officers.[21] My clothes were so wet that the water could be wrung out of them and my first care was to dry them. That done, I set out for the camp at Valley Mountain three miles distant, and reached it on the morning of Friday the 23rd of August, which happened to be the first clear day I had seen for more than a week.

The following Sunday I began my duties as chaplain, and had services in camp which were well attended. That week our scouts had a running fire with the enemy's pickets, and one of our lieutenants captured a Federal soldier. As it was the first achievement of the kind by any of our regiment, our camp was greatly enlivened by it. About this time I was appointed Assistant Surgeon, but I did not wish to accept the office as I felt that it might separate me from my regiment. I do not remember, however, any time throughout the war, when there was any opportunity offered for me to assist the work of the surgeons that I did not do it.

One afternoon a courier arrived at Colonel Maney's headquarters with orders for the regiment to report to General Loring.[22] While Colonel Maney was reading the order, a sudden volley of small arms resounded through the mountain, and some one, thinking the Federal forces had attacked General Lee's position, ordered the long roll beaten. This startled the camp, every man seized his gun and cartridge box, and the regi-

20. Alfred S. Fulton was colonel of the 8th Tennessee. Lindsley, *Military Annals*, 265.
21. Brig. Gen. Samuel Read Anderson (1804–1883) of Nashville would command a brigade in the coming campaign which would include the 1st Tennessee. Brig. Gen. Daniel Smith Donelson (1801–1863) of Sumner County, Tennessee, also would command a brigade. Warner, *Generals in Gray*, 10–11, 74–75. "Major" Duval appears to have been Lt. Henry Duval, Donelson's aide. Crute, *Confederate Staff Officers*, 51.
22. Brig. Gen. William Wing Loring (1818–1886) of Florida, then commanding the "Northwestern Army." OR 2:986–87.

ment was at once in line. For at that time the boys were spoiling for a fight.

I well remember how good Mrs. Sullivan, the wife of an Irish private and a kind of "daughter of the regiment," drew off her shoes and gave them to a soldier who was barefoot. The boys started off for General Lee's headquarters without rations, without blankets, and many of them without coats or shoes. In this plight they reported for duty. It was altogether a false alarm. A regiment had been on picket duty and was firing off guns in order to clean them. Nevertheless it happened that the action of our boys was in conformity to an order received regularly enough about five minutes later, requiring our regiment to take position within a very short distance of the enemy's entrenchments, and the regiment remained out in consequence from Friday morning until Sunday, in full view of the enemy.

A few days after this General Loring determined on a movement on the enemy holding a fortified position on Cheat Pass. The camp became a scene of great animation in anticipation of an important impending battle. To me it was a memorable week beginning on Monday September 8th—a week of such experiences as I had never dreamed would fall to my lot, and of such fatigues as I never imagined myself capable of enduring.

General Lee's plans were undoubtedly well and skillfully laid, but "the wisest schemes of mice and men gang aft aglee." The plan, to my mind, was somewhat complicated inasmuch as it demanded concerted action on the part of too many commanders far removed from each other. Thus General Henry R. Jackson of Georgia, with Rust of Arkansas, was to attack the enemy at Cheat Pass where he was strongly entrenched. General Loring with Donelson was to engage the enemy at Crouch's and Huttonville and force his way up to Cheat Pass, while Anderson with his brigade was to pass over Cheat Mountain and engage the enemy in the rear.[23]

The Rock City Guard, with the regiment, left camp at Valley Mountain on Monday, and moved to a new camp three or four miles in ad-

23. Brig. Gen. Henry Rootes Jackson (1820–1898) of Georgia commanded a small division. Col. (later Brig. Gen.) Albert Rust (1818–1870) of Arkansas commanded the 3rd Arkansas Regiment. While CTQ is correct as to the complicated nature of the Confederate attack plan, General Robert E. Lee's complex plan appears to have been the most practical means of seizing the initiative in the wet and difficult terrain. CTQ's description of the Confederate plan is somewhat inaccurate in that Anderson was to occupy a blocking position rather than attacking the Federals at Cheat Pass. D. S. Freeman, *R. E. Lee: A Biography*, 4 vols. (New York: Charles Scribner's Sons, 1934), 1:562–63.

vance. I remained behind for a day to care for the sick and then followed the regiment. At nine o'clock on Tuesday morning General S. R. Anderson's Brigade, consisting of Colonel Maney's regiment and two others, started on. The route was not by a road but through fields and over mountains the most precipitous, in going up which we had to wind single file along the sides and reach the top by very circuitous paths. The paths were exceedingly steep, rocky and rough, and our horses had to be taken to the rear. At one time I reached the top of the mountain and sat down for a little rest under a great boulder that projected out into the pathway. An officer in front called out to me, "Tell them that the order is to 'double quick!'" I passed the command to another officer, who turned to those behind him who were struggling up the mountain pass and called out to them, "The order is to 'double quick' back there!" Whereupon the rear of the regiment turned and rushed down the mountain. In the flight the Major was upset, and flat on his back and with heels in the air he poured forth benedictions of an unusual kind for a Presbyterian elder.[24]

Our first night out, after I had traveled twelve miles on foot, (I had lent to a less fortunate officer the horse that had been presented to me but a few days previously), we halted at 10 o'clock. Soon after it began to rain heavily. I had been carrying the blankets of Lieutenant Joe Van Leer, who had been exceedingly kind to me throughout the march, and when I came up to him he said, "I have a capital place where we may sleep. I'll put my blankets on the ground and we'll cover with yours, as they are heavier."[25] So he cleaned out a hollow on the side of the mountain, and there we lay down for the night. We had my blanket and his rubber coat for a covering. Shortly after midnight a little river began running down my neck. The rain was pouring in torrents, and the basin Van Leer had scooped out was soon filled; so I spent the night as did the Georgia soldier who said that he had slept in the bed of a river with a thin sheet of water over him. This was not altogether a unique experience for me as we shall soon see.

The next morning, after breaking our fast on cold meat and "gutter percha" bread, we took up our line of march and had gone but a mile or

24. Presumably, the major was Maj. A. M. Looney of the 1st Tennessee Regiment. See note 5 in this chapter.

25. Joseph H. Vanleer was lieutenant of Company B, 1st Tennessee. CWCCT, *Tennesseans in the Civil War: A Military History of Confederate and Union Units with Available Rosters of Personnel*, 2 vols. (Nashville: Civil War Centennial Commission, 1964–1965), 2:411.

so when we heard the fire of musketry at our left.[26] We supposed this was by the scouts sent out by General Donelson. This day, (Wednesday), was the severest of all upon our men. We made slow progress and the march was very toilsome. We kept perfect silence, expecting every moment to come up with scouting parties of the enemy. At about three o'clock the order was passed along the line, just as one half the regiment had reached the top of the mountain, to "double-quick forward!"

The drums of the enemy were distinctly heard, and we moved as rapidly as possible, and were about an hour in descending. All the horses were left behind, as the mountain was found so steep and rocky that it was impossible for them to go any further. We clambered down the rocks, clinging to the bushes and jumping from rock to rock, and at nine o'clock we halted for the night.

Not a word was spoken above a whisper, nor a fire lighted, although it was very cold. Van Leer arranged our blankets as on the previous night, and with much the same result. For soon after we lay down the rain came as though the windows of heaven were opened, and about eleven o'clock we were thoroughly saturated. A rivulet ran down my back and Joe and I actually lay in a pool of water all night. I thought it impossible for me to stand it, but as there was no alternative, I kept quiet and thought over all I had ever read of the benefits of hydropathy. I consoled myself with the reflection that the water-cure might relieve me of an intense pain I had suffered for some hours in my left knee, — and so it did. At the same time I would hesitate long before recommending the same treatment for every other pain in the left knee.

In the morning I was well soaked, my finger ends were corrugated and my whole body chilled through. I was very hungry also, but all I could get to eat was one tough biscuit that almost defied my most vigorous assaults. We were ordered to be on the Parkersburg Pike that day, (Thursday), at daybreak. To show how little we understood the art of war at that time, soon after we started, a well mounted horseman passed halfway down the line of the regiment without detection. He proved to be a Fed-

26. "Gutter percha" bread is an obvious joke. "Gutta percha" is a rubbery substance, derived from tropical trees, used in the Civil War for insulation and waterproofing. *The American Heritage Dictionary of the English Language*, 3rd ed., s.v. "gutta-percha"; Levi S. White, "Confederate Ordnance: The Good Work Done by General Gorgas in His Department," SHSP 29 (1901): 319.

eral courier. Lieutenant-Colonel Sevier finally halted him and said in surprise: "Why, you're a Yankee!" To which the courier coolly replied: "I'm so thankful you found me out; I was so afraid of being shot."

The Colonel took from him a fine pair of pistols, sword, carbine and his horse, which he gave to Major Looney who was thoroughly knocked up. Half a mile further on brought us to the Parkersburg Pike, three miles and a half from Cheat Mountain Pass. The brigade was, as rapidly as possible, put in position. The First Tennessee was at the head of a column towards Cheat Pass. In about ten minutes a body of the enemy, about one hundred strong, in ambush on the opposite side of the road and only about twenty-five yards from our troops, began firing into our left, composed of the companies from Pulaski, Columbia and Murfreesboro. The enemy were completely concealed but our men stood the fire nobly. Not a man flinched. After two or three volleys had been fired, Captain Field ordered a charge and the enemy fled.[27]

We lost two killed, two missing and sixteen wounded. We captured Lieutenant Merrill of the Engineer Corps, U.S.A., attached to General Rosecrans' command.[28] I fell into conversation with him, and found him not only a most intelligent gentleman but also a most genial and pleasant companion,—as most West Pointers are. We also captured seven privates, and left on the roadside two wounded men of the enemy who were so disabled that they could not be moved, though we dressed their wounds and made them as comfortable as possible. The enemy lost some eight or ten killed,—how many wounded I do not know.

My first experience in actual battle was very different from what I had anticipated. I had expected an open field and a fair fight, but this bushwhacking was entirely out of my line. The balls whistled in a way that can never be appreciated by one who has not heard them. We held our position until four o'clock in the afternoon, anxiously listening for General H. R. Jackson's fire, upon which the whole movement depended; but not a gun was heard in that direction. General Donelson, however, met a party of the enemy and engaged them, killing seventeen and taking sixty-

27. Capt. (later Maj. and then Col.) Hume R. Feild of Tennessee, who at this time commanded Company K of the 1st Tennessee, the "Martin Guards" of Giles County, Tennessee. CWCCT, *Tennesseans*, 1:172.

28. William E. Merrill, U.S. Army Corps of Engineers, United States Military Academy class of 1859. OR 2:284.

eight prisoners. He then waited for us,—of course waited in vain, and like us withdrew.[29]

When we left the turnpike, we took with us our wounded, all but five of whom were carried on horses, the others on litters. About two miles from the highway we came to the house of a Mr. White, where we deposited seven of our wounded men and left them. The brigade halted in a meadow. After attending to the wounded, I lay down by a wheat-stack with Joe Van Leer, who made a very comfortable bed for us. At daylight I returned to the house to assist the surgeons in dressing the wounds of our men. This occupied us until nine o'clock.

The brigade in the meantime had moved forward and left us. We supposed that they had stationed a guard for our protection, but it had been neglected, and when we left, a man suggested to us that we better remove the white badges from our caps, for we might come across some scouting party of the enemy. We took his advice and in addition I took the precaution to tie a white handkerchief to a stick, and so I led the way. After winding about over the hills for a mile or so, we came upon a body of men behind a fallen tree with their guns pointed at us ready to fire. We heard the click of the locks and I instantly threw up the white flag, and this possibly saved our party from being shot down *by our own men*. It was a detachment that had been sent back for us, and as they saw us winding along without our badges, they supposed us a party of the enemy on the trail of our forces. One man was very much overcome when he found out who we were.

About a mile further on we came up with the main body of our troops, which had been halted for us by Colonel Hatton, who, on discovering that we were in the rear, ran the whole length of the column to inform General Anderson of the fact.[30] It felt mighty good to get with the brigade again.

In less than half an hour after we left Mr. White's house, a party of the

29. Jackson's column, led by Colonel Rust, had stealthily approached the Federal position on Cheat Mountain in preparation for the anticipated attack. Several pickets were captured and deceived Rust with a tale that four to five thousand Yankees occupied the position, when the actual number was closer to three hundred. Deterred by this alarming intelligence and the impressive looking Federal works, Rust moved away without making the attack. Freeman, *R. E. Lee*, 1:570–71.

30. Ohio-born Robert Hopkins Hatton of Lebanon, Tennessee, was colonel of the 7th Tennessee. Hatton was later promoted to brigadier general and killed at the Battle of Seven Pines on May 31, 1862. Warner, *Generals in Gray*, 128.

enemy was in possession there. At half past twelve word was passed along the line that the enemy were following us. Immediately a line of battle was formed, but very shortly we moved on to get a more advantageous position. We rolled down one precipice and climbed up another and again the line of battle was formed. Then it was discovered that a small part of the enemy's forces was on its way by a route that crossed ours to reinforce Crouch's, so there was no fighting.

Friday night we camped about one mile from the place we occupied our first night out. I had no provisions, but various persons gave me what made up a tolerably good supper, to wit,—a roasting ear, a slice of bacon and a biscuit; and in the morning I found on a log a good sized piece of fresh meat, not strikingly clean, but I sliced off a piece of it and cooked it on a long stick. The fire, I reckon, removed all impurities; and Joe Van Leer brought me half a cup of coffee and another biscuit. We rested here until seven o'clock at night, when we took up our march for Brady's Gate. At about eleven o'clock we rested for the night and had the pleasure of meeting two men from Nashville who had brought out a couple of ambulances loaded with nick-nacks for the Rock City Guard. Out of their supplies we had a comfortable breakfast, and again started for Brady's Gate and reached it at 1 P.M.

At this point the enemy had been in great numbers,—some three or four thousand. Everywhere in the woods they had erected comfortable booths and rustic benches. Our brigade took position expecting an attack, and waited until half-past six, and then once more started on our march. About eight o'clock the rain poured down in torrents and once more we were thoroughly drenched. The brigade remained all night in an open meadow, but Colonel Sevier insisted upon my taking his horse, and so I rode forward with Major Looney and some other officers to a house half a mile further on, and Dr. Buist, Van Leer, myself and five others took up quarters for the night in a smoke-house. Unfortunately the shingles were off just over my head and the rain came through pretty freely. The next morning we started for our old camp at Valley Mountain, which we reached at eleven o'clock. It really seemed like getting home. The tents looked more than familiar,—inviting even. I rested well and ate well and felt well generally.

The march left many of our men bare-footed. Some of them made the last of the tramp in their stocking feet, and when we reached our quarters they had not even a thread to cover them. One of Captain Jack Butler's men made the remark that if the enemy took the Captain prisoner they would not believe him if he told them his rank; and when I looked at the dear fellow, ragged and barefooted, with feet cut and swollen, I thought so too.[31] But then when I looked down at my own feet and saw my own toes peeping,—nay, rather boldly showing themselves,—as plain as the nose on my face—and found that almost a majority of our regiment were bootless and shoeless by the hardness of the march, I realized what we had gone through.

The path by which we ascended to the top of Cheat Mountain was one which the foot of man probably never trod before. The guide said that he knew that he could cross it but did not think that the brigade could. I would not have undertaken the march, I presume, could I have foretold what it would be. I made the whole trip, with the exception of a few miles, on foot; for the morning we started out, Lieutenant John House, of Franklin, a noble fellow, was very weak from an attack of fever from which he had not entirely convalesced.[32] I insisted upon his taking my horse and so I did not ride at all until Sunday the 15th. My horse proved a most valuable one. On our return one of the wounded men rode her down the steepest hills and she did not once miss a foot. Being raised in that region she had the faculty of adapting herself to the provender, while other Tennessee horses grew thin and became useless.

As a result of the expedition, our forces had driven in all the outposts of the enemy, made a thorough survey of all their works, had killed, wounded and captured about two hundred of their men, and all with a loss of less than thirty on our side. But the campaign in that section was abandoned and all our forces were transferred to another section.[33]

I was very glad to believe that my labors among the soldiers as their chaplain were not all thrown away. It was very delightful to see how well our regular daily evening service in camp was attended. And I was greatly pleased to find so many of the young men anxious to receive the Holy

31. John S. Butler was captain of Company F, 1st Tennessee, the "Railroad Boys" of Nashville. CWCCT, *Tennesseans*, 1:172.

32. Lt. (later Capt. and Lt. Col.) John L. House of Company D, 1st Tennessee, the "Williamson Grays." Ibid.

33. CTQ is putting the best face on the failure of Lee's plan. General Lee termed the affair a "grievous disappointment." R. E. Lee to John Letcher, September 12, 1861, in *The Wartime Papers of R. E. Lee*, ed. Clifford Dowdy and Louis H. Manerin (New York: Bramhall House, 1961), 75. CTQ wrote a friend to the effect that Cheat Mountain would be something to talk about the rest of his life. See J. B. Craighead to CTQ, October 13, 1861, Quintard Papers, DU.

Communion when I celebrated on the fifteenth Sunday after Trinity, the day before we started on the expedition. The whole regiment seemed devoted to me. One of the Captains told the Major that he believed every man in his company would lay down his life for me. Certainly I met nothing but kindness from officers and men. And so I was led to hope that some good would yet grow out of the seed sown in those wild mountains.[34]

On Friday the 13th of September, General Loring was anxious to have a reconnaissance made, and assigned the duty to Major Fitzhugh Lee, son of General Robert E. Lee.[35] Colonel J. A. Washington, a brother-in-law of General Lee and one of his personal aides, asked permission to accompany the party, which was granted.[36] They had advanced a considerable distance when Major Lee told the Colonel that it was unsafe for them to proceed further. But the Colonel was anxious to make a thorough exploration. Major Lee, however, decided not to endanger the lives of his men by taking them along, and so halted them and rode on with Colonel Washington, accompanied by two privates.

They had not gone far when they were fired upon by a large picket guard lying in ambush by the roadside. Colonel Washington was instantly killed, being pierced by three balls through the breast. Major Lee's horse was shot under him and one of the privates also lost his horse. Major Lee escaped on Colonel Washington's horse. A flag was sent to the Federal camp the next day by General Lee, and Colonel Washington's body was given up. The enemy offered to send it the whole distance in an ambulance, but this offer Colonel Stark, the bearer of the flag, declined.

This sad occurrence was the occasion of my first acquaintance with General Lee, the most conspicuous character in the struggle between the States. I saw him at Cheat Mountain when he had just learned of the death of Colonel Washington. He was standing with his right arm thrown over the neck of his horse,—(a blooded animal, thoroughly groomed),—and I was impressed first of all by the man's splendid physique, and then

34. A member of the regiment wrote that each man was given a New Testament by CTQ, on the flyleaf of which was written, "God is our sun and our shield." Marcus B. Toney, *The Privations of a Private* (Nashville: M. E. Church, South Publishing House, 1907), 19.

35. Maj. (later Maj. Gen.) William Henry Fitzhugh "Rooney" Lee (1837–1891).

36. Col. John Augustine Washington (1820–1861) was the last member of the Washington family to own Mount Vernon.

by the look of extreme sadness that pervaded his countenance. He felt the death of his relative very keenly and seemed greatly dispirited.

It was my high privilege later on to be brought in contact with this great and good man and to learn most thoroughly to appreciate his exalted character and to understand why his life is to-day an enduring inheritance of his country and the Church of Christ. Personally he was a man of rare gifts, physical and mental. To these were added the advantages of finished culture. He was a very Bayard in manner and bearing. The habits of temperance, frugality and self-control, formed by him in youth, adhered to him through life.

CHAPTER III

Personal Narrative—
Big Sewell Mountain, Winchester and Romney

From Valley Mountain I was sent with the sick of our brigade to a place named Edrai where a number of our troops were encamped.[1] I think it was about sixteen miles distant, but on account of the condition of the roads, I was fully three days in making the trip. I had given up my horse to Lieutenant Van Leer and I was busy each day of the march administering to the wants of the sick, several of whom died on the way. A cup of strong coffee was made for me by the sergeant in command of our escort, (we had coffee in those days, later our ingenuity was taxed to discover substitutes for it), which was the only thing that refreshed me on the march. Instead of a coffee mill, a hatchet handle was used to beat up the grains which were then boiled in a tin cup. I was a long time drinking that cup of coffee.

The last day of the journey I felt myself breaking down and determined to reach Edrai as soon as possible. Accordingly I took the middle of the road, not avoiding the holes which were abundant, and walked through slush and mud, reaching Edrai just in the gloaming. There was one brick house in the place, to which I made my way. To my delight I found there Major Looney of my regiment, who received me with great cordiality. I was so exhausted that I was obliged to support myself in my chair, and the

1. Edray was a small town in Pocahontas County, Virginia (now West Virginia).

Major, seeing how greatly prostrated I was, gave me a large drink of brandy. It produced not the slightest effect on me, and so in fifteen minutes more he repeated the dose, and "Richard was himself again." I went out at once, borrowed a horse of a friend who was a Lieutenant in a Virginia Regiment, and rode back to meet my sick train. The next day I officiated at the burial of those who had died en route.[2]

Shortly after this, General Lee ordered us to reinforce General John B. Floyd, who was strongly intrenched at Big Sewell Mountain, facing the Federal Army under General Rosecrans and only a mile distant.[3] I passed through the Hot Springs on the way to Big Sewell Mountain; and from there, making our way was very gradual, for rains had been destructive of the roads. In some places every trace of the road had been so completely washed away that no one would dream that any had ever been where were then gullies eight or ten feet or even fifteen feet deep. Fences, bridges and even houses had been washed away, farms ruined, and at White Sulphur Springs the guests had to be taken from the lower story of the hotel. Major Looney, Captain Foster and myself were detained at this point for several days, and I went back and forth to hold services and visit the sick.[4]

At Big Sewell Mountain I was brought into very pleasant relations with General Lee. At White Sulphur Springs, Mrs. Lee had entrusted me with a parcel to deliver to the General at my first opportunity. Upon my arrival I at once called upon him and spent several hours with him in most delightful intercourse. From his headquarters we could see the whole Federal encampment. With the audacity of ignorance, I said to him: "Why, General, there are the Federals! why don't we attack them?" In his gentle voice, he replied: "Ah, it is sometimes better to wait until you are attacked."

From the camp at Big Sewell Mountain I was sent, in the latter part of October, to accompany a detachment of our sick men to the hospitals at White Sulphur and Hot Springs, Virginia. When I reached the latter place, being only fifteen miles from a railroad, I determined to run down

2. As a testament to CTQ's tireless efforts as a surgeon and minister during this time, he received a letter from a grateful mother who felt "that under the good Providence of God she owe[d] the life of her son to him." C. C. Hardin to CTQ, January 23, 1862, Quintard Papers, DU.

3. The officers referred to are Brig. Gen. John Buchanan Floyd (1806–1863) of Virginia and Brig. Gen. (later Major General) William Starke Rosecrans (1819–1898) of Ohio.

4. Robert C. Foster was captain of Company C, 1st Tennessee, part of CTQ's own Rock City Guards.

to Staunton to get, if possible, some clean clothing. My visit was timely, for a few hours after my arrival in Staunton I received by train two boxes,—one from Rome, Georgia, and one from Nashville. In the latter box were two pairs of heavy winter boots, a pair of winter pants, flannel under-clothing and a great variety of useful articles, and my wardrobe was now so generally well supplied that I could help along some who were in worse condition than I was in.

My visit to Staunton was otherwise a rich treat. Somehow or other everybody seemed to have heard of me or to know me, and all extended to me the most overflowing cordiality and hospitality. I was first the guest of the Rev. Mr. Latané and afterwards of Dr. Stribling, the Superintendent of the Insane Asylum.[5] Mrs. Stribling and her daughter sent by me two trunks filled with things for our regiment, and a lady met me on the street and handed me ten dollars for the use of the sick.

About the middle of November I received orders from General Loring to proceed from Huntersville to the Lewisburg line and to transport all the sick and convalescent belonging to his division to the hospitals at Warm, Hot and Bath Alum Springs.[6] I accordingly left General Loring's headquarters one Friday at noon, and crossing the Greenbrier Bridge, six miles above Huntersville, took the road to Hillsboro, a little hamlet ten miles distant, where I spent the night very pleasantly, without charge, at the home of Mr. Baird. Thence I rode to the residence of Mr. Renick, sixteen miles, and found three of our regiment who had been sick for some weeks but were then greatly improved and glad to get away under my protection.[7] On Sunday morning I rode five miles to the town of Frankford and my name (and fame) having preceded me, I was urged to have services in the Presbyterian Church. Of course I was very glad to do so and had a good and very attentive congregation.

5. Francis T. Stribling, 50, is listed in the 1860 census for Augusta County, Virginia, as a physician and the superintendent of the Western Insane Asylum.

6. Special Order No. 46 of the Army of the Northwest, dated November 8, 1861, provided that CTQ was to proceed to the "Lewisburg line of operations for the purpose of collecting the sick & others of this army to their Reg't & such other Hospitals on this line as he may find best suited for them." CTQ CSR, Confederate General and Staff Officers, RG 109, M-331, NA.

7. No "Mr. Baird" is listed in the 1860 census for Pocahontas County, Virginia. From the 1860 census for the Falling Springs District of Greenbriar County, Virginia, "Mr. Renick" appears to have been either James H. Renick, age sixty-one, a farmer, or R. W. Renick, age fifty, a farmer.

At Frankford there lived a Dr. Renick who had been extremely kind to all of our Tennessee soldiers. He turned his home into a hospital and he and his wife devoted themselves most assiduously to the welfare of the sick, refusing any remuneration. I stopped at his house and at his request baptized his youngest child, a little girl about eighteen months old, born on Easter Sunday. The parents were quite unacquainted with the ecclesiastical calendar, yet the father said: "I'm going to give her a good Episcopal name, Doctor," and so he had me give her in baptism the name of "Margaret Easter Sunday." I was glad she was not born on Quinquagesima Sunday for I might in that case have had to give her that name.[8]

The following day I went to Lewisburg and thence to White Sulphur Springs, hoping to be in part relieved by one of the surgeons, whom I ordered to join his regiment with the sick men belonging to it. There were more than one thousand patients at White Sulphur Springs and there had been forty deaths within the past thirteen days.

I shall never forget the dinner we had in camp one Sunday about the last of November. It was the best of the season. Beef, venison, preserved peaches, raspberries and plums, rice, fine old Madeira, currant wine and many other things,—most of which had been sent by Dr. Stribling,—made a real feast quite in contrast with our usual camp fare. At that time the boys were going into winter quarters and were building very snug, roofed cabins.

One Sunday early in December, after having service in the camp near Huntersville, with a pass from General Loring to go to Richmond and return at the public charge, I started first for Staunton to look after the interests of a young man from Maury County, Tennessee, who while in a state of intoxication, killed another man by the accidental discharge of his pistol. That I arrived safely in Staunton I felt to be a matter of special congratulation on account of the roads I had to travel. The mud was from two to three feet deep.

The young prisoner was a noble fellow to whom I had become very much attached, and was clear of an intentional wrong, I was sure. After calling upon him in Staunton and consulting with his lawyer, we concluded to engage the services of the Hon. Alexander H. Stuart, formerly Secretary of the Interior under President Fillmore, and I went to Rich-

8. "Quinquagesima" is the Sunday before Ash Wednesday. *Oxford Dictionary of the Christian Church*, s.v. "Quinquagesima." Dr. Renick cannot be identified in the 1860 Federal census for Greenbriar County.

mond to see that eminent man.[9] On my return to Staunton I had the trial put off until the January term of court. When it was finally held, I was called upon to testify to the good character of the accused and I am glad to say that the verdict of the jury was in the end: "not guilty."

Our regiment's stay at Big Sewell was not long. There was a good deal of marching to and fro, and Rosecrans finally escaped Lee and Jackson. From Big Sewell, General Loring, to whose division we were attached, was invited to join General Thomas J. Jackson at Winchester.[10] There for the first time I met that distinguished General and I was very cordially received by the Rev. Mr. Meredith, the rector of the parish, and was made to feel quite at home in the rectory.[11]

This was the beginning of a severe and disastrous campaign. The weather was bitterly cold and during the second night of our encampment a severe snowstorm arose. I can never forget the appearance of the troops as they arose the next morning from their snowy couches. It suggested thoughts of the Resurrection morn. In spite of it all, the troops were very cheerful, and as they shook the snow from their uniforms, began singing a song, the chorus of which was:

> "So let the wide world wag as it will,
> We'll be gay and happy still!"

After some delay we began our march against Bath on New Year's day 1862. It was one of the coldest winters known to the oldest inhabitant. Snow, sleet and rain came down upon us in all their wrath. We had a skirmish on the march. General Jackson wished to drive the enemy's forces from the gap in Capon Mountain opposite Bath where they were posted. I begged him to allow me to bring up the First Tennessee regiment. They were some distance in the rear, but I brought them forward in short time. As they passed by in double-quick, the General said to me: "What a splendid regiment!"

9. Alexander H. H. Stuart (1807–1891) was a noted Virginia lawyer who had been secretary of the interior, a congressman, and a member of the Virginia secession convention who opposed secession. *Dictionary of American Biography*, s.v. "Stuart, Alexander Hugh Holmes."

10. Maj. Gen. (later Lt. Gen.) Thomas Jonathan "Stonewall" Jackson (1824–1863) of Virginia, commanding the Army of the Valley.

11. W. C. Meredith remained rector of the parish at Winchester throughout the war. Margaret Barton Colt, *Defend the Valley: A Shenandoah Family in the Civil War* (New York: Orion Books, 1994) 329.

In his report of the engagement, General Jackson said: "The order to drive the enemy from the hill was undertaken with a patriotic enthusiasm which entitles the First Tennessee and its commander to special praise."[12] It was here that Captain Bullock issued his unique command: "Here, you boys, just separate three or four yards, and pie-root!" (pirouette).[13] They did pirouette and made the enemy dance as well.

As the Federal troops retreated through the gap in the mountain, they came face to face with a brigade of the Virginia Militia. Each fired a volley and fled as fast as legs could carry them, in opposite directions. To the boys looking down upon the scene from the mountain, it was a comical sight. As the infantry put the Federals to flight on Capon Mountain, Captain Turner Ashby drove the Federal cavalry along the highway in the valley like leaves before the wind.[14]

We reached Romney without further obstruction. On Sunday I officiated in a church which was crowded to its utmost capacity. I shall never forget the grave attention which "Stonewall" Jackson paid to my discourse. The text from which I preached was: "Be sure your sin will find you out."

The march from Winchester to Romney was one of great hardship and was utterly fruitless of military results. The situation in our camp in the latter part of January, 1862, was rather disturbed. The two Generals, Stonewall Jackson and Loring, did not work well together. Their commands were separate. Jackson commanded the Army of the Valley District; Loring the Army of the North West. The former had written begging the Secretary of War to send Loring and all his forces to co-operate with him (Jackson), in that section and expressing the opinion that the two could drive the enemy from the whole region. The Secretary of War enclosed Jackson's letter to Loring, leaving the movement to his (Loring's) discretion, but at the same time expressing his opinion and that of the President, as decidedly in favor of it.

Accordingly Loring went expecting some prompt and decided work. But no sooner had he arrived in Winchester, than General Jackson began to work to merge the two armies into one and to take General Loring's command under his control. Jackson had but one brigade, while Loring

---

12. The report appears at OR 5: 390–91.

13. Apparently J. Lee Bullock, who was actually lieutenant, Company G, 1st Tennessee. CWCCT, *Tennesseans*, 2:65.

14. Capt. (later Col. and Brig. Gen.) Turner Ashby (1828–1862) of Virginia.

had three under his control. The troops of the latter, from the highest officer to the lowest private, were perfectly devoted to their General. Of course a vast amount of ill feeling was stirred up, and the affair reached a climax when an order was issued for our troops to build winter quarters in Romney, while Jackson's brigade marched back to ease and comfort in Winchester.

I cannot begin to tell all that our troops suffered through the stupidity and want of forethought, (as I then thought it), of Major-General Jackson. It is enough to say that we were subjected to the severest trials that human nature could endure. We left Winchester with 2,700 men in General Anderson's Brigade of Tennesseans. That number was reduced to 1,100. When we reached the position opposite the town of Hancock, Maryland, the First Regiment numbered 680. In Romney, it mustered only 230 men fit for duty. I felt that General Loring ought to demand that he might be allowed to withdraw his forces from the command of Major-General Jackson.

So far as the personal staff of General Loring (including myself) was concerned, it was comfortably situated in a very pleasant new house.[15] But no one could possibly imagine the horrible condition of affairs at Romney among the troops; and when Stonewall Jackson took his command back to Winchester, the men of Loring's command shouted to them: "There go your F. F. V.'s!"[16] The "pet lambs" of the Stonewall Brigade were comfortably housed at Winchester while the troops of Loring's command were left behind in Romney to endure the bitter, biting weather.

This movement on the part of Jackson was the subject of much bitter comment. A report thereof was taken to Richmond and laid before the Secretary of War. He was greatly surprised that Jackson should have withdrawn his forces to Winchester, leaving the reinforcing column behind,—or as it was expressed at the time, "leaving the guests,—the invited guests,—out in the cold." As a result of the controversy that ensued, General Jackson was required by the Secretary of War to direct General Loring to return with his command to Winchester. This we did on the 1st of February, and while in Winchester I was called to officiate at the funerals

15. It is at this point we learn that CTQ became a member of Loring's staff. On January 1, 1862, Loring assigned CTQ as aide-de-camp. CTQ therefore resigned as chaplain of the 1st Tennessee and was appointed lieutenant to rank from January 10, 1862. CTQ CSR, Confederate General and Staff Officers, RG 109, M-331, NA.

16. First Families of Virginia, a jibe at the "privileged" status of Jackson's Brigade.

of a number of our men who had died from sickness and exposure. And it was while there that we received the news of the fall of Fort Donelson.[17] Although Jackson complied with the order of the Secretary of War, he regarded it as a case of interference with his command and took umbrage. It was by the exercise of great tact on the part of General Joseph E. Johnston, Commander-in-Chief of the Department, and of Governor John Letcher, of Virginia, that Jackson was prevailed upon to withhold his resignation, and his valuable services were preserved to the army of the Confederacy.[18]

On the 10th of February, 1862, the First and Third Regiments, Tennessee Volunteers, with a Georgia Regiment, were by the command of the Secretary of War, ordered to proceed to Knoxville, Tennessee, and to report for duty to General Albert Sidney Johnston. A different disposition was made of the Seventh and Fourteenth Tennessee Volunteers and of an Arkansas Regiment, and all the remainder of the command of Brigadier-General Loring was to proceed to Manassas, Virginia, to report for duty to General Joseph E. Johnston. It was with a sad heart that "the boys" of the First Tennessee bade farewell, on the 7th of February, to the Seventh and Fourteenth Regiments and to their warm-hearted and hospitable Virginia friends.[19]

During the march against Romney, General Loring had me commissioned by the Secretary of War as his aide-de-camp.[20] I was very strongly opposed to holding such a commission, and declined to accept, but I could not leave General Loring in the troubles and anxieties that dis-

17. Fort Donelson, on the Cumberland River near Dover, Tennessee, surrendered on February 16, 1862. As a direct result of this calamity, Nashville fell on February 25, 1862.

18. Jackson's threat of resignation achieved the desired result of severing his military relationship with Loring, but he could hardly be considered the prevailing party. Jackson had actually preferred charges against Loring, but these were dismissed, and Loring was promoted and transferred. James I. Robertson, Jr., *Stonewall Jackson: The Man, the Soldier, the Legend*, (New York: Macmillan, 1997) 313–22.

19. For the order making the transfer, see OR 5:1068. The 1st Tennessee's return to Tennessee was required by the defeat of the Confederate army covering East Tennessee in February, 1862. The transfer was part of the complete removal of Loring's command away from Jackson, caused in part by the "unhappy discordance" between Jackson's men and those of Loring. OR 5:1066–67.

20. While CTQ deemed Loring the "noblest of men & most gallant of soldiers," he later termed the resignation of his chaplaincy and the acceptance of the aide position as a temptation of Satan. CTQ to Blulove (?), May 31, 1862, CTQ CSR, Confederate General and Staff Officers, RG 109, M-331, NA.

tressed him, and so as a member of his staff, I traveled around considerably at that time, going from camp to camp, attending the trial of my friend at Staunton, and going to Richmond on military business. To get from Romney to Staunton on one occasion I had to take a horse-back ride of forty-three miles to Winchester, then go by stage eighteen miles to Strasburg, and thence by rail via Manassas and Gordonsville. This was a roundabout way but was preferable at the time to a much shorter route down the valley from Winchester.

On the 21st of February, I went with General Loring to Norfolk, to which point he had been ordered, instead, as I had hoped, to Georgia, where I would have been nearer my family. At this time he was promoted to Major-General. We went, of course, by way of Richmond where I called with him on President Jefferson Davis and was very agreeably disappointed in his personal appearance and bearing. I might have witnessed the ceremonies of his inauguration, but as the day set for that function proved very inclement, I was glad that I chose to spend it on the cars between Richmond and Norfolk. On that day General Loring had a very severe chill followed by congestion of the right lung, which was the precursor of an attack of pneumonia affecting both lungs. I watched by his bedside in Norfolk through all his illness, which prolonged my visit in that city for several weeks.

CHAPTER IV

Personal Narrative—Norfolk

At Norfolk I had the pleasure of intercourse with such friends as John Tattnall, son of Commander Tattnall; Benjamin Loyall and Lieutenant Walter Butt of the ironclad "Virginia," with the clergy of the city and with many charming families.[1] How can I ever forget the old-time Virginia hospitality that was meted out to me—the enthusiastic reception I had from all kinds and conditions of men? How well I remember Mr. Tazewell Taylor![2] He was well up in genealogy, and not only knew all of the old families of Virginia, but the principal families of the whole South. It was quite delightful to hear him, "in the midst of war's alarums," talk over "old times" and old folks. Those days before the war were all so different

---

1. "Commander" Tattnall was Commodore Josiah Tattnall, veteran of the War of 1812, who resigned his commission in the United States Navy to accept a Confederate commission. A. A. Hoehling, *Thunder at Hampton Roads* (Englewood Cliffs, N.J.: Prentice-Hall, 1976), 176. Lt. Benjamin Pollard Loyall of Virginia, formerly a lieutenant in the U.S. Navy, was at this time on parole after being captured in North Carolina earlier that year. Lt. Walter R. Butt of Virginia, formerly a midshipman in the U.S. Navy, was as CTQ indicates a member of the *Virginia*'s crew. Naval War Records Office, *Register of Officers of the Confederate States Navy, 1861–1865* (1931; reprint, Mattituck, N.Y.: J. M. Carroll & Co., 1983), 27, 117.

2. The 1860 federal census for Norfolk County, Virginia, lists Taylor, age 50, as a lawyer.

from what we have known since. No one born since the war can write intelligently of the blessed old days in the South.

But if any one would read a true account of the trials and woes of a Southern household during the dreadful war-time, let him read "The Diary of a Southern Refugee During the War," written by Mrs. Judith W. McGuire for the members of her family, "who were too young to remember those days." Mrs. McGuire's book is a wonderful record of hope, joys, sorrows and trials, and of the way in which, amid it all, the faithful women of the South cheered the hearts of the heroes in the field.[3]

One Sunday in March I preached a sermon at St. Paul's Church, (old St. Paul's, built in 1739), exhorting the people to the work before them, reminding them that in the conflict in which we were engaged, not only the rights of our people and the glory of our nation, but the Church of God was imperiled. It was my "old war sermon," rearranged for Virginia. At the solicitation of clergy and people formally presented, I repeated it several times in Norfolk. On Ash Wednesday I preached again in St. Paul's to a fine congregation and was requested to repeat my sermon, which was on the Good Samaritan, the following Sunday in the same church and subsequently in Christ Church.

I met many persons of distinction in the city. General Huger, who was in command in Norfolk, called upon me. General Howell Cobb was there as Commissioner on the part of the Confederate Government to arrange with General Wood on the part of the United States, about the exchange of prisoners.[4]

In the latter part of February, I became interested in the transformation by which the "Merrimac" became the "Virginia" of the Confederate Navy. One day I slipped off from my patient, General Loring, while he was sleeping, and went to Portsmouth to visit the wonderful craft. The

3. Mrs. McGuire's diary notes that on Sunday, February 16, 1862, she heard an "excellent sermon" by CTQ at St. Paul's Church in Richmond. "He wore the gown over the Confederate gray—" she wrote; "it was strange to see the bright military buttons gleam beneath the canonicals." Judith W. McGuire, *Diary of a Southern Refugee During the War*, 3rd ed. (Richmond: J. W. Randolph and English, 1889), 93.

4. The Confederate officers identified here are Maj. Gen. Benjamin Huger (1805–1877) and Brig. Gen. Howell Cobb (1815–1868), a Georgia politician. No Federal "General Wood" appears to have been present in the area of Norfolk or Fort Monroe during this time. Probably CTQ is referring to the venerable Maj. Gen. John Ellis Wool (1784–1869), then the Federal commander at Fortress Monroe. Ezra Warner, *Generals in Blue* (Baton Rouge: Louisiana State University Press, 1964), 573–74.

part that appeared above water suggested to me a book opened at an angle of forty-five degrees and the fore edges of its cover placed on a table. At the bow as a sharp projection by which it was expected to pierce the side of any ship it might run against.

All the machinery was below water. The roof was about thirty-eight inches in thickness, of timber very heavily plated with iron. The fore and aft guns were the heaviest, carrying shot and shell eighty-five and ninety pounds in weight. The others were very heavy also and magnificent of their kind. She carried ten guns in all. Her new steel-pointed and wrought iron shot were destined to do some terrific work. She was likely to escape injury unless struck below the water-line, and there was not much danger of that occurring as she was in a measure protected below that line also. She drew rather too much water, as Lieutenant Spotswood told me at the time of my visit.[5]

While I was at Norfolk, the great battle between the "Virginia" and the "Monitor" and ships of war "Congress" and "Cumberland" took place. I witnessed the destruction of the "Congress" and the "Cumberland." The first day's fight was on the 8th of March. By special invitation, the Rev. J. H. D. Wingfield, (who afterwards became Bishop of Northern California), celebrated the Blessed Sacrament in his church, (Trinity Church, Portsmouth), for the officers of the "Virginia" before they went into battle.[6]

When the "Virginia" cast off her moorings at Norfolk Navy Yard and steamed down the river, the "Congress" and the "Cumberland" (frigates) had been lying for some time off Newport News. Officers and men on the "Virginia" were taking things quietly as if they were really on an ordinary trial trip. As they drew near the "Congress," Captain Buchanan, the Commander of the "Virginia," made a brief and stirring appeal to his crew, which was answered by cheers.[7] He then took his place by the side of the pilot near the wheel.

5. CTQ appears to have been mistaken. No Lieutenant Spotswood is identified as a member of *Virginia's* company. *ORN*, Series 2, 1:308–11.

6. John Henry Ducachet Wingfield (1833–1898) of Virginia was ordained a priest in 1859 after a career in education. At this time he was assistant to his father, who was rector of Trinity Church in Portsmouth. Wingfield was elected missionary bishop of northern California in 1874 and stayed in that area through the end of his career, declining an appointment as bishop of Louisiana in 1879. Tyler, Lyon Gardiner, ed., *Encyclopedia of Virginia Biography*, 5 vols. (1915; reprint, Baltimore: Genealogical Publishing, 1998), s.v. "Wingfield, John Henry Ducachet."

7. Franklin Buchanan (1800–1874) of Maryland, who resigned from the United States Navy in 1861, anticipating Maryland would secede. When Maryland did not, Buchanan tried to rescind his resignation but was rebuffed. He later joined the Confederate navy and

My friend Lieutenant J. R. Eggleston commanded the nine-inch broadside guns next abaft the engine-room hatch, and he was ordered to serve one of them with hot shot.[8] Suddenly he saw a great ship near at hand bearing down upon the "Virginia." In a moment twenty-five solid shot and shell struck the sloping side of the "Virginia" and glanced high into the air, many of the shells exploding in their upward flight.

In reply to this broadside from the "Congress" one red hot shot and three nine-inch shells were hurled into her and the "Virginia" steamed on without pausing. Suddenly there was a jar as if the vessel had run aground. There was a cheering forward and Lieutenant Eggleston passed aft, waving his hat and crying: "We have sunk the 'Cumberland.'" She had been struck about amidship by the prow of the "Virginia," and in sinking tore the prow from the bow of her assailant and carried it down with her. The "Virginia" then moved some distance up the river in order to turn about in the narrow channel.

As soon as the "Congress" saw her terrible foe coming down upon her, she tried to escape under sail, but ran aground in the effort. The "Virginia" took position under her stern and a few raking shots brought down her flag. Captain Porcher, in command of the Confederate ship "Beaufort," made an effort to take the officers and wounded men of the "Congress" prisoners.[9] Two officers came on board the "Beaufort" and surrendered the "Congress." Captain Porcher asked them to get the officers and wounded men aboard his vessel as quickly as possible as he had been ordered to burn the "Congress." He was begged not to do so as there were sixty wounded men on board the "Congress," but his orders were peremptory.

While he was making every effort to move the wounded, a tremendous fire was opened on the "Beaufort" from the shore. The Federal officers begged him to hoist a white flag lest all the wounded men should be killed. The fact that the Federals were firing on a white flag flying from the mainmast of the "Congress" was brought to the attention of the Fed-

---

was both captain of the *Virginia* and commander of the Confederate fleet that unsuccessfully defended Mobile Bay in 1864. William C. Davis, *Duel between the First Ironclads*, (Garden City, N.Y.: Doubleday, 1975) 39–40.

8. Lt. (later Capt.) John R. Eggleston later published an account of the battle between the ironclads. J. R. Eggleston, "Captain Eggleston's Narrative of the Battle of the Merrimac," *SHSP* 41 (1916):166.

9. CTQ is mistaken. The commander of *Beaufort* was Lt. William H. Parker. *ORN*, Series 1, 7:44–45.

eral officers, who claimed, however, that they were powerless to stop the fire as it proceeded from a lot of volunteers who were not under the control of the officers on the "Beaufort." The fire continuing, Captain Porcher returned it, but with little effect. He estimated the loss in the Federal fleet, in killed, drowned, wounded and missing, of nearly four hundred men. The total loss of Confederates did not exceed sixty. Captain Buchanan and his flag-lieutenant were wounded and taken to the Naval Hospital at Norfolk. Catesby Jones succeeded to the command of the "Virginia."[10] About an hour before midnight the fire reached the magazine of the "Congress" and she blew up.

The next day the "Virginia" steamed out towards the "Minnesota," when the "Monitor" made her appearance.[11] The latter came gallantly forward, and then began the first battle ever fought between ironclads. It continued for several hours, neither vessel, so far as could be ascertained at the time, inflicting by her fire any very serious damage on the other.

The "Virginia" then got ready to try what ramming would do for the "Monitor." What it did was to silence the latter forever in the presence of the "Virginia." Unfortunately, just before the "Virginia" struck the "Monitor," the former stopped her engine under the belief that the momentum of the ship would prove sufficient for the work. Had the "Virginia" kept at full speed, she would undoubtedly have run the "Monitor" under. As it was, the latter got such a shaking up that she sought safety in shoal water whither she knew the "Virginia" could not follow her. It should be remembered that the "Virginia" drew twenty-two feet of water and was very hard to manage, whereas the "Monitor" was readily managed and drew but ten feet of water.

The following day the Rev. Mr. Wingfield was called upon to offer up prayers and thanksgiving for the victory, on board the gallant ship. It was a solemn, most impressive and affecting scene, as those valiant men of war fell upon their knees on the deck and bowed their heads in reverence and godly fear. The weather-beaten faces of many of the brave seamen

10. Lt. Catesby ap Roger Jones (1821–1877) also wrote an account of his experiences on *Virginia.* Catesby ap R. Jones, "Services of the *Virginia (Merrimac),*" *SHSP* 11 (February–March, 1883): 65. The odd name "ap" was a Welsh idiom meaning "son of." Davis, *Duel between the First Ironclads,* 30.

11. The dramatic arrival of the *Monitor* saved the wooden-hulled Federal fleet at Hampton Roads. Ironically, CTQ's brother George William Quintard was in the shipping business and appears to have been involved in the construction of the *Monitor.* Quintard Genealogy File, Quintard Papers, U of S.

were observed to be bathed in tears and trembling with emotion under the influence of that memorable service.

After this Commodore Tattnall was placed in command of the "Virginia," and on the morning of the 11th of April the "Virginia" went down Hampton Roads with the design of engaging the enemy to the fullest extent. I received a concise cypher telegram, ("Splinters," was all it said), from my dear friend John Tattnall, son of the Commodore, and I at once set out to see what was going on. With General Loring, (who was by that time fully recovered from his illness), and quite a party of friends and officers, I went down the bay in a cockle-shell of a steamer, to witness the engagement. In order to provoke the enemy, Commodore Tattnall ordered two of his gunboats to run into the transport anchorage and cut out such of the vessels as were lying nearest the "Virginia." This was successfully done within sight of and almost within gun-shot of the "Monitor," but she could not be drawn into an engagement. Although the enemy refused to fight, the "Monitor" threw a number of shells, several of which passed over our little steamer. We deemed it, therefore, good military, (and naval) tactics to withdraw and let the contestants attend to their own business.

CHAPTER V

Personal Narrative—Perryville

Hearing about this time of the extreme illness of my Bishop, the Right
Reverend James Hervey Otey, in Jackson, Mississippi, I left Norfolk, with
considerable regret, for the society of that city I had found most charming,
and my stay there had been very pleasant. I went by way of Mobile, having
for my traveling companion from Montgomery, Alabama, to that city,
Captain J. F. Lay, a brother of the then Bishop of Arkansas. The Captain
was a member of Beauregard's staff.[1]

General Forney was in command at Mobile and I had a very pleasant
chat with him. His left arm was almost useless from a severe wound received in the Dranesville fight.[2] I met also the Rev. Mr. Pierce, who afterwards became Bishop of Arkansas; and Madame Le Vert, one of the most

1. John F. Lay was assistant adjutant general on the staff of Gen. Pierre Gustave Tou-
tant Beauregard (1818–1893) of Louisiana. Beauregard assumed command of the Confederate Army of the Mississippi on April 6, 1862, on the battlefield of Shiloh, after the death
of Gen. Albert Sidney Johnston. In June 1862, Beauregard took an unauthorized leave of
absence on a surgeon's certificate and was replaced by Gen. Braxton Bragg. See OR
17(2):601, 614.

2. Brig. Gen. (later Maj. Gen.) John Horace Forney (1829–1902). On December 20,
1861, at Dranesville, Virginia, 1,750 Confederates under Brig. Gen. J. E. B. Stuart unexpectedly encountered a Federal force of approximately 4,000 under Brig. Gen. E. O. C.
Ord, with the Federals getting the advantage. Emory M. Thomas, *Bold Dragoon: The Life
of J. E. B. Stuart* (New York: Harper & Row, 1986), 97–99.

distinguished of Southern writers.[3] I had a drive down the bay over one of the finest shell roads in the world. And on the Sunday that I spent in Mobile, I preached my "war sermon," — adapted, of course, to the people of Mobile.

I found my beloved Bishop at the residence of Mrs. George Yerger, in Jackson, and remained in attendance on him for several weeks. He was then removed from Jackson to the residence of Mrs. Johnstone at Annandale.[4] There he enjoyed all that kindness and wealth could give. He was able to drive out after a time, and I remember how thoroughly he enjoyed the music of the spring birds. There was one bird that he called the "wood-robin," whose notes were especially enjoyed, and the carriage was frequently stopped that he might listen to the warbling of this bird.[5]

From Annandale I went to visit my family in Rome, Georgia, and spent some time in attendance upon the hospitals there. Then I returned to General Loring's headquarters for a brief visit to the General to whom I was warmly attached, and to make farewell visits to sundry officers and bid my old military companions a final adieu. For my intention it then was to leave the army.

General Loring's headquarters were at New River, Virginia, at a place called the Narrows, because the river gashed through Peter's Mountain, which rises abruptly from the banks on either side.[6] The General and all the staff gave me a most cordial greeting, but the former told me that I had no business to resign and that he had kept the place open for me. If I would not be his aide he had a place for me as chaplain. But my resigna-

3. Rev. Henry Niles Pierce (1820–1899), consecrated as bishop in 1870. Fay Hempstead, *Historical Review of Arkansas: Its Commerce, Industry, and Modern Affairs*, 3 vols. (1911; reprint, Easley, S.C.: Southern Historical Press, 1978), 3:1196. Octavia Walton LeVert (1810–1877) wrote *Souvenirs of Travel* (1857), an account of her experiences during two trips to Europe in the 1850's. Lina Mainiero, ed., *American Women Writers: A Critical Reference Guide from Colonial Times to the Present*, 5 vols. (New York: Frederick Ungar, 1979–1994), 2:565–67.

4. Sally M. Yerger is identified in the 1860 federal census for Hinds County, Mississippi, as age 49 and as having a substantial estate. Mrs. Johnstone cannot be identified.

5. CTQ wrote a friend that Otey "will probably rally from his present attack — but never recover. His *active* life as Bp. of Tenn. is over. Where will we look for his successor?" CTQ to ———, May 31, 1862, CTQ CSR, Confederate General and Staff Officers, RG 109, M-331, NA.

6. Loring was assigned to command the new Department of Southwestern Virginia. James W. Raab, *W. W. Loring: Florida's Forgotten General* (Manhattan, Kans.: Sunflower University Press, 1996), 67–69.

tion had already been accepted on the 14th of June by the Secretary of War. As soon as I had determined to resign, I forwarded to the Secretary of War a copy of my resignation to General Loring and the former had accepted it.[7]

The General, Colonel Myer, Colonel Fitzhugh and myself, with a cavalry escort, went for a little outing to the Salt Sulphur Springs, dining on our way at the Gray Sulphur Springs.[8] The former place was really one of the pleasantest of all the watering places I visited in Virginia. The grounds were rolling, well laid out and very well shaded. The houses were principally of stone and capable of accommodating about four hundred guests.

There were two springs of great value there, the Salt Sulphur and the Iodine. The first possessed all the sensible properties of sulphur water in general; its odor, for instance, was very like that of a "tolerable egg," and might be perceived at some distance from the Spring; and in taste it was cousin-german[9] to a strong solution of Epsom salts and magnesia. Like most of the sulphurous, this water was transparent and deposited a whitish sediment composed of its various saline ingredients mingled with sulphur.

The Iodine Spring was altogether remarkable and was the only one possessing similar properties in all the country round. It was peculiarly adapted to cutaneous eruptions[10] and glandular diseases. The Salt Sulphur Spring was hemmed in on every side by mountains.

General William Wing Loring, of whom I was then taking my leave, was not only a very charming companion but he was altogether a remarkable man. A braver man never lived. He was a North Carolinian by birth, and only a few years older than myself. Yet he was already the hero of three wars—the Seminole War, the War with Mexico and that in which

7. The space of over thirty years seems to have disrupted CTQ's recollection of this sequence of events. CTQ's letter to Secretary of War George Wythe Randolph resigning his commission as a lieutenant on Loring's staff was written from Annandale on May 31, and in that letter he also asked that he be returned his commission as a chaplain. CTQ felt "that my services can be much more efficient as a Chaplain." CTQ to George W. Randolph, May 31, 1862, CTQ CSR, Confederate General and Staff Officers, RG 109, M-331, NA.

8. "Colonel Myer" is more accurately Maj. William B. Myers, who, along with Col. Henry H. Fitzhugh, was Loring's assistant adjutant general. Crute, *Confederate Staff Officers*, 125.

9. First cousin.

10. Skin eruptions.

we were then engaged. And in 1849 he had marched across the continent to Oregon with some United States troops as an escort for a party of gold-seekers. He had also engaged in Indian warfare and had taken part in the Utah Expedition in 1858. His frontier services in the United States Army were equaled only by those of that grand soldier, Albert Sidney Johnston. The following year, he had leave of absence from the army and visited Europe, Egypt and the Holy Land. He was in command of the Department of New Mexico in May 1861 and resigned to accept a commission as a Brigadier-General in the Confederate Army.

As Major-General he served to the end of the war, leading a Division and frequently commanding a corps—always with credit to himself and to the service in which he was engaged.[11] It was at Vicksburg, in 1863, that he received the familiar nickname of "Old Blizzard." After the war he took service with the Khedive of Egypt as General of Brigade and was decorated in 1875 with the "Imperial Order of Osmariah," and was promoted to be General of a Division. Four years later he was mustered out of the Egyptian service. In 1883 he published "A Confederate Soldier in Egypt,"—a most readable book. He died in New York city three years later at the age of sixty-eight.

I officiated at his funeral in St. Augustine, Florida, on the 19th of March, 1886. The commanding General of the Army post at St. Augustine acted as one of the pall-bearers, and at the cemetery the body was borne from the gun-carriage to the grave by three Federal and three ex-Confederate soldiers. A salute was fired at the grave by a battery of United States Artillery.

I had looked toward the Diocese of Alabama for some parochial work,

11. Some would debate CTQ's evaluation of Loring, especially insofar as his performance at the Battle of Champion Hill (May 16, 1863), when Loring's division was cut off from the rest of the Confederate army. Loring commanded a corps in the Army of Tennessee in the interval between Leonidas Polk's death on June 14, 1864, and Alexander P. Stewart's assumption of command on July 7, 1864. Loring competently led the corps during the Battle of Kennesaw Mountain (June 27, 1864) and expected permanent command of the corps. See Raab, *Florida's Forgotten General*, 158–60. It does not appear Loring got any serious consideration in Richmond. In response to a request by President Davis for a recommendation for the vacant corps command, Robert E. Lee stated: "I should think [the corps] would require a commander at once as I understand Genl Loring is the Senior present." R. E. Lee to Jefferson Davis, June 21, 1864, in Douglas S. Freeman, ed., *Lee's Dispatches: Unpublished Letters of General Robert E. Lee, C.S.A., to Jefferson Davis and the War Department of the Confederate States of America, 1862–65*, new ed., with additional dispatches and foreword by Grady McWhiney (New York: Putnam, 1957) 256–57.

but the Bishop of Alabama, the Rt. Rev. Dr. Wilmer, not only could offer me no work in his jurisdiction, but strongly advised me to go back to the army as chaplain and surgeon, assuring me that there was work for me in that capacity.[12] In June, I had a petition from my old regiment to rejoin it.[13] I had no difficulty in getting a chaplain's commission. General Loring wrote me a strong letter, and that, with the aid of a telegram from General (and Bishop) Polk, secured it.[14] So I returned to the Army of Tennessee at Chattanooga, and was enthusiastically received by the officers and members of my regiment; and especially General Polk and his staff, upon which I found my dear friends Colonel Harry Yeatman, Colonel William B. Richmond and Colonel William D. Gale.[15]

In August 1862 we advanced into Kentucky, crossing over Walden's Ridge and the Cumberland Mountains by way of Pikeville and Sparta, Tennessee. My first intention was to leave Chattanooga with General Polk and his staff, but on finding that Dr. Buist was going alone, I concluded to accompany him. So we two started off at 10 A.M. on the 28th of August,

12. Rt. Rev. Richard Hooker Wilmer (1816–1900) was the only Episcopal bishop consecrated by the Confederate church. The ratification of his consecration by the reunited national church in 1865 was seen as a sign of reunion. Chitty, *Reconstruction at Sewanee*, 87. In light of CTQ's letter of May 31 to Randolph (see note 7 in this chapter), his discussion with Wilmer obviously occurred before that date.

13. CTQ's papers at Duke University include four petitions, three bearing the date of June 27, 1862, from Companies B, C, G, and H. Company H's document bears the signature of future author Sam R. Watkins. Petitions to CTQ, June 27, 1862, Quintard Papers, DU. On August 10, 1862, a newspaper reporter noted CTQ's presence in Chattanooga and observed that there would be "great rejoicing" on his return to his regiment and that "No one has been more self-sacrificing in his efforts to be useful, and no one is more universally beloved in that portion of the army with which he has been connected. The services of such a man are invaluable to the country." *Chattanooga Daily Rebel*, August 10, 1862.

14. Maj. Gen. (soon to be Lt. Gen.) Leonidas Polk (1806–1864), Confederate general and Episcopal bishop of Louisiana. CTQ's resignation from Loring's staff was accepted June 14, 1862, and his reappointment as chaplain occurred on July 28, 1862, to rank from June 14. CTQ CSR, Confederate General and Staff Officers, RG 109, M-331, NA.

15. The reference to the Army of Tennessee is anachronistic. The army CTQ joined was the Army of the Mississippi, which was not renamed the Army of Tennessee until November, 1862. Stanley F. Horn, *The Army of Tennessee: A Military History* (1941; reprint, Wilmington, N.C.: Broadfoot Publishing, 1987), 192. Lt. Col. Henry C. Yeatman was the stepson of 1860 presidential candidate John Bell and was Leonidas' brother Lucius Polk's son-in-law. William D. Richmond only attained the rank of lieutenant. William D. Gale was Leonidas Polk's son-in-law and, at this time, only a voluntary aide. Joseph H. Parks, *General Leonidas Polk, C.S.A.: The Fighting Bishop* (Baton Rouge: Louisiana State University Press, 1962), 307; Crute, *Confederate Staff Officers*, 154–56.

and following the route of our immense wagon train, which stretched out for miles along the road, we supposed we were all right and knew nothing to the contrary until we reached the top of Walden's Ridge where we found General Bragg, General Buckner and Governor Harris.[16] The Governor put us right as to our way and we had a long ride back to get into the road taken by our Brigade, which was quite different from that taken by the wagon train.

We rode until after four o'clock in the afternoon, and then stopped at a house that was crowded with soldiers and refugees. We had a bed made on the floor for us and, with many others, slept well until 1 A.M., when we started on, and after a couple of hours learned that the army had halted. We rode into camp, about thirty miles from Chattanooga, at dinner time with ravenous appetites. We were having pretty good living just then, for the country was admirably watered. A great many country women visited our camp to hear our band play.

We continued our march to Mumfordville, Kentucky, where the Louisville and Nashville Railroad crosses Green River. There on the 16th of September, with a loss of fifty killed and wounded, we captured some four thousand prisoners with as many guns and much ammunition, besides killing and wounding seven hundred of the enemy. The Federal forces were commanded by General Wilder, since the war a most prominent citizen of Chattanooga, for whom I entertain the heartiest and most cordial regard.[17] General Chalmers, one of General Bragg's brigadiers, was conspicuous in this fight for the gallantry and skill with which he handled his troops.[18] When the Federal forces surrendered on the 17th, I stood beside the road and saw them lay down their arms. Though there were but four thousand, I thought as they passed by me that the whole Federal Army had surrendered to General Bragg. The night following this battle I found a sleeping place in a graveyard.[19]

16. Gen. Braxton Bragg (1817–1876) of North Carolina and Louisiana commanded the Army of the Mississippi, soon to be renamed the Army of Tennessee. Maj. Gen. Simon Bolivar Buckner (1823–1914) of Kentucky commanded a division in the army. Isham Green Harris (1818–1897) was Governor of Tennessee.

17. Colonel John T. Wilder (1830–1917) of New York and Ohio, who later commanded the Spencer repeating rifle–armed "Lightning Brigade" of the Federal Army of the Cumberland.

18. Brig. Gen. James Ronald Chalmers (1831–1898) of Mississippi.

19. Among those CTQ shared the graveyard with that night was Pvt. Sam Watkins, who rode CTQ's horse much of the next day. Watkins, "Co. Aytch" 61.

On the 23rd of September we reached Bardstown, Kentucky, and took possession. In the meantime General Buell, leaving a strong guard at Nashville, marched to Louisville where his army was increased to fully one hundred thousand men.[20] It was not until October and after he had reorganized his army and was in danger of being superseded in the command thereof that he began his campaign against General Bragg's forces. The latter had collected an immense train, mostly of Federal army wagons loaded with supplies. And it being clear that the two great objects of our invasion of Kentucky—the evacuation of Nashville and the inducement of Kentucky to join the Confederacy—would fail, Bragg decided only to gain time to effect a retreat with his spoils. He harassed the advance of Buell on Bardstown and Springfield, retired to Danville and thence marched to Harrodsburg to effect a juncture with General Kirby-Smith.[21]

On the 7th of October he moved to Perryville, where on Wednesday, the 8th, a battle was fought between a portion of Bragg's army and Buell's advance, commanded by General McCook.[22] At this battle of Perryville our regiment captured from the Federals four twelve-pounder Napoleon brass guns, which were afterwards, by special order, presented to the battery of Maney's Brigade.

The night before the battle I shared blankets in a barnyard with General Leonidas Polk, Bishop of Louisiana. The battle began at break of day by an artillery duel, the Federal battery being commanded by Colonel Charles Carroll Parsons and the Confederates by Captain William W. Carnes. Colonel Parsons was a graduate of West Point and Captain Carnes was a graduate of the Naval Academy at Annapolis. I took position upon an eminence at no great distance, commanding a fine view of the engagement, and there I watched the progress of the battle until duty called me elsewhere.

20. Maj. Gen. Don Carlos Buell (1818–1898) of Ohio, commanding the Federal Army of the Ohio.

21. Maj. Gen. Edmund Kirby Smith (1824–1893) of Florida, commanding the Confederate Department of East Tennessee, led a column of approximately twelve thousand men, which he designated the Army of Kentucky. Bragg expected Kirby Smith to cooperate with his operations in Kentucky, but was largely disappointed. See Thomas L. Connelly, *Army of the Heartland* (Baton Rouge: Louisiana State University Press, 1967) 235–37, 254–56, 261.

22. Maj. Gen. Alexander McDowell McCook (1831–1903) of Ohio, commanding the 1st Corps of Buell's Army of the Ohio.

Captain Carnes managed his battery with the greatest skill, killing and wounding nearly all the officers, men and horses connected with Parsons' battery. Parsons fought with great bravery and coolness and continued fighting a single gun until the Confederate infantry advanced. The officer in command ordered Colonel Parsons to be shot down. As the muskets were leveled at him, he drew his sword and stood at "parade rest," ready to receive the fire. The Confederate Colonel was so impressed with this display of calm courage that he ordered the guns lowered, saying: "No! you shall not shoot down such a brave man!" And Colonel Parsons was allowed to walk off the field.

Subsequently I captured Colonel Parsons for the ministry of the Church in the Diocese of Tennessee. He was brevetted for his bravery at Perryville and he performed other feats of bravery in the war. At Murfreesboro he repelled six charges, much of the time under musketry fire. He was often mentioned in official reports of battles. After the war he was on frontier duty until 1868 when he returned to West Point as a Professor. Shortly after my consecration as Bishop of Tennessee, I preached in the Church of the Holy Trinity, Brooklyn, New York, on "Repentance and the Divine Life." This sermon made a deep impression upon Colonel Parsons, as he told me when I subsequently met him at a reception at the residence of the Hon. Hamilton Fish.[23]

I visited him twice at West Point by his invitation, and a correspondence sprang up between us. In 1870 he resigned his commission in the army to enter the ministry. He studied theology with me at Memphis, and it was my privilege to ordain him to the diaconate and advance him to the priesthood. His first work was at Memphis. Then for a while he was at Cold Spring, New York. He returned, however, to Memphis and became rector of a parish of which Mr. Jefferson Davis was a member and a vestryman. He remained heroically at his post of duty during the great epidemic of yellow fever in 1878. He was stricken with the fever and died at my Episcopal residence on the 6th of September.[24] Captain Carnes

23. Probably the elder Hamilton Fish (1808–1893) of New York, prewar United States Senator and United States Secretary of State, 1869–1877, and a prominent Episcopalian layman.

24. A lieutenant who received brevet promotions during the war to captain and lieutenant colonel, Parsons went on to fight with his command (Batteries H and M, Fourth U. S. Artillery) in the crucial struggle for the Round Forest at Murfreesboro. See OR 20(1):523. During the latter part of the war, however, he saw little action on account of poor health. CTQ indeed seems to have influenced Parsons into the priesthood, as Parsons wrote the bishop in 1870: "It gives me sincere satisfaction to tell you that I believe God has blessed your good counsel." Parsons also experienced wide variety in his friends, being

was the first man I confirmed after my consecration to the Episcopate of Tennessee.[25]

With the advance of Cheatham's division the battle of Perryville began in good earnest. General Cheatham was supported by General Cleburne and General Bushrod Johnson, but it was not long before the whole Confederate line from right to left was advancing steadily, driving back the enemy.[26] It was a fierce struggle. Until nightfall the battle raged with unexampled fury,—a perfect hurricane of shell tore up the earth and scattered death on all sides, while the storm of musketry mowed down the opposing ranks. Maney's Brigade did the most brilliant fighting of the day. It was in the charge by which the Federal Battery was captured that Major-General Jackson of the Federal Army was killed.[27]

It was shortly after noon that the battle began with a sudden crash followed by a prolonged roar. I was resting at the time in the woods, discussing questions of theology with the Rev. Dr. Joseph Cross, a Wesleyan chaplain whom I had first met on the march into Kentucky.[28] I sprang to my horse at once and said to him: "Let us go! There will be work enough for us presently!" He mounted his horse and followed me up a hill where

close to his 1861 United States Military Academy classmate George Armstrong Custer. John Henry Davis, "Two Martyrs of the Yellow Fever Epidemic of 1878," *West Tennessee Historical Society Papers* 26 (1972): 20–36.

25. Like Parsons, Carnes left the field artillery in the middle of the war. Having seen very hard fighting at Chickamauga, he transferred to the Confederate navy after the retreat from Chattanooga. Carnes lived in Macon, Georgia, for a period of years after the war. Later, like Parsons, Carnes enjoyed the esteem of the citizens of Memphis, where he enjoyed a life of business and politics. Upon retirement, he moved to Bradenton, Florida, but grew restless and started an insurance business in old age. *CMH* 10:395–97; "Capt. W. W. Carnes—A Worker," *CV* 31 (June 1923): 205.

26. The officers named were Maj. Gen. Benjamin Franklin Cheatham (1820–1886) of Tennessee, commanding a division in Polk's Corps; Brig. Gen. (later Maj. Gen.) Patrick Ronayne Cleburne (1828–1864) of Ireland and Arkansas, commanding a division in Hardee's Corps, and Brig. Gen. (later Maj. Gen.) Bushrod Rust Johnson (1817–1880) of Ohio and Tennessee, commanding a brigade in Buckner's Division.

27. Brig. Gen. James Streshly Jackson (1823–1862) of Kentucky, commanding the Army of the Ohio's 10th Division.

28. Affiliated with the Methodist Episcopal Church, Joseph Cross was born in England on July 4, 1813, landed in America on July 4, 1824, joined the church on July 4, 1826, preached his first sermon on July 4, 1829, was married on July 4, 1834, and was commissioned chaplain of the 2nd Tennessee Regiment on July 4, 1861. Thomas A. Head, *Campaigns and Battles of the Sixteenth Regiment, Tennessee Volunteers* (1885; reprint, McMinnville, Tenn.: Womack Printing, 1961) 385–87.

we paused in full view of the enemy's line. I dismounted and sat down in the shelter of a large tree, saying as I did so: "You better get off your horse! The enemy is training a battery this way and there will be a shell here in a short time!"

Scarcely were the warning words uttered than a shell struck the tree twenty feet above my head and a shower of wooden splinters fell about me. I jumped into my saddle again and rode at full speed down the hill, followed by my friend, who shouted with laughter at what he called my resemblance to an enormous bird in flight, with my long coat-skirts like wings lying horizontal on the air. When he overtook me at the creek, I said to him: "This is the place. You will remain with me and I shall give you something more serious to do than laughing at a flying buzzard." Dr. Cross assisted me that fearful day. We met many times subsequently during the war and afterwards, I ordained him deacon and priest, and he was for a time on my staff of clergy in the Diocese of Tennessee.

When the wounded were brought to the rear, at three o'clock in the afternoon, I took my place as a surgeon on Chaplain's Creek, and throughout the rest of the day and until half past five the next morning, without food of any sort, I was incessantly occupied with the wounded. It was a horrible night I spent, — God save me from such another. I suppose excitement kept me up. About half past five in the morning of the 9th, I dropped, — I could do no more. I went out by myself and leaning against a fence, I wept like a child. And all that day I was so unnerved that if any one asked me about the regiment, I could make no reply without tears. Having taken off my shirt to tear into strips to make bandages, I took a severe cold.

The total loss of the Confederates, (whose force numbered of all arms only 16,000), was 510 killed, 2635 wounded and 251 captured or missing, and of this loss a great part was sustained by our regiment. How well I remember the wounded men! One of the Rock City Guard, brought to me mortally wounded, cried out: "Oh, Doctor, I have been praying ever since I was shot that I might be brought to you." One of the captains was wounded mortally, it was thought at first, but it was afterwards learned that the ball which struck him in the side, instead of passing through his body, had passed around under the integuments.[29] Lieutenant Woolridge had both eyes shot out and still lives.[30] A stripling of fifteen years fell in

29. The skin.
30. "Lieutenant Woolridge" was John H. Woldridge of Company K. Toney, *Privations of a Private*, 45.

the battle apparently dead, shot through the neck and collar-bone, but is still living. Lieutenant-Colonel Patterson was killed at his side.[31] The latter was wounded in the arm early in the action. He bound his handkerchief around his arm and in the most gallant and dashing style urged his men forward until a grape shot struck him in the face killing him instantly.

Two days after the battle I went to the enemy's line with a flag of truce. And the following day General Polk, (who had won the hearts of the whole army), asked me to go with him to the church in Harrodsburg. I obtained the key and as we entered the holy house, I think that we both felt that we were in the presence of God. General Polk threw his arms about my neck and said: "Oh for the blessed days when we walked in the house of God as friends! Let us have prayer!"

I vested myself with surplice and stole and entered the sanctuary. The General knelt at the altar railing. I said the Litany, used proper prayers and supplications, and then turned to the dear Bishop and General and pronounced the benediction from the office for the visitation of the sick. "Unto God's gracious mercy and protection I commit thee. The Lord bless thee and keep thee. The Lord make His face to shine upon thee and be gracious unto thee. The Lord lift up the light of His countenance upon thee and give thee peace, both now and evermore. Amen."

The Bishop bowed his head upon the railing and wept like a child on its mother's breast. Shortly after this service, General Kirby-Smith begged me that he might go to the church with me, so I returned, and he too was refreshed at God's altar.

General Kirby-Smith was a most remarkable character. A few years later it was my pleasure to have him as one of my neighbors at Sewanee, Tennessee, where he did much towards making the University of the South what it is. He was kindly, big-hearted, and no man was a better friend. He was a very devoted communicant of the church, and during the war, whenever opportunity offered, he held services and officiated as lay-reader. In an epidemic of cholera at Nashville, some years after the war, he was called upon to say the burial office over his own rector who had died of the dread disease. He entered upon his duties in the University of the South in 1875, as Professor of Mathematics and gave a great deal of attention to botany and natural science.

31. Lt. Col. John Patterson of the 1st Tennessee. Lindsley, *Military Annals*, 159.

His end on the 28th of March, 1893, was very peaceful. He died as he had lived—bright, strong in his Christian faith and hope. One of his last connected utterances was on the fourth verse from the twenty-third Psalm. On Good Friday, the 31st of March, 1893, it was my high privilege to commit his body to the earth in the cemetery at Sewanee.

CHAPTER VI

Personal Narrative—Murfreesboro

After the battle of Perryville, both Bragg and Kirby-Smith were compelled to retreat by way of Cumberland Gap to Chattanooga. During this retreat I was in charge of the regiment as surgeon, Dr. Buist having been left behind to care for our sick and wounded. Every morning I filled my canteen with whiskey and strapped it to the pommel of my saddle to help the wearied and broken down to keep up in the march. I was riding a splendid bay which had been brought from Maury County and presented to me by members of the regiment. He was the best saddle horse I ever rode. One day the colonel commanding the regiment rode up to me on his old gray nag and said: "Doctor, this horse of mine is very rough. Would you mind exchanging with me for a little while?"

I was off my horse before he had finished speaking. With a smiling countenance and a look of great gratitude he mounted my bay and rode off some hundred yards or more to the front, accompanied by the lieutenant-colonel, the major and one or two other officers—when they wheeled and saluted me, the colonel holding aloft my canteen of whiskey and waving it with great glee, each one taking a drink. When that canteen was returned to me every drop of the whiskey had disappeared. I was an "innocent abroad."[1]

1. The colonel of the 1st Tennessee at this time was Hume R. Feild.

From Chattanooga I went to Rome, Georgia, to visit my family and to obtain some fresh clothing of which I was sorely in need. There were many hospitals established there and among them was one named for me, "Quintard Hospital." I spent much of my time in the hospitals, and also went to Columbus, Georgia, to secure clothing for my regiment.[2] Mr. Rhodes Brown, President of one of the principal woolen mills in Columbus, gave me abundant supplies of the very best material.[3] Besides this generous donation, he gave me a thousand dollars to use as I saw fit.

After some weeks I rejoined the army which had moved on to Murfreesboro. On my way up, I met at Stevenson, Alabama, Captain Jack Butler of my regiment, who informed me that a telegraphic dispatch from General Polk had just passed over the line ordering me to Murfreesboro. I asked how he knew it, and he told me that he had caught it as it clicked over the wire, which seemed very wonderful to me then. Immediately on reaching Murfreesboro I reported to General Polk and said: "General, I am here in response to your telegram." He was greatly astonished and asked how it was possible for me to have made the journey from Rome, Georgia, in so brief a time.

General Bragg, who was in command at Murfreesboro, was attacked by Rosecrans on the last day of the year 1862. A great battle resulted and the fighting continued until the 2d day of January, 1863. I was on the field dressing the wounded, as usual, when an order came for me to repair to the hospitals. While crossing the fields on my way to the hospitals in town, a tremendous shell came flying towards me, and I felt sure it would strike me in the epigastric region. I leaned down over the pommel of my saddle and the shell passed far above my head. As I rose to an upright position, I found that my watchguard had been broken and that a gold cross which had been suspended from it, was lost. I never expected to see it again. The next day, a colonel, moving with his command at "double quick" in line of battle, picked up the cross and returned it to me the day following. It is still in my possession—a valued relic of the Battle of Murfreesboro.

As Dr. Buist was still in Perryville, Kentucky, I was practically surgeon of the regiment. As the wounded of the First Tennessee were brought in,

2. During this time, CTQ was noted in his service record and on the 1st Tennessee's rolls as being on detached service at hospitals as Chaplain. CTQ CSR, Confederate Soldiers Who Served in Organizations from the State of Tennessee, RG 109, M-268, NA; CTQ CSR, Confederate General and Staff Officers, RG 109, M-331, NA.

3. In the 1860 federal census for Muscogee County, Georgia, Brown, originally of Massachusetts, is listed as a factory agent.

they always called for me, and it was my high privilege to attend to nearly, if not quite all, the wounded of my regiment. Some of them were desperately wounded; among these was Bryant House, nicknamed among the boys, who were artists at bestowing nicknames, "Shanty." He had been shot through the body. The surgeon into whose hands he had first fallen told him that it was impossible to extract the ball and that there was no hope for him.[4] "Well, send for my chaplain," he said, doubtless thinking that I would offer up a prayer in his behalf. Instead of that, however, I went in search of the ball with my surgical instruments, and was successful. "Shanty" died in September, 1895. He was for years after the war a conductor on the Nashville, Chattanooga and St. Louis Railway, and took great delight in telling this story.

I continued at work in the hospital located in Soule College[5] until the army was about to fall back to Shelbyville, when I was sent for by General Polk, who asked if I would go to Chattanooga in charge of Willie Huger, whose leg had been amputated at the thigh. He was placed in a box car with a number of other wounded men and I held the stump of his thigh in my hands most of the journey. When we reached Chattanooga I was more exhausted than my patient. I remained with him for some time. The dear fellow finally recovered, married a daughter of General Polk, and now resides in New Orleans.[6]

General James E. Raines, a member of my parish in Nashville, fell while gallantly leading his men at the battle of Murfreesboro. General Hanson of Kentucky, likewise gave up his life. His last words were: "I am willing to die with such a wound in so glorious a cause!" Here it was that

4. A private in the 1st Tennessee, House wrote that he was told that the surgeons "had better devote their attention to some one less hurt than I was that would be some use to the Confederacy as I could not last long wounded in the hip." In writing his memoirs, CTQ corresponded with a number of coparticipants such as House for assistance with various details. Thomas B. House to CTQ, July 4, 1895, Quintard Papers, DU.

5. Chartered in 1854, Soule Female College was affiliated with the Methodist Episcopal Church and was used at various times during the war as a Confederate and Federal hospital. John C. Spence, *Annals of Rutherford County*, 2 vols. (Nashville: Williams Printing, 1991), 2:102–5.

6. William E. Huger married Elizabeth Polk a few weeks prior to General Polk's death on June 14, 1864. Parks, *General Leonidas Polk*, 381. At some point during the week after the battle, CTQ spent some time with Brig. Gen. John Hunt Morgan and his new bride, Mattie Ready Morgan. CTQ to Catherine H. Quintard, January 7, 1863, Quintard Papers, DU.

Colonel Marks, afterward Governor of Tennessee, was severely wounded and lamed for life.[7]

After the first day's fight, General Bragg sent a telegram to Richmond in the following words: "God has indeed granted us a happy New Year." But subsequently hearing that Rosecrans was being heavily reinforced from Nashville, he retired to Shelbyville, carrying with him his prisoners and the spoils of battle, for the Confederates captured and carried off 30 cannon, 6,000 small arms, and over 6,000 prisoners, including those captured by cavalry in the rear of the Union army. Wheeler's cavalry also captured and burned 800 wagons.[8]

7. The officers referred to were Brig. Gen. James Edwards Rains (1833–1862); Brig. Gen. Roger Weightman Hanson (1827–1863), commander of the famed "Orphan Brigade"; and Col. Albert S. Marks (1836–1891) of the 17th Tennessee, Governor of Tennessee from 1879 to 1881.

8. These numbers appear to be derived from Bragg's report of the battle. See OR 20(1):669. CTQ seems to be putting the best possible spin on a Confederate defeat.

Personal Narrative—Shelbyville

Having placed Willie Huger in comfortable quarters in Chattanooga and watched over him as long as I was able to, I returned to the army.[1] At Shelbyville, I found General Polk's headquarters occupying the grounds of William Gosling, Esquire.[2] The Gosling family were old friends of mine and insisted upon my making their house my home. General Polk had his office in the house. Mrs. Gosling was an ideal housekeeper and made me feel in every respect at home.

We remained nearly six months in Shelbyville, most of the army being camped about Tullahoma. Soon after the Battle of Murfreesboro, General

1. CTQ apparently was not in Chattanooga very long. On January 7, he wrote Catherine that he had just had a visit with Brig. Gen. John Hunt Morgan and his wife, Morgan having just returned from a raid. CTQ to Catherine B. Quintard, January 7, 1863, Quintard Papers, DU. The raid ranged into Kentucky and extended from December 22, 1862 to January 2, 1863. Morgan wrote: "The results of the expedition may be summed up as follows: The destruction of the Louisville and Nashville Railroad from Munfordville to Shepherdsville, within 18 miles of Louisville, rendering it impassable for at least two months; the capture of 1,877 prisoners, including 62 commissioned officers; the destruction of over $2,000,000 of United States property, and a large loss to the enemy in killed and wounded." OR 20(1):154–58.

2. The 1860 Federal census for Bedford County, Tennessee, lists Gosling, a native Englishman, as a "factoryist."

Bragg was removed from the command of the Army of the Tennessee and General Johnston was sent to Shelbyville.[3]

On the 7th of February, 1863, we had a grand review by General Johnston, who rode my horse—to me the most interesting item of the review.[4] For I had seen so much of marching and countermarching that I was tired of it all—thoroughly disgusted indeed. It was a brilliant pageant, nevertheless. The troops looked and marched well, and General Johnston expressed the greatest satisfaction with what he witnessed. He said he had never seen men he would rather trust.

I found General Johnston a charming man. I was constantly with him at General Polk's headquarters and enjoyed his visit to the army very much. He was of perfectly simple manners, of easy and graceful carriage and a good conversationalist. He had used his utmost endeavor to keep General Bragg in command of the Army of the Tennessee; though when he was ordered, in May, to take command of the forces of Mississippi, General Bragg remarked to me, "Doctor, he was kept here too long to watch me!" Afterwards in command of the Army of the Tennessee, no man enjoyed a greater popularity than he did. Soldiers and citizens alike recognized that General Johnston possessed a solid judgment, invincible firmness, imperturbable self-reliance and a perseverance which no difficulties could subdue.

It was my privilege to be frequently with the General after the war and more and more he entered into the religious life, illustrating in his daily walk and conversation the highest type of the Christian gentleman. He was one of the pall-bearers at the funeral of General Sherman at a time

3. Gen. Joseph Eggleston Johnston (1807–1891) of Virginia. CTQ oversimplifies the complex maneuvers that resulted in Bragg's brief "relief" by Johnston in the spring of 1863. President Davis intended to remove Bragg as a result of discontent in the army's officer corps, but Johnston's reluctance to be the agent of that relief foiled Davis' plan. See Thomas L. Connelly, *Autumn of Glory: The Army of Tennessee, 1862–1865* (Baton Rouge: Louisiana State University Press, 1971), 77–87. "Army of the Tennessee" is a misnomer used by CTQ (or Noll) more than once. The name of the Confederate army at Tullahoma and Shelbyville was the Army of Tennessee.

4. This was possibly the new thoroughbred horse presented to CTQ by the members of the Rock City Guard and the Maury Grays on January 31. The animal was presented "as a slight testimonial of regard, with our deepest gratitude for the many disinterested and most invaluable services we have increasingly been made the recipients of, at your hands during our whole intercourse." *Chattanooga Daily Rebel*, February 7, 1863.

when his health was far from strong. He caught cold and died of heart failure in March, 1891.

The weather was at times very inclement while we were in Shelbyville and I suffered much illness. I kept at my work as well as I could, however, and often I preached before distinguished congregations; as, for example, when Generals Johnston, Polk, Cheatham and nearly all the general officers and staffs were present. The congregations were usually large.[5]

I recall reading with a great deal of zest, one day when the weather was very inclement and I was by illness kept in the house, a publication entitled "Robinson Crusoe." Perhaps my readers may have heard of such a book. And one night in February, General Polk and I remained up until two o'clock, and the Bishop-General gave me a detailed account of the manner in which his mind was turned to serious things while he was at West Point—practically the same story that may be found in Dr. William M. Polk's recently published life of his father.[6]

On another occasion the General and I were riding out together and he mentioned the following odd incident to me: His eldest son when at college in the North purchased a gold-headed walking-stick as a present to the Bishop. Wishing his name and seal engraved upon it, the son took it to an engraver in New York, giving him a picture of the Bishop's seal as published in a Church Almanac. The seal was a simple shield having for its device a cross in the center, with a crosier and key laid across it. By some hocus pocus the artist engraved a crosier and a *sword* instead of the key. The Bishop had the cane still when he told me this, and I think it was his intention to adopt that device as his seal thenceforth. But, of course, as we all know, the Bishop's death before the close of the war prevented his adopting a seal for his future work in the Episcopate.

It must not be supposed, however, that my time was idly spent in Shelbyville or in reading such books as "Robinson Crusoe" and listening to the charming conversation of General Polk and others. On the 2nd of March, at the request of my fellow-chaplains, General Bragg issued an order to the effect that I was assigned to duty at the general hospitals of

5. For a discussion of the revivalism that occurred in the Army of Tennessee in the spring of 1863, see Larry J. Daniel, *Soldiering in the Army of Tennessee* (Chapel Hill: University of North Carolina Press, 1991), 116–19.

6. Polk was converted by the military academy's chaplain, Dr. Charles Pettit McIlwane, later Episcopal bishop of Ohio. The story is related in William M. Polk, *Leonidas Polk: Bishop and General*, 2d ed., 2 vols. (New York: Longmans, Green & Co., 1915), 1:88–104.

Polk's corps, and was to proceed to a central point and there establish my office.[7] With the approval of Medical Officers, I was to visit the different hospitals, rendering such services and affording such relief and consolation to the sick and wounded as a minister only could give.

On my copy of this order was endorsed "'Transportation furnished in kind from Wartrace to Atlanta, Mch. 3, '63." So I went off and was gone several weeks, visiting my family in Rome, Georgia, before my return.[8] I also made a trip to Columbia, Tennessee, on business relating to my new appointment—a distance of forty miles from Shelbyville, over roads none of the best at that time.

While I was in Rome I received a very characteristic letter from my friend, Colonel Yeatman, on Polk's staff, which gave me an amusing account of the services held in Shelbyville on the day appointed by the President of the Confederate States to be observed as a day of fasting and prayer. The chaplain of an Alabama regiment preached a very good sermon, the letter says, and then "your brother—wound up with a prayer—eminently a *war prayer*—in which he prayed that their (the Yankees') moral sensibilities might be awakened by the 'roar of our cannon and the gleam of our bayonets and that the *stars and bars* might soon wave in triumph through these beleaguered states!' and then after prescribing a course which he desired might be followed by the Lord, he quit." It is such a good example of the manner in which some persons attempt to preach to the people while they pray to God, that it is quite worth quoting here.[9]

7. On February 18, 1863, ten chaplains met and discussed the lack of "Bibles, testaments, tracts, etc." and the fact that some regiments were without chaplains. It was decided that a department agent was needed for Polk's Corps, "to visit hospitals in the rear and secure post and regimental chaplains, secure donations for religious reading, and otherwise promote the spiritual interests of the army." S. M. Cherry to J. William Jones, March 8, 1888, in J. William Jones, *Christ in the Camp; or, Religion in Lee's Army* . . . (Richmond: B. F. Johnson & Co., 1888), 573. To these chaplains, it was "rather appalling" that there were only fifteen regimental chaplains in a corps of forty regiments. W. T. Bennett to CTQ, March 25, 1863, Quintard Papers, DU. CTQ was assigned to his new duty on March 2, 1863. Special Order 55/6, Department and Army of Tennessee, March 2, 1863, CTQ CSR, Confederate Soldiers from Organizations from the State of Tennessee, RG 109, M-268, NA.

8. While in Rome, CTQ addressed a meeting of the town's Ladies Hospital Association, whose president was his mother-in-law, Mrs. Nicholas J. Bayard. Roger Aycock, *All Roads to Rome* (Roswell, Ga.: Wolfe Associates, 1981), 104–5.

9. About this time CTQ was informed by a member of Polk's staff (possibly Yeatman) that the post of brigade chaplain of Maney's Brigade (of which the 1st Tennessee was a component) was to be created and that a Mr. Elliott of the Nashville Female Academy had applied. CTQ wrote Confederate Senator Gustavus A. Henry of Tennessee that his claim

The visit of Bishop Elliott, of Georgia, to Shelbyville was a great event.[10] He arrived on the 23rd of May and was most affectionately welcomed by his friend General Polk, and remained with us at Mr. Gosling's house two weeks. Services were held every day and the Bishop preached. Everywhere he was received most enthusiastically. The Presbyterian Church in Shelbyville, was by far the largest church building in the town, and as it was without a pastor at the time, I had been invited to occupy it and had accepted the very kind invitation. We accordingly held services there on Sunday, the 24th of May. In the morning I said the service and the Bishop preached one of his most eloquent sermons, and I presented a class of ten persons for confirmation. It included Colonel Yeatman; Colonel Porter (of the Sixth Tennessee); Major Hoxton, Chief of Artillery on Hardee's staff; Lieutenant Smith, on General Cheatham's staff; Surgeon Green, (Fourth Tennessee); four privates of my own regiment; one private of the Fifty-first Alabama Cavalry; and a lady.[11]

It was a very novel sight to see a large Church crowded in every part with officers and soldiers. Scarcely a dozen of the gentler sex were to be seen. The attention of this large body of soldiers was earnest and like that of men who were thoughtful about their souls.

Being anxious for the Bishop to officiate for my regiment, I made an appointment with him for the following day, to preach to the brigade under General George Maney, at their camp. The service was held at the headquarters of Colonel Porter of the Sixth Regiment. The attendance was very large and the Bishop said he had never had a more orderly or attentive congregation in a church. I conducted the service and the Bishop preached.

On Tuesday I was very unwell but felt it my duty to drive six miles to

was superior, stating: "I have, as you know, endured all the hardships of the war as Chaplain of the 1st Tenn. Regt.—have shrunk from no duty & faced many dangers. I do not like the idea of having such a man as Elliott put over me." CTQ to G. A. Henry, April 24, 1864. Henry obliged by recommending CTQ to President Davis for the position on April 30, 1863, stating that CTQ was "an able divine & a gallant soldier." G. A. Henry to J. Davis, April 30, 1863. CTQ CSR, Confederate General and Staff Officers, RG 109, M-331, NA. CTQ did not assume the post, but there is no record anyone else did, either.

10. Rt. Rev. Stephen Elliott (1806–1866), Episcopal bishop of Georgia.

11. The officers named other than Yeatman were Col. George C. Porter, who commanded the consolidated 6th and 9th Tennessee Regiments; Capt. (later Major) Llewellyn Hoxton; Lt. J. Webb Smith, one of Cheatham's aides; and S. P. Green, assistant surgeon of the 4th Tennessee. Lindsley, *Military Annals*, 186, 215; Crute, *Confederate Staff Officers*, 35, 79.

the front and visit, with the Bishop, the Brigade of General Manigault, of South Carolina.[12] He was on outpost duty and was only a few miles from the pickets of General Rosecrans' army. The service was at five o'clock. The whole brigade was in attendance, having been marched to the grove arranged for the service, under arms. I assisted in the service and undertook to baptize a captain of the Twenty-eighth Alabama, but was taken ill, and being unable to proceed, the Bishop took my place.[13]

It was a very solemn service indeed. The Captain knelt in the presence of his brother soldiers and enlisted under the banner of Christ Crucified. After which the Bishop preached to the assembled officers and soldiers seated on the ground in concentric circles. It was an admirable extempore discourse which fell with great effect upon the hearts of all who heard it.

On returning to Shelbyville, I betook myself to bed, and using proper remedies, I had a comfortable night. The following day, I fasted and lounged about headquarters. Mr. Vallandigham, who had been sent to us by the Federal authorities because of what were regarded as disloyal utterances made in political speeches in Ohio, dined with us, and my great desire to see him gave me strength to endure a long sitting at table, though I ate nothing.[14]

Mr. Vallandigham was altogether a different man from what I had expected. He was about my own age and height, had remarkably fine features, a frank, open countenance, beautiful teeth and a color indicating very high health. He wore no side-whiskers nor moustache but a beard slightly tinged with gray, on his chin. In manner he was extremely easy

12. Brig. Gen. Arthur Middleton Manigault (1824–1886) of South Carolina commanded a brigade of Alabama and South Carolina troops in the division of Maj. Gen. Jones Withers. See A. M. Manigault, *A Carolinian Goes to War: The Civil War Narrative of Arthur Middleton Manigault*, ed. R. Lockwood Tower (Columbia: University of South Carolina Press, 1983), ix–xii, 72–79.

13. Elliott's sketchy diary, which corroborates CTQ's narrative, notes that on this occasion, he baptized "for D. Quintard one Captain." Bishop Stephen Elliott diary, May 26, 1863, microfilm in GDAH. Manigault later wrote asking CTQ to present his young brother-in-law William E. Huger, closing with the "hope that you have entirely recovered from your late indisposition." A. M. Manigault to CTQ, May 28, 1863, Quintard Papers, DU. Lieutenant Huger is to be distinguished from the Willie Huger mentioned at the beginning of this chapter. See Manigault, *A Carolinian Goes to War*, 79.

14. Representative Clement Laird Vallandigham (1820–1871) of Ohio, leader of the Peace Democrats or "Copperheads." After leaving the Army of Tennessee, he ran the blockade and went on to Canada before returning to Ohio. *Dictionary of American Biography*, s.v. "Vallandigham, Clement Laird."

and polite; in conversation very fluent and entertaining. He was greatly pleased with the kind reception he had met from the officers of the army and the citizens of Shelbyville, but was very desirous of avoiding all public demonstration.

On Thursday morning, feeling much better, I accompanied Bishop Elliott to Wartrace, the headquarters of General Hardee.[15] General Polk and Colonel Richmond accompanied us. Later Colonel Yeatman brought Mr. Vallandigham over in General Polk's ambulance and we had a "goodlie companie." At eleven o'clock we held a service in the Presbyterian Church, the use of which was kindly tendered me.[16] There was a large congregation, consisting of officers, soldiers and ladies. The Bishop read part of the morning service and I preached an extempore sermon. I had not expected to say anything, but the Bishop having declined to preach, I was determined not to disappoint the congregation altogether. And I had great reason to be thankful that I did preach, for it gave me the opportunity to have a long and very delightful conversation with General Hardee about confirmation. In the afternoon, services were to have been held for the brigades of General Wood and General Lucius Polk, but rain coming on, and the services having been arranged for the open air, it was thought best to postpone them to a future occasion.[17]

The train that evening brought a very agreeable addition to our party in the person of Lieutenant-Colonel Freemantle of the Coldstream Guard of the British Army. The Guard was the oldest regiment in the British service. Colonel Fremantle was only about eight and twenty, and was on furlough,—just taking a hasty tour through the Confederacy to look at our army and become acquainted with our officers. He was very intelligent and very companionable. His grandfather and his father were adjutants of the Coldstream Guard, and he had held the same office. His family was an ancient and honorable one, and he seemed worthy to wear his ancestral honors. He accompanied General Polk and myself to Shel-

15. Lt. Gen. William Joseph Hardee (1815–1873) of Georgia commanded one of the Army of Tennessee's two corps. See Nathaniel Cheairs Hughes, Jr., *General William J. Hardee: Old Reliable* (Baton Rouge: Louisiana State University Press, 1965).

16. Bishop Elliott's diary notes that he read the service at Beth Salem Presbyterian Church, with "D. Quintard addressing audience." Elliott Diary, May 28, 1863, GDAH.

17. Brig. Gen. Sterling Alexander Martin Wood (1823–1891) of Alabama, who commanded a brigade of Alabama and Mississippi troops, and Brig. Gen. Lucius Eugene Polk (1833–1892) of Tennessee, who commanded a brigade of Tennessee and Arkansas troops. Both brigades were in Cleburne's Division.

byville the next day, and was for a while the General's guest. He had left
England three months before and had come into the Confederacy by way
of Texas.[18]

The following Sunday I held services again in the Presbyterian
Church at Shelbyville, preached to a crowded congregation, and presented another class to the Bishop for confirmation. In the afternoon we
drove to Wartrace where I said Evening Prayer at the headquarters of
General Wood, and the Bishop preached to an immense concourse. Between four and five thousand persons were present and the services were
most impressive and solemn.[19]

On Monday morning, (June 1st), we attended a review of General Liddell's brigade.[20] After the review, General Hardee had the brigade formed
in a hollow square and the Bishop addressed it briefly upon the religious
aspects of the struggle in which we were engaged.

A memorable incident of Bishop Elliott's visit to our army was General
Bragg's baptism and confirmation.[21] As soon as I found that the Bishop
was able to give us a visit, I made very earnest appeals to the officers and
soldiers of our army to confess Christ before men. But there was one man
in the army whom I felt I could never get at. He was the Commander-in-
chief, General Braxton Bragg. He had the reputation of being so stern
and so sharp in his sarcasm, that many men were afraid to go near him.
Yet I had often thought of him in connection with my work. He never
came to the Holy Communion, and I never heard of his being a member
of any religious denomination.

Immediately after I received notice of Bishop Elliott's proposed visit, I

18. On May 29, 1863, Fremantle recorded in his journal: "I took a walk before breakfast
with Dr. Quintard, a zealous Episcopal chaplain, who began life as a surgeon, which en-
ables him to attend to the bodily as well as the spiritual wants of the Tennessean regiment
to which he is chaplain." Arthur J. L. Fremantle, *Three Months in the Southern States*
(New York: John Bradburn, 1864), 141.

19. Bishop Elliott's diary records that he confirmed seven persons presented by CTQ
at Shelbyville and that he preached at Wartrace that afternoon to three thousand soldiers
of Wood's Brigade. Elliott Diary, May 31, 1863, GDAH.

20. Liddell's Brigade of Arkansas troops was commanded by Brig. Gen. St. John Richardson Liddell (1815–1870) of Mississippi and Louisiana. See St. John Richardson Liddell,
Liddell's Record, ed. Nathaniel Cheairs Hughes, Jr. (Baton Rouge: Louisiana State University Press, 1997).

21. Bishop Elliott's diary records that Bragg was baptized and confirmed in the Episcopal Church at Shelbyville on Tuesday evening, June 2, 1863. Elliott diary, June 2, 1863,
GDAH.

determined to have a talk with General Bragg. It was late one afternoon when I started for his headquarters. I found two tents and a sentry at the outer one, and when I asked for General Bragg the sentry said: "You cannot see him. He is very busy, and has given positive orders not to be disturbed, except for a matter of life and death."

That cooled my enthusiasm and I returned to my own quarters; but all the night long I blamed myself for my timidity.

The next day I started out again, found the same sentry and received the same reply. This time, however, I was resolved to see the General, no matter what happened, so I said:

"It *is* a matter of life and death."

The sentry withdrew and in a few minutes returned and said: "You can see the General, but I advise you to be brief. He is not in a good humor."

This chilled me, but I went in. I found the General dictating to two secretaries. He met me with: "Well, Dr. Quintard, what can I do for you? I am quite busy, as you can see."

I stammered out that I wanted to see him alone. He replied that it was impossible, but I persisted. Finally, he dismissed the secretaries, saying to me rather sternly: "Your business must be of grave importance, sir."

I was very much frightened, but I asked the General to be seated, and then, fixing my eyes upon a knot-hole in the pine board floor of the tent, talked about our Blessed Lord and about the responsibilities of a man in the General's position. When I looked up after a while I saw tears in the General's eyes and took courage to ask him to be confirmed. At last he came to me, took both my hands in his and said: "I have been waiting for twenty years to have some one say this to me, and I thank you from my heart. Certainly, I shall be confirmed if you will give me the necessary instruction."

I had frequent interviews with him subsequently on the subject and he was baptized and confirmed. The latter service took place in Shelbyville, on the afternoon of our return from Wartrace. Wishing to make the usual record, I asked the General to give me the names of his parents and the date of his birth. In reply he sent me the following note:

My dear Doctor: I was born in the town of Warrenton, Warren County, North Carolina, on the 21st of June, 1817, son of Thomas Bragg and Margaret Crossland, his wife. Though too late in seeking, [but not,] I hope, in obtaining the pardon offered to all who penitently confess, I trust time will yet be allowed me to prove the sincerity with which I have at last undertaken the task. For the kindness and consideration of yourself and the good and venerable Bishop, for whom my admiration has ever been very great, I shall never cease to be grateful. My mind has never been so much at ease, and I feel renewed strength for the task before me.

Faithfully yours,
Braxton Bragg

Toward the end of our stay in Shelbyville, it was my privilege to assist in getting two ladies through the enemy's lines. The Rev. Mr. Clark, rector of St. Paul's Church, Augusta, Georgia, had been appointed by the Bishop of Georgia, a Missionary to the Army,—that is, sort of a Chaplain under diocesan control and for whose support the Confederate Government was in no way responsible.[22] The plan was intended to continue the work which the Bishop had begun by his visit to our army. Mr. Clark desired to send his mother and sister to Nashville, and communicating with me in advance, I made all necessary arrangements for their transit through the lines before they arrived in our camp at Shelbyville. I obtained a pass from General Bragg and his permission for Mr. Edmund Cooper, of Shelbyville, to write such letters to Federal officers as he saw fit. Mr. Cooper was in a position to be a great service to us, for although a Union man and afterwards private secretary to President Johnson and Assistant Secretary of the United States Treasury, his brothers were in the Confederate Army.[23] He accordingly gave us letters to General Rosecrans and Governor Andrew Johnson. General Wheeler wrote to Colonel Webb, in command of our outposts, requesting him to do all in his power for the welfare of the party.[24]

22. Rev. William H. Clarke (d. 1877). Charles C. Jones, Jr., and Salem Dutcher, *Memorial History of Augusta, Georgia* (Syracuse, N.Y.: D. Mason, 1890), 371.

23. Harvard-educated Edmund Cooper (1821–1911) was at this point a Unionist lawyer in Shelbyville, although he had served a term as a Whig in the 28th Tennessee General Assembly (1849–1851). After the war, he served not only as President Andrew Johnson's private secretary and as assistant secretary of the treasury, but also in Congress and again in the Tennessee General Assembly. McBride and Robison, *Biographical Directory of the Tennessee General Assembly*, 1:164.

24. Maj. Gen. Joseph Wheeler (1836–1906) of Georgia, commander of the Confederate cavalry in that sector. Lt. Col. James D. Webb commanded the 51st Alabama Cavalry Regiment. Webb was mortally wounded in a skirmish during the Army of Tennessee's retreat from Middle Tennessee in July. *OR* 23(1):574.

In the morning the two ladies, accompanied by the Rev. Mr. Clark, my old class-mate Dr. Frank Stanford, then General Wheeler's Medical Director, and myself, left Shelbyville in a fine four-horse ambulance.[25] On our way "to the front," nine miles out, we reached General Martin's headquarters, where our passports were examined and approved.[26] Three miles further on, we reached Colonel Webb, who gave us a note to Lieutenant Spence of the outer picket, still three miles further in advance. Lieutenant Spence conducted us to a house where we were kindly received and made to feel quite at home. He sent one of his scouts forward to the residence of Colonel Lytle, two miles further on the "neutral ground," to inform him of our arrival and to take letters to him from Mr. Cooper and myself asking his assistance in conveying the ladies through the enemy's lines.[27]

About two o'clock Colonel and Mrs. Lytle arrived in their carriage. The latter kindly offered to accompany the ladies through the Federal lines to the house of a friend where they could remain until they could communicate with General Rosecrans. At this point we made our adieus and on returning to camp stopped for dinner at Colonel, (afterward General) Strahl's headquarters.[28] The day was a pleasant one and the whole party was greatly pleased with the trip. The Rev. Mr. Clark remained with me over the following Sunday and held services for one of our regiments.

25. Frank A. Stanford of Georgia, surgeon and medical director of Wheeler's Cavalry Corps, originally mustered in as surgeon of the 15th Alabama Infantry. Stanford CSR, Confederate General and Staff Officers, RG 109, M-331, NA.

26. Brig. Gen. William Thompson Martin (1823–1910) commanded a division of Confederate cavalry.

27. Otherwise unidentified, Colonel Lytle was apparently a Union sympathizer. On June 6, 1863, Federal Brig. Gen. Jefferson C. Davis reported information that Lytle had related relative to Confederate troop movements. OR 23(1):364.

28. Col. Otho French Strahl (1831–1864) of Ohio and Tennessee, commander of the 4th Tennessee Regiment. That spring, Strahl commanded Alexander P. Stewart's brigade of Cheatham's Division while Stewart exercised temporary command of Maj. Gen. John P. McCown's division after McCown's arrest. A few days after Stewart returned to the brigade, he was elevated to command a new division in Hardee's Corps, and Strahl received command of the brigade permanently, earning a promotion to brigadier general on July 28, 1863. OR 23(2):654; Charles M. Cummings, "Otho French Strahl: Choicest Spirit to Embrace the South," *Tennessee Historical Quarterly* 24 (Winter 1965): 341, 349.

CHAPTER VIII

Personal Narrative—A Dramatic Episode

A short time before we left Shelbyville I was a participant in one of the most solemn, and at the same time one of the most dramatic, scenes of my whole life.

I was requested one day by General Polk to visit two men who were sentenced to be shot within a few days for desertion. One of them belonged to the Nineteenth Tennessee Regiment and the other to the Eighth Tennessee. The former was a man forty-seven years of age, the latter not more than twenty-three.

I cannot describe the feelings which oppressed me on my first visit in compliance with the General's request. I urged upon both men, with all the powers of my persuasion, an attention to the interests of their souls. The younger man was, I believe, really in earnest in endeavoring to prepare for death, but the other seemed to have no realizing sense of his condition. I found that the younger man had a Cumberland Presbyterian minister for a Chaplain for whom I sent and who would minister to him.

I called upon Governor Harris and begged him to see the judges of the Court and find if there was any possibility of having the men pardoned. I never begged so hard for anything in my life as for the lives of these men. I had a special sympathy for the older man, for he had deserted to visit his wife and children. However, the day came for their execution.

The Cumberland Presbyterian Chaplain baptized the man belonging to his regiment. I remained in town the night preceding the day appointed for the execution, and from eight o'clock to nine, the Cumberland Presbyterian Chaplain and myself engaged in prayer privately in behalf of the condemned men.

At seven in the morning I gave them the most comfortable Sacrament of Christ's Body and Blood. Both prisoners seemed deeply and profoundly penitent and to be very much in earnest in preparing for death. The room in which they were confined was a very mean and uncleanly one. Half the window was boarded up, and the light struggled through the dirt that begrimed the other half. But the Sacrament Itself and the thought that the prisoners would so soon be in Eternity, made it all very solemn. The prisoners made an effort to give themselves up to God, and seemed to feel that this was the occasion for bidding farewell to earth and earthly things. I pronounced the benediction, placing my hand upon the head of each, and commending them to the mercy of God.

At eight o'clock, the older man, to whom I was to minister in his last moments, was taken from his cell, ironed hand and feet. He was placed in an ambulance, surrounded by a guard, and we started for the brigade of Colonel Strahl, seven miles out of town. On reaching Strahl's headquarters, the prisoner was placed in a room and closely guarded until the hour fixed for his execution,—one o'clock,—should arrive. A squad of twenty-four men was marched into the yard, and stacking arms, was marched off in order that the guns might be loaded by an officer,—one half with blank cartridges.

Leaving headquarters preceded by a wagon bearing the prisoner's coffin and followed by the squad which was to do the execution, we arrived on the ground precisely at one o'clock. The brigade was drawn up on three sides of a square. Colonel Strahl and his staff, Captain Stanford; Major Jack, General Polk's Adjutant; and Captain Spence of General Polk's staff, rode forward with me. A grave had been dug. The coffin was placed beside the grave, the prisoner was seated on it and I took my place by his side. Captain Johnston, Colonel Strahl's Adjutant, advanced and read the sentence of the Court and the approval of the General.[1] The

---

1. Other than the previously identified Strahl, the officers named include Capt. Thomas J. Stanford of Mississippi, commander of the artillery battery attached to Strahl's (Stewart's) brigade; Maj. (later Col.) Thomas M. Jack; Lt. P. B. Spence, Polk's assistant inspector general; and Capt. James W. Johnston, adjutant of the 4th Tennessee Regiment. Crute, *Confederate Staff Officers*, 154–55, 187.

prisoner was then informed that if he wished to make any remarks, he had now an opportunity. He requested me to cut off a lock of his hair and preserve it for his wife. He then stood up and said: "I am about to die. I hope I am going to a better world. I trust that one and all of my companions will take warning by my fate."

He seated himself on his coffin again and I began on the Psalm: "Out of the deep have I called unto Thee, O Lord," and after that the "Comfortable words." We then knelt down together, and I said the Confession from the Communion Office. Then I turned to the office for the Visitation of Prisoners, and used the prayer beginning, "O Father of Mercies and God of all Comfort," and so on down to the benediction, "Unto God's gracious mercy and protection I commit you." I then shook hands with him and said: "Be a man! It will soon be over!"

The firing squad was in position, the guns were cocked, the order had been given to "take aim," when Major Jack rode forward and read "Special Order, No. 132," the purport of which was that since the sentence of the Court-martial and order for the execution of the prisoner, facts and circumstances with regard to the history and character of the man had come to the knowledge of the Lieutenant-General Commanding which in his judgment palliated the offence of desertion of which the man had been condemned and warranted a suspension of his execution. The sentence of death was therefore annulled, and the man was pardoned and ordered to report to his regiment for duty.

The poor fellow did not understand it at first, but when the truth burst upon him, he exclaimed: "Thank God! thank God!" and the tears streamed down his face. The whole scene was most impressive, and was calculated to have a good effect upon all who were present. The other prisoner was executed at high noon in another locality.

Personal Narrative—Chickamauga

On the last day of June, 1863, Rosecrans began to advance on Bragg.[1] That was the signal for our leaving Shelbyville. On the 3rd of July the Union army entered Tullahoma.

On the morning of the 2nd, as I left the headquarters of General Bragg, I met my friend Governor Isham G. Harris. He looked very bright and cheerful and said to me: "To-morrow morning you will be roused up by the thunder of our artillery." But instead of being thus aroused I found myself in full retreat toward Winchester. Thence I rode to Cowan, where I found General Bragg and his staff, and General Polk with his staff. I rode up to them and said to General Bragg: "My dear General, I am afraid you are thoroughly outdone."

"Yes," he said, "I am utterly broken down." And then leaning over his saddle he spoke of the loss of Middle Tennessee and whispered: "This is a great disaster."

I said to him: "General, don't be disheartened, our turn will come next."[2]

1. Rosecrans actually began his advance on June 24, 1863.

2. The nine days between June 24 and July 3, 1863, were indeed a time of "great disaster" for Bragg and the Army of Tennessee. Rosecrans and his army brilliantly executed a plan that deprived the Confederacy of many hundreds of square miles of Middle Tennessee with a minimum of casualties. For discussions of the campaign, see Connelly, *Autumn*

I found Colonel Walters, his Adjutant-General, lying in the corner of a rail fence, with his hands under his head, look the very picture of despair.[3] I said to him: "My dear Colonel, what is the matter with you?" His reply was: "How can you ask such a question, when you know as well as I do what has happened?"

Our troops were at this time moving rapidly across the Sewanee Mountain, over country which subsequently became very familiar to me in times of peace. I said to him; "My dear Colonel, I am afraid you've not read the Psalms for the day." "No," he answered. "What do they say?"

I replied in the words of the first verse of the Eleventh Psalm: "In the Lord I put my trust; how say ye then to my soul, that she should flee as a bird unto the hill?"

I gave my horse to one of "the boys," and at the request of General Bragg, I accompanied him by rail to Chattanooga. On the 21st of August, a day appointed by the President of the Confederate States for fasting, humiliation and prayer, while I was preaching in a church, the Union army appeared opposite Chattanooga and began shelling the town. I think my sermon on that occasion was not long.[4] Early in September, General McCook and General Thomas moved in such a way as to completely flank the Confederate position.[5] General Bragg immediately began his retreat southward, and having been joined by General Longstreet and his forces, attacked General Thomas at Lee and Gordon's Mills, twelve miles south of Chattanooga, on the 19th of September. It was a bitter fight, but the day closed without any decisive results to either side.[6]

---

of Glory, 121–34; Steven E. Woodworth, *Six Armies in Tennessee: The Chickamauga and Chattanooga Campaigns* (Lincoln: University of Nebraska Press, 1998) 19–46.

3. Lt. Col. Harvey Washington Walter, Bragg's judge-advocate, as well as his "excellent friend and Brother soldier." Braxton Bragg to Fredonia B. Walter, May 7, 1863, Harvey Washington Walter Papers, UNC.

4. CTQ was not alone in the brevity of his devotions that day. At another service in Chattanooga, the Rev. D. M. Palmer, D.D., of New Orleans, was praying when a shell came near the church. He continued with the prayer, but when finished, he "noticed a perceptible diminution of his congregation." Daniel Harvey Hill, "Chickamauga—The Great Battle in the West," in *Battles and Leaders of the Civil War,* 4 vols., ed. Robert Underwood Johnson and Clarence Clough Buel (1887–1888; reprint, New York: Youseloff, 1956), 3:640.

5. Maj. Gen. Alexander McDowell McCook of Ohio commanded the Union 20th Corps; Maj. Gen. George Henry Thomas of Virginia commanded the Union 14th Corps.

6. Lt. Gen. James Longstreet, commander of the 1st Corps of the Confederate Army of Northern Virginia, had been dispatched to Bragg's aid with two divisions. CTQ is somewhat mistaken relative to the fighting on September 19, 1863. Longstreet and the greater

After this the great battle of Chickamauga was fought.[7] Undoubtedly General Thomas saved the Union army from utter ruin, but Longstreet, by his prompt action in seizing an opportunity, won the victory for the Confederate army.[8]

The troops led by Brigadier-General Archibald Gracie fired the last gun and stormed the last strong position held by the enemy at the battle of Chickamauga, and so memorable was his conduct on that day, that the people in that vicinity have given the hill the name of Gracie Hill. It was a great privilege to know General Gracie as I did. He was a character that old Froissart would have delighted to paint. Chivalrous as a Bayard, he had all the tenderness of a woman. A warrior by nature as well as a soldier by education, (he graduated at West Point in 1852), and profession, he had a horror of shedding blood and would almost shed tears in the hour of victory over the thin ranks of his brigade. A few months before his death he became a communicant of the Church.[9]

One great personal loss I sustained in the battle of Chickamauga was that of my dear friend, Colonel W. B. Richmond, a member of General Polk's staff. He was a true friend, a thoroughly well rounded character and a most gallant soldier. He was the Treasurer of the Diocese of Tennessee, before the war.[10]

Brigadier-General Helm of Kentucky was killed at Chickamauga, as was also Brigadier-General Preston Smith. Among the dead was my cousin, Captain Thomas E. King, of Roswell, Georgia, who had suffi-

---

number of his brigades were not on the field during the day's fighting, and the battle occurred along Chickamauga Creek north of Lee and Gordon's Mill. Hill, "Chickamauga," 649.

7. The Battle of Chickamauga was the subject of another of CTQ's letters seeking particular information. He inquired of Alexander P. Stewart, then serving on the Chickamauga and Chattanooga National Military Park Commission, the strength of the Army of Tennessee during the battle. Stewart replied that he did not have any definitive knowledge, but that he felt the army's numbers may have been as low as forty thousand (a figure that seems too low) based on a conversation he had had with Bragg shortly after the battle. A. P. Stewart to CTQ, October 18, 1895, Quintard Papers, DU.

8. "The great battle of Chickamauga" CTQ somewhat narrowly refers to is the fighting on September 20, 1863. Longstreet launched an attack that fortuitously exploited a gap in the Federal lines, resulting in the rout of a portion of the Army of the Cumberland. Maj. Gen. George Henry Thomas earned the sobriquet "Rock of Chickamauga" for his stand with a portion of the Union army until nightfall.

9. Brig. Gen. Archibald Gracie, Jr. (1832–1864), of New York and Alabama.

10. Richmond was shot through the head near the Federal breastworks. Polk, *Leonidas Polk*, 2:284.

ciently recovered from his fearful wounds at the first battle of Manassas, to act as honorary aid-de-camp to General Smith.[11] Here also General Hood lost a leg.[12]

The day after the battle I was sent to the field with one hundred and fifty ambulances to gather up the wounded. It was a sad duty. I saw many distressing sights. I was directed to convey the Federal wounded to the Field Hospitals fitted up by the Federal surgeons that had been captured to the number of not less than fifty, I think. I labored all the day and at nightfall I came upon a wretched hut into which a half dozen wounded men had dragged themselves. I found there among them, a young fellow about seventeen years of age. He had a severe wound in his leg and a small bone had been torn away. I chatted with him pleasantly for a while and promised to take him to the hospital early the next morning.

Early the next day when I went to fulfill my promise, I saw a surgeon's amputating knife on the head of a barrel by the door of the hut, and found that my young friend had been weeping bitterly. When I asked him what was the matter, he replied: "The surgeon has been examining my wound and says that my leg must be amputated. I would not care for myself, but my poor mother—" and then he burst into an agony of tears.

"Nonsense!" I said to him. "They shall not take off your leg." And lifting him up bodily, I placed him in an ambulance and took him to the Hospital, where the next day I found him bright and cheerful. I learned subsequently that the "surgeon" who was about to amputate his leg unnecessarily, was a doctor who had come up from Georgia to get a little practice in that line. The boy subsequently became a railway conductor

11. Brig. Gen. Benjamin Hardin Helm (1831–1863), whose wife was Emily Todd, half sister of Mary Todd Lincoln. Helm commanded the Kentucky "Orphan Brigade." Brig. Gen. Preston Smith (1823–1863) commanded a Tennessee brigade in Cheatham's Division. Smith and Catherine Quintard's cousin Thomas E. King were killed when they mistakenly rode into the Federal lines during a night attack on September 19, 1863. Pratt, "Captain Thomas E. King," 511–14. CTQ received letters from members of King's family inquiring as to his last moments and "his Christian expressions, if any." James R. King to CTQ, October 1, 1863, C. B. King to CTQ, October 1, 1863, Quintard Papers, DU. Later, CTQ composed a small book dedicated to King's memory, with "many personal eulogies of him." Copies were presented to his wife, Mary Read Clemens King, and to his three children, John, Thomas, and Evelyn. *Coat of Arms Certification Concerning the Family Name of King/Barrington* (n.p., n.d.), available at GDAH.

12. Maj. Gen. (later Gen.) John Bell Hood (1831–1879) of Kentucky, who commanded Longstreet's Corps when Longstreet assumed command of the Left Wing, Army of Tennessee.

and used to say many years later, "You know I belong to Bishop Quintard. He saved my leg and perhaps my life at Chickamauga. The leg young Saw-bones was going to amputate is now as good as the other."

Another warm friend of mine, John Marsh, was horribly wounded at the battle of Chickamauga; so sorely wounded that he could not be removed from the field. A tent was erected over him and I nursed him until he was in a condition to be taken to the hospital.[13] On the 1st of October, I obtained leave of absence from my duties as Chaplain of Polk's corps, volunteered my services as an Assistant Surgeon, was assigned to duty as such at Marietta, Georgia, and reported as promptly as possible to Surgeon D. D. Saunders, who was in charge of the hospitals at that post.[14]

I took Marsh with me and there he slowly recovered his health. I prepared him for baptism and it was my great pleasure to baptize him and present him to Bishop Elliott for confirmation. When he was to be baptized, knowing that it would be painful for him to kneel because of his recent and scarcely healed wounds, I told him that he might sit in his chair. "No," he said. "Let me kneel; let me kneel." And so he knelt, as I placed upon his brow the sign of the cross.

Our victory was complete at Chickamauga and Rosecrans' army threw down their arms and retreated pell-mell in the direction of Chattanooga. The Confederates followed on the 21st of September and took possession of Missionary Ridge and Lookout Mountain. For two months the two armies confronted each other at Chattanooga.

13. Lt. John H. Marsh moved to Hardeman County, Tennessee, from North Carolina in his infancy. Appointed to West Point, he resigned after having been at the academy for a short time when the war came. He served as an artillery officer at Shiloh and Perryville. Marsh is variously reported as serving on the staff of either Brig. Gen. Preston Smith or Brig. Gen. Otho F. Strahl at the time of Chickamauga. A battlefield marker, however, states Marsh commanded Scott's Tennessee Battery there. Marsh's left arm was shattered in the fighting on September 19, 1863. As CTQ relates, he and Marsh formed a close attachment, Marsh writing CTQ on one occasion: "If possible, my heart, and affection goes out to you, stronger and stronger every day." John Marsh to CTQ, April 16, 1864, Quintard Papers, DU. See also "Tribute to Lieut. John Marsh," CV 5 (December 1897): 599–600; Lindsley, Military Annals, 793; Bromfield Ridley, Battles and Sketches of the Army of Tennessee (1906; reprint, Dayton, Ohio: Morningside Bookshop, 1995), 422–23.

14. Dudley D. Saunders, originally of Alabama, went into the Confederate service from his medical practice in Memphis and served in large hospital posts and as chief surgeon of the reserve surgical operating corps, which assisted the field medical corps on the battlefield. Saunders was described as "a man of great energy, resourceful and alert," with widely recognized professional skill. CMH, 10:695–96.

Matters remained quiet in both armies until November, when the Confederate lines extended around Chattanooga from the mouth of Chattanooga Creek above, to Moccasin Point below the town. To my great regret, General Polk was relieved of his command on the 29th of September, in consequence of a misunderstanding with General Bragg, the Commanding General. His application for a Court of Inquiry was dismissed and a month later he was assigned to a new field of duty, alike important and difficult—the best evidence that President Davis could offer of his appreciation of the Bishop-General's past services and of his expectations of his future career.[15]

It was while we were in Chattanooga, before the battle of Chicka-mauga, that the "Order of the Southern Cross" was organized. There came to General Polk's headquarters, (on whose staff I was serving), several officers, who stated that they had been considering the propriety if not the necessity of instituting an organization within the army, both so-cial and charitable in its character, whose aim would be a military broth-erhood, to foster patriotic sentiment, to strengthen the ties of army fellowship and at the same time to provide a fund, not only for the mutual benefit of its members, but for the relief of disabled soldiers and the wid-ows and orphans of such as might perish in the Confederate service.[16]

They requested Bishop Polk to attend a meeting that evening to con-sider the subject further, and he finding it inconvenient to attend, asked me to go as his representative. So I went. Some six or eight of us met at Tyne's Station, about nine miles northwest of Chattanooga.[17] After suffi-cient discussion and explanation to bring us to a common understanding of the purposes of the proposed order, General Pat Cleburne, General John C. Brown, General Liddell and myself were appointed a committee

15. Problems between Bragg and Polk had been building for almost a year. When Polk failed to launch a timely attack on the morning of September 20, 1863, Bragg seized the opportunity to remove Polk from command of his corps. See Woodworth, *Six Armies in Tennessee*, 138–40.

16. Membership in the Comrades of the Southern Cross required one to be "a com-missioned officer or enlisted soldier in the Confederate States service, a free white male over eighteen years of age, intelligent in his military duties and of known patriotism and integrity." Howell Purdue and Elizabeth Purdue, *Pat Cleburne, Confederate General: A Definitive Biography* (Hillsboro, Tex.: Hill Junior College Press, 1973), 229, n. 9. The obli-gation assumed in the ritual "was to remain in the army if necessary for life, and fight it out to the bitter end." Roger Q. Mills to J. P. Douglas, January 10, 1901, in "Concerning Re-Enlistment at Dalton," *CV* 9 (January 1901): 13.

17. The correct name was "Tyner's Station."

to draft a constitution and a plan of organization.[18] We met every day, I think, for a week or ten days, and the outcome of our labors was a little pamphlet, in appearance similar to the catechisms of our Sunday School days. It was in fact three by five inches in size, contained twenty-five pages and was from the press of Burke, Boykin & Co., Macon, Georgia. It was entitled "Constitution of the Comrades of the Southern Cross, adopted August 28, 1863."

Several "companies" were at once organized and but for the unfavorable course of events, I do not doubt that the order would have rapidly extended throughout the armies of the Confederacy. But active military operations were very soon afterward begun, and the army was kept constantly on the move until the "bottom dropped out," and the "Order of the Southern Cross"—like the Southern Confederacy—went to pieces. The Confederate Veterans' Organization subsequently embodied some of the features which it was intended that the Comrades of the Southern Cross should possess.

18. The officer previously unidentified here was Brig. Gen. (later Major General) John Calvin Brown (1827–1889) of Tennessee, who, at the time of this meeting, commanded a brigade in Maj. Gen. Alexander P. Stewart's division.

CHAPTER X

Personal Narrative—Atlanta

General Bragg was defeated by General Grant at Chattanooga in November 1863, and early in the following month he was, at his own request, relieved of the command of the Confederate army. He was called to Richmond to act for a while as military adviser to President Davis. His life subsequent to the war was quiet. He was a God-fearing man in peace and in war. He died in 1876.

He was succeeded in the command by General Joseph E. Johnston, whose army was encamped in and around Atlanta.[1] Soon afterward I secured the use of a Methodist Church building on the corner of Garnet and Forsyth Streets, assembled a congregation, held services and instituted a work which resulted in the establishment of St. Luke's Parish.

A suitable lot was soon obtained and with the help of men detailed from the army, a building was speedily erected. It was a most attractive building, handsomely furnished, and although somewhat "Confederate" in style, would have compared favorably with most churches built in the days of peace and prosperity.[2]

1. When Johnston assumed command on December 27, 1863, the Army of Tennessee was camped around Dalton, Georgia, on the Western and Atlantic Railroad about eighty miles north of Atlanta.

2. Known as the "Little Refugee Church," St. Luke's was situated between Marietta and Walton Streets in Atlanta and was "a symmetrical and imposing edifice, ornamented with a tasteful belfry, appropriately surmounted with a cross." Inside, the depth of the church was eighty-five feet, "containing three rows of neatly finished pews, eighty-eight in

Within its portals devout worshippers,—many distinguished Confederate officers among them,—were delighted to turn aside from the bloody strife of war and bow themselves before the Throne of Grace. On the 8th of May, 1864, while I was in Atlanta in charge of St. Luke's Church and in attendance upon the hospitals, the following telegram came to me from Major Henry Hampton: "Can't you come up tomorrow? General Hood wishes to be baptized." It was impossible for me to go, but it was a great pleasure for me to learn afterwards that General Polk arrived with his staff that day and that night he baptized his brother General. It was the eve of an expected battle. It was a touching sight, we may be sure,—the one-legged veteran, leaning upon his crutches to receive the waters of baptism and the sign of the cross. A few nights later, General Polk baptized General Johnston and Lieutenant-General Hardee, General Hood being witness. These were two of the four ecclesiastical acts performed by Bishop Polk after receiving his commission in the army.[3]

I was then Chaplain-at-Large under the appointment of the General Commanding.[4] Being anxious for the Bishop of Georgia to consecrate the new church, I arranged for him to visit that portion of the army then at Dalton. At Dalton I baptized Brigadier-General Strahl in his camp in the presence of his assembled brigade, and at night we held services in the Methodist Church at Dalton.

---

number, and double aisles leading down to the chancel, which [was] ten feet by twelve in dimensions." "Consecration of St. Luke's Church," *Atlanta Southern Confederacy*, April 23, 1864; Robert S. Davis, Jr., ed., *Requiem for a Lost City: Sallie Clayton's Memoirs of Civil War Atlanta* (Macon, Ga.: Mercer University Press, 1999), 96.

3. Polk's delight in these baptisms is described in Parks, *General Leonidas Polk*, 374, 377–78. Hardee appears to have been confirmed, rather than baptized, and at a different time. Parks, *General Leonidas Polk*, 377; Hughes, *Hardee*, 209; Ridley, *Battles and Sketches*, 422.

4. When Polk was relieved after the Battle of Chickamauga and sent to Mississippi, he wanted CTQ to follow him to Mississippi, a member of his staff writing CTQ in November, 1863, that "the General wants you with him but doesn't know how to arrange it." Henry C. Yeatman to CTQ, November 5, 1863, Quintard Papers, DU. Perhaps Polk's enemy and CTQ's friend Bragg had something to do with Polk's frustration. On December 31, 1863, with Bragg gone, CTQ was relieved from duty with the Army of Tennessee and ordered to report to Polk. Special Orders No. 77, Army of Tennessee, December 31, 1863, Quintard Papers, DU. CTQ's duty with Polk was short-lived, as CTQ was assigned to duty in Atlanta by order of Joseph E. Johnston dated February 3, 1864. CTQ CSR, Confederate General and Staff Officers, RG 109, M-331, NA. As chaplain at large, CTQ had permission to pass through the camps of the Army of Tennessee at will and use the army's railroad transportation. Order, Headquarters, Army of Tennessee, April 12, 1864, Quintard Papers, DU.

The church was so densely packed that it was impossible for Bishop Elliott and myself to enter by the front door. Fortunately there was a small door in the rear of the Church, opening into what I should call the Chancel. We were obliged to vest ourselves in the open air. I crawled through the little doorway first, and then taking the Bishop by his right hand, did all I could to help him through.

I read Evening Prayer and the Bishop preached; after which I presented a class for confirmation in which were General Hardee, General Strahl, two other Generals, a number of officers of the line and many privates.

The next day I accompanied the Bishop to Marietta where he held an ordination service at which I preached the sermon. And the day following he consecrated to the service of Almighty God, St. Luke's Church, Atlanta.[5] In the afternoon of that day I presented a class of five persons to the Bishop for confirmation,—the first-fruits of my labors in St. Luke's parish.

It was about this time that I prepared some little books adapted to the use of the soldiers as a convenient substitute for the Book of Common Prayer. I also prepared a booklet, entitled, "Balm for the Weary and Wounded."[6] It was through the great kindness and generosity of Mr. Jacob K. Sass, the treasurer of the General Council of the Church in the Confederate States, that I was enabled to publish these two little volumes. The first four copies of the latter booklet that came from the press were forwarded to General Polk and he wrote upon three of them the names of General J. E. Johnston, Lieutenant-General Hardee and Lieutenant-General Hood, respectively, and "With the compliments of Lieutenant-General Leonidas Polk, June 12, 1864." They were taken from the breast-

5. Here, CTQ's narrative is not strictly chronological. The consecration took place on April 22, 1864. Bishop Elliott's text was "The way of the Lord is in his sanctuary." A newspaper account noted that CTQ had erected the church in the "almost incredibly short period of six weeks." CTQ was extolled as having "entered into the spirit of the work before him with that energy, and industry, and patience, which have ever been chief among his leading characteristics." "Consecration of St. Luke's Church," Quintard Papers, DU.

6. The two volumes were *The Confederate Soldier's Pocket Manual of Devotions* (1863), a soldier's manual of prayers, scriptural passages, meditations and hymns compiled by CTQ, and *Balm for the Weary and Wounded* (1864), "arranged for such of our soldiers as have, by reason of wounds or disease, been compelled to exchange active service in the field for the harder and more wearying service in the hospital, or on the bed of sickness and pain." *Balm* was dedicated to the memory of Thomas E. King.

pocket of his coat, stained with his blood, after his death, and forwarded to the officers for whom he had intended them.[7]

On the 14th of June, I telegraphed to General Polk from Atlanta that I would visit him at his headquarters and give him the Blessed Sacrament. Two telegrams came to me that day. One was from Major Mason and read as follows: "Lieutenant-General Polk's remains leave here on the 12 o'clock train and will go directly through to Augusta." The other was as follows: "To the Rev. Dr. Quintard, Atlanta, Georgia. Lieutenant-General Polk was killed to-day by a cannon ball. His body goes down to Atlanta to-day. Be at the depot to meet it and watch the trains. Douglas West, A.A.G." I was never more shocked and overwhelmed.[8]

On reaching Atlanta the body of the dead Bishop and General was escorted to St. Luke's Church, and placed in front of the altar. He was dressed in his gray uniform. On his breast rested a cross of white roses and beside his casket lay his sword.

Throughout the following morning, thousands of soldiers and citizens came to pay their last tribute of affection. At noon, assisted by the Rev. John W. Beckwith, of Demopolis, (afterwards Bishop of Georgia), I held funeral services and made an address.[9] The body was then escorted to the railway station by the dead General's personal staff, together with General G. W. Smith, General Wright, General Ruggles, General Reynolds, Colonel Ewell and many officers of the army, soldiers and citizens, and a committee representing the city of Atlanta.[10]

7. Polk was not the only high-ranking officer to whom CTQ provided a copy of the work. Mrs. Robert E. Lee wrote CTQ thanking him for "the little volumes which will form a valuable addition to my soldier's library." Mary Lee to CTQ, June 20, 1864, Quintard Papers, DU. CTQ also sent several copies to Braxton Bragg, who sent them to one of the hospitals in Richmond. Braxton Bragg to CTQ, June 6, 1864, Quintard Papers, U of S.

8. On the morning of June 14, 1864, Johnston, Polk, and Hardee were atop Pine Mountain, northwest of Marietta, Georgia, viewing the position of the Confederate lines. The presence of these high-ranking officers gathered a crowd, which drew Union artillery fire. As described by Johnston: "Lieutenant-General Polk unconsciously exposed by his characteristic insensibility to danger, fell by the third shot, which passed from left to right through the middle of his chest." Joseph E. Johnston, *Narrative of Military Operations Directed During the Late War Between the States* (New York: D. Appleton & Co., 1874), 337. Richard M. Mason and Douglas West were members of Polk's staff. A copy of West's telegram is in Quintard's papers at Duke University.

9. CTQ's address was reported to be "an eloquent and impressive eulogy." "The Fall of Lieutenant General Polk," *Atlanta Southern Confederacy*, June 16, 1864.

10. The officers named include Maj. Gen. Gustavus Woodson Smith (1821–1896), commander of the Georgia militia around Atlanta; Brig. Gen. Marcus J. Wright (1831–1922), commander of the post of Atlanta; Brig. Gen. Daniel Ruggles (1810–1897), "awaiting

At Augusta the body remained two days at St. Paul's Church and lay in state at the City Hall until St. Peter's day, June 29th, when the final rites were held in St. Paul's Church. The Bishops of Georgia, Mississippi and Arkansas officiated. The sermon was by the Bishop of Georgia. The burial was in the chancel of the church.[11]

Bishop Polk's was the first funeral to take place in St. Luke's Church, Atlanta. There was but one other, that of a child named after and baptized by Bishop Elliott, for whom Bishop Polk had stood as sponsor but a short time before.

In August, 1864, I was in Macon, Georgia, not knowing precisely what to do or where to go. The times were very distressing. I took charge of the church and parish in Macon for the rector who had been sick but was slowly recovering. This was in accordance with a letter from the Bishop of Georgia, who had written me about the middle of the previous month, that I had been sadly tossed about and needed rest and that I might go to Macon for that purpose. But a few days later I was with Bishop Lay of Arkansas, in Atlanta, and with the army again, though compelled to go on Sundays to Macon to officiate for the sick rector at that place.[12]

I remained at General Hood's headquarters in Atlanta, expecting to move with the General into Tennessee. The city was being shelled by the Federals, and some of the shells fell very thickly about the General's headquarters. I thought the locality seemed very unhealthy, but as the General and his staff did not seem in the least disturbed, Bishop Lay and I concluded that everything was going on all right according to the art of war and we stood it with the best of them. On one particular day when

---

orders" at Atlanta (see OR 38[4]:781, 38[5]:882); Brig. Gen. Alexander Welch Reynolds (1816–1876), commander of a brigade in Stevenson's Division, wounded at New Hope Church (see OR 38[3]: 814); and Col. Benjamin S. Ewell, General Johnston's assistant adjutant general. Crute, *Confederate Staff Officers*, 103. CTQ was among the committee representing the city of Atlanta that accompanied the corpse to Augusta. *Atlanta Southern Confederacy*, June 19, 1864. In 1945, Polk's remains were reinterred at Christ Church Cathedral in New Orleans.

11. Among those who cast earth on Polk's coffin was James Longstreet, in Georgia to recuperate from his own wounding in the Battle of the Wilderness on May 6, 1864. Polk, *Leonidas Polk*, 2:386.

12. CTQ's narrative omits the great battles that occurred after Bishop Polk's death, Kennesaw Mountain (June 27, 1864), Peachtree Creek (July 20, 1864), Atlanta (June 22, 1864), and Ezra Church (July 28, 1864). Also omitted is the immensely controversial relief of Gen. Joseph E. Johnston by Gen. John B. Hood on July 17, 1864. Bishop Lay was the Rt. Rev. Henry Champlin Lay, missionary bishop of Arkansas from 1859 to 1869.

more shells were thrown in than in all the other days put together, there were, strange to say, no casualties.

On the 10th of August, at headquarters, I presented a class to Bishop Lay for confirmation. It included General Hood and some officers of his staff. In speaking to me the night before his confirmation, the General said: "Doctor, I have two objects in life that engage my supreme regard. One is to do all I can for my country. The other is to be ready and pre-pared for death whenever God shall call me."

Learning that St. Luke's Church had been injured in the bombard-ment of the city, Bishop Lay and I made a visit to it. We looked in wonder at the sight that met our eyes upon our entering the sacred edifice. One of the largest shells had torn through the side of the building and struck the prayer desk on which the large Bible happened to be lying. The prayer desk was broken and the Bible fell under it and upon the shell so as appar-ently to smother it and prevent its exploding. I lifted up the Bible and removed the shell and gathered up all the prayer books I could find for the soldiers in the camps.

Before leaving the church I sat in one of the seats for a few moments and thought of the dear friends who had assisted in the building of the church, and who had offered up the sacrifice of praise and thanksgiving in that place; of the Bishop who had but a short time before consecrated it; of the Bishop-General over whom I had said the burial service there; of the now scattered flock and the utter desolation of God's house. As I rose to go, I picked up a handkerchief that had been dropped there at the child's funeral, which was the last service held there. I wrote a little story subsequently about "Nellie Peters' Pocket Handkerchief, and What It Saw," and it was published in the columns of the "Church Intelligencer."

This was the last time I visited St. Luke's Church of which I have such tender memories. It was destroyed in the "burning of Atlanta."

On the 6th of September, 1864, a general pass was issued to me by order of General Hood and signed by General F. A. Shoup, his Chief of Staff. This pass is an interesting relic of my early associations with one who subsequent to the war came under my jurisdiction as a priest of the Church when I was Bishop of Tennessee. He married a daughter of Bishop Elliott, took orders in the Church, so distinguished himself in the ministry as to receive the degree of Doctor of Divinity, and was for a long time my neighbor at Sewanee, where he was a Professor in the University of the South.[13]

13. Brig. Gen. Francis Asbury Shoup (1834–1896) of Indiana and Florida.

CHAPTER XI

Personal Narrative—Columbus (Georgia) and the Journey into Tennessee

When the fall of Atlanta seemed imminent, General Johnston advised me to remove my family from the city and I decided to go to Columbus, Georgia.[1] The rector of Trinity Church in that town was ill, and the Bishop of Georgia appointed me a Missionary to the Army, at a stipend of $3,000 per year, to be paid as long as the churches in Georgia remained open, and to be continued to me while I was in Columbus and while the Rev. Mr. Hawks, rector of Trinity Church, was ill.[2] My appointment was subsequently made that of Permanent Missionary to the Army.[3]

1. Johnston's advice to CTQ is similar to a recommendation he made to Braxton Bragg on July 12, 1864, that the prisoner of war camp at Andersonville be broken up and the prisoners redistributed elsewhere. This request was perhaps one of the factors in the decision to replace Johnston with Hood in July 1864. Thomas L. Connelly, *Autumn of Glory*, 404.

2. Rev. William N. Hawks had at that point been rector of Trinity Church for approximately ten years. His illness was apparently part of a downward progression, as Hawks died at age fifty-six on December 9, 1865. Buster W. Wright, comp., *Burials and Deaths Reported in the Columbus (Georgia) Enquirer, 1832–1872* (n.p., 1984), 205; Mary Kent Berry, comp., *Records of Marriage, Baptism and Burial from the First Register of Trinity Parish (1836–1903)* (n.p., 1985), 100. Both compilations may be found at GDAH.

3. CTQ's service record does not reflect any capacity with the Confederate government after April 1864. There is no indication, however, that he resigned in order to take his ecclesiastical appointment.

So in October, 1864, I rented a very comfortable house two miles from town, for which I paid rent in advance for nine months—twenty-five hundred dollars Confederate money. But everything seemed to be on the same generous scale, for when on the Sunday after my arrival, I preached in Trinity Church, the offerings for the poor amounted to one thousand dollars. We met with great cordiality from all the people of the town, especially from Mr. J. Rhodes Brown, who placed me under great obligations by his kindness.[4]

We met in Columbus the musical prodigy, "Blind Tom," who belonged to one of our neighbors, General Bethune.[5] I had heard him in a public performance two years previously. I was calling on the Bethunes one day, and on hearing my voice, Tom came into the parlor and in the most uncouth way paid his respects to the ladies and myself. He was not as much as usual in the humor for playing, having already spent four hours at the piano that day for the amusement of some cavalrymen who had visited him. Nevertheless he cheerfully sat down to the piano and gave us some delightful music, and sang us some French songs, in which his powers of mimicry were wonderfully displayed. His playing was most marvellous. It seemed as though inspired. He was then a lad of fifteen. His musical talents were exhibited in his earliest childhood.[6]

During all the month of October I was in constant attendance upon the sick and wounded in the hospitals of Columbus and holding daily religious services in my capacity of Missionary to the Army. My brother-in-law, Dr. H. M. Anderson, having been ordered to Selma with the Polk Hospital to which he was attached, spent a week with me and did much to assist me in my medical services.[7] Greatly to my satisfaction he afterwards received orders to report for duty to the hospitals in Columbus.

4. As seen in Chapter 6, Brown had already been a great supporter of CTQ's efforts.

5. James Neil Bethune was the founder of one of the first "states' rights" newspapers in Georgia, the *Corner Stone*. Bethune derived his "rank" either from having been solicitor general in 1825 or from having been brigadier general of the Georgia militia in 1827–28. Nancy Telfair, *A History of Columbus, Georgia, 1828–1928* (Columbus: Historical Publishing, 1929), 92–93; L. F. Hays, comp., *Georgia Service Records* (n.p., 1936), 229.

6. Thomas Greene Bethune, "Blind Tom" (1849–1908), was the slave of General Bethune and had toured the country before the war as a musical novelty. At the outbreak of the war, "Blind Tom" returned to the South and performed for invalid Confederate soldiers and regular civilian audiences. When the war ended, "Blind Tom" resumed his lucrative tour schedule. Kenneth Coleman and Charles Steven Gurr, *Dictionary of Georgia Biography* (Athens: University of Georgia Press, 1983), s.v. "Bethune, Thomas Greene."

7. Originally from Maryland, Henry Martin Anderson was the husband of Catherine Quintard's sister, Julia Isabella Hand. *Coat of Arms Certification Concerning King/Barrington*, available at GDAH. His service record lists him as a "contract physician" attached to

One day, at the Carnes Hospital, in the presence of a large number of surgeons and convalescents, I baptized an infant. That day was made ever memorable by the generous donation of my friend, Mr. J. Rhodes Brown, who handed me a thousand dollars to be appropriated to the purchase of reading matter for the army. He also presented me with a pair of blankets for my own use, and subsequently with three hundred yards of excellent cloth to clothe my regiment. To this he thoughtfully added buttons, thread and lining and three hundred pairs of socks. The cloth at that time was valued at forty-five dollars a yard. "The liberal soul shall be made fat."[8]

About the middle of October, General G. P. T. Beauregard assumed command of the Military Division East of the Mississippi River, including the Department of Tennessee and Georgia commanded by General Hood, who, however, was to retain command of his department.[9] On assuming command, General Beauregard published an address to his army in excellent tone and taste, promising a forward movement. It caused great enthusiasm. The General was very popular with his troops and his name was a tower of strength.

On the 8th of November, Captain Wickham informed me that he would leave for the army on the morrow and I immediately made my arrangements to accompany him.[10] Leaving Columbus on a freight train, after a long and wearying journey we reached Montgomery, Alabama, and found accommodations, or what passed for such, in the topmost story of the principal hotel. While in Montgomery I dined at Dr. Scott's in company with a number of Tennessee friends, among whom were Colonel Battle, late in command of the Twentieth Tennessee, and then State Treasurer; Colonel Ray, Secretary of State; General Dunlap, Comptrol-

the Polk Hospital. H. M. Anderson CSR, Confederate General and Staff Officers, RG 109, M-331, NA.

8. CTQ planned to leave for the Army of Tennessee with the clothes Brown provided, noting that he had supplied his "boys" every winter. Writing a friend at the end of October, he stated: "I do not know where I shall find General Hood—in Nashville I hope." CTQ to "Dear Friend," November 1, 1864, Quintard Papers, U of S. At that juncture, the headquarters of the Army of Tennessee was near the Tennessee River at Tuscumbia, Alabama, preparatory to moving into Middle Tennessee. OR 39(1): 808.

9. P. G. T. Beauregard was appointed to "command the two military departments and the troops therein, known as the Department of Tennessee and Georgia and the Department of Alabama, Mississippi and East Louisiana" on October 3, 1864. OR 39(3):785.

10. Previously on the staff of Gen. Albert Sidney Johnston, Capt. W. L. Wickham was apparently en route to join Maj. Gen. B. F. Cheatham's staff as a paymaster. Crute, *Confederate Staff Officers*, 36, 102.

ler; Henry Watterson, and Albert Roberts who then edited the *Montgomery Mail*.[11] Colonel Battle followed me after I left the house, and handed me a roll of bills, which he begged me to accept from Colonel Ray, General Dunlap and himself, to assist me in defraying my expenses. The money came very opportunely and I thanked him very heartily, for I had not five dollars in my pocket at the time.

I took a steamer for Selma. The vessel was crowded to excess—in the cabin, on the deck and all about the guards. Still I had a much pleasanter night than I anticipated—on the floor of the cabin.

At Selma, I met the Rev. Mr. Ticknor, who handed me a letter from my dear friend, the Bishop of Alabama, containing a check for five hundred dollars, which he begged me to accept for my own comfort.[12]

I left for Demopolis at eight the following morning, in company with Captain Wickham and my friend Major Thomas Peters, formerly of General Polk's staff.[13] At Demopolis I had the pleasure of seeing the Rev. John W. Beckwith, who had officiated with me at the funeral of General Polk and who was afterwards to become the Bishop of Georgia.

Continuing on our journey we sailed down the Tombigbee river to the terminus of the railway, where we took cars and started for Meridian, Mississippi. It was a most tedious trip on the river, taking up about ten hours to make fifty miles. And when we reached the cars we found them crowded to excess.

11. Col. Joel B. Battle commanded the 20th Tennessee until he was stunned by a falling tree limb at Shiloh and captured. After his exchange, he was appointed state treasurer. Lindsley, *Military Annals*, 383. John Edward R. Ray (1824–1879) and James Trimble Dunlap (1812–1879) apparently got their military titles from prewar state militia positions. McBride and Robison, *Biographical Directory of the Tennessee General Assembly*, 1:217, 609. Henry Watterson, of Louisville, Kentucky, served on the staffs of Nathan Bedford Forrest and Leonidas Polk and published the *Chattanooga Daily Rebel. CMH* 11:570–71. Like Battle, Albert Roberts was a veteran of early service with the 20th Tennessee and had later seen service with John Hunt Morgan's cavalry. In 1863, Roberts joined Watterson on the staff of the *Rebel*, and in 1864 they both went to Atlanta to write for the *Southern Confederacy* and the displaced *Memphis Appeal*. When Atlanta fell, they traveled to Montgomery, where they were employed by the *Mail*. In Montgomery, Roberts boarded with Dr. and Mrs. John Godwin Scott, an expatriate English couple. James Summerville, "Albert Roberts, Journalist of the New South, Part I," *Tennessee Historical Quarterly* 42 (Spring 1983): 18, 24–28.

12. Rev. J. H. Ticknor was the rector of St. Paul's Church in Selma, Alabama. The Bishop was Rt. Rev. Richard Hooker Wilmer of Alabama. William A. Clebsch, ed., *Journals of the Protestant Episcopal Church in the Confederate States*, III-215.

13. Capt. W. L. Wickham has been identified previously. Maj. Thomas Peters was at this point quartermaster on the staff of Lt. Gen. Richard Taylor. Crute, *Confederate Staff Officers*, 36, 191.

I stopped at Macon, Mississippi, to visit Captain Yates who had lost his leg at Atlanta and to whom I had ministered there.[14] I met the heartiest of welcomes, and found the Captain greatly improved and getting about a little on crutches. His nephew, who had lost a leg at Murfreesboro, was visiting him.

I started off from Macon with abundant supplies furnished by Mrs. Yates, among which were two roast turkeys, a ham and "all the et ceteras." When the train came along I found Major Winter, of the Engineers, in the car with his baggage and implements.[15] He kindly invited me to a seat and I had a comfortable ride to Okolona, Mississippi. It having been decided not to go forward until General Cheatham could be heard from, Captain Wickham, Captain Bradford and I went on to Columbus, Mississippi, where I was very cordially received by Bishop Green of Mississippi.[16]

Wednesday, the 16th of November, having been set apart by the President of the Confederate States as a day of supplication and prayer for God's blessing on our cause, I officiated in St. Paul's Church, Columbus, and preached from the text: "Think not that I am come to send peace on earth: I came not to send peace, but a sword."

General Cheatham telegraphed me to go forward. So I left West Point, Mississippi, on the 19th of November, in a car loaded with corn. The party on our car included Brigadier-General Quarles, Sterling Cockrill, of Nashville, Captains Shute, Wickham, Bradford, Jones, Mayrant and Colonel Young of the Forty-ninth Tennessee Regiment, besides some ladies and young people.[17] The day wore away pleasantly enough in such com-

14. The 1860 Federal census for Noxubee County, Mississippi, lists R. E. V. Yates, then age 25, a physician. Robert Elliot Valentine Yates was captain of the Noxubee Guards, Company D, 41st Mississippi Regiment. Yates actually commanded the regiment as its senior officer present for a brief time in January 1864. Dunbar Rowland, *Military History of Mississippi, 1843–1898* (1908; reprint, Spartanburg, S. C.: Reprint Co., 1978), 344–51; H. Grady Howell, Jr., comp., *For Dixie Land I'll Take My Stand!: A Muster Listing of All Known Mississippi Confederate Soldiers, Sailors, and Marines*, 3 vols., (Madison, Miss.: Chickasaw Bayou Press, 1998), 3:3280.

15. Major D. Wintter of the engineers had previously been on Leonidas Polk's staff and was at this point in charge of the engineers in the District of Mississippi and East Louisiana. *OR* 45(1):1229.

16. Captain Bradford was possibly Capt. James M. Bradford of the 33rd Tennessee. Rt. Rev. William Mercer Green (1798–1887) was bishop of Mississippi.

17. Brig. Gen. William Andrew Quarles (1825–1893) was commander of a Tennessee brigade in Maj. Gen. Edward C. Walthall's division. Sterling Cockrill, a prominent citizen

pany and about 8 o'clock at night we reached Corinth, Mississippi, where the Rev. Mr. Markham, an excellent Presbyterian minister from New Orleans, shared my blankets with me.[18] Here we had information that General Sherman was making his way to the seaboard and was within thirty miles of Macon, Georgia.

Captain Wickham and myself passed on with others, and at half-past four in the evening of Thursday, the 22nd of November, we crossed the line into Tennessee. In consequence of the wretched condition of the roads and the rough weather, we had a hard time of it. I made my way with all possible speed, through Mount Pleasant to Ashwood and to the house of my dear friend, General Lucius Polk.[19]

Such greetings as I received! How I thanked God for the friends He had given me! General Chalmers and his staff were guests at General Polk's, and the next day we had many happy meetings. All day long there was a constant stream of visitors to Hamilton Place, the residence of General Polk. General Hood and Governor Harris came early in the day as did also General Cheatham. Then came General John C. Brown, Gen-

---

of Nashville, purportedly coined the phrase "Cotton is the King that will shake the jewels of Queen Victoria." Isabel Howell, "John Armfield of Beersheba Springs," *Tennessee Historical Quarterly* 3 (March 1944): 60; John G. Frank, "Adolphus Heiman: Architect and Soldier," *Tennessee Historical Quarterly* 5 (March 1946): 38–39. Capt. James Shute of Louisiana was a member of General Quarles' staff. Lindsley, *Military Annals*, 519. Jones cannot be identified. Robert W. Mayrant served in the 3rd Alabama, and was later assistant quartermaster of the 22nd Alabama. On August 16, 1864, Maj. Gen. James Patton Anderson requested that he be appointed paymaster of his division—which in November, 1864, was commanded by Maj. Gen. Edward Johnson. R. W. Mayrant CSR, Confederate General and Staff Officers, M-331, NA. Col. William F. Young (d. 1899) commanded the 49th Tennessee of Quarles' Brigade. He was severely wounded at Ezra Church on July 28, 1864, which occasioned the loss of his right arm. Although Young was able to return to his regiment, Quarles relieved him on account of his feeble condition just as it formed on the field at Franklin. *CMH*, 10: 327–29, 804–5.

18. Rev. Thomas Railey Markham (1828–1894), of the Lafayette Street Church in New Orleans. E. C. Scott, *Ministerial Directory of the Presbyterian Church, U.S., 1861–1941* (Austin, Tex: Von Boeckman-Jones Co., 1942), 430.

19. Because CTQ refers in the next paragraph to Hamilton Place, the "General Lucius Polk" referred to here is probably the house's owner, Lucius Julius Polk (1802–1870), Leonidas Polk's brother. Lucius Julius bore the title "general" for his service as a prewar adjutant general of the State of Tennessee. His nephew, Brig. Gen. Lucius Eugene Polk, was at this point recuperating from his fourth wound of the war, received at Kennesaw Mountain. William Bruce Turner, *History of Maury County, Tennessee* (Nashville: Parthenon Press, 1955), 246–47, 252–253; Warner, *Generals in Gray*, 244.

eral Gibson, General Bate, handsome Frank Armstrong, and General Walthall, who with his staff, spent the night with us.[20] I offered a special prayer of Thanksgiving to God for our return to Tennessee, and the following day was one of supreme enjoyment. I did not move out of the house but just rested and tried to realize that I was once more in Tennessee.

On the 27th, Advent Sunday, I had Morning Prayer at the residence of General Lucius Polk, and baptized two children, making a record of the same in the Parish Register.

On the following day our forces entered Columbia. I accompanied them and found the good people of the town in a state of the wildest enthusiasm. Almost the first person I met was my dear friend, the Rev. Dr. Pise who went with me to call on several families.[21] These were days of great hopefulness. General Beauregard telegraphed to General Hood that Sherman was making his way rapidly to the Atlantic coast and urged Hood to advance to relieve General Lee. General Hood proposed to press forward with all possible speed, and said to me confidentially that he would either beat the enemy to Nashville or make the latter go there double quick. So the race began to see who would get to Nashville first. That night the enemy was still on the opposite side of Duck River, but it was thought he would withdraw next morning. At all events our forces were to cross at daylight.

General Hood urged me to go with the ambulance. When he told me "Good-bye," I prayed God's blessing, guidance and direction on him. "Thank you, Doctor," he replied, "that is my hope and trust." And as he turned away he remarked: "The enemy must give me fight or I will be in Nashville before to-morrow night."

20. The previously unidentified officers in this paragraph include Brig. Gen. Randall Lee Gibson (1832–1892), commanding a Louisiana brigade in Maj. Gen. Henry D. Clayton's division; Maj. Gen. William Brimage Bate (1826–1905), commanding a division in Maj. Gen. B. F. Cheatham's corps; Brig. Gen. Frank Crawford Armstrong (1835–1909), commanding a cavalry brigade in Brig. Gen. William H. Jackson's division; and Maj. Gen. Edward Cary Walthall (1831–1898), commanding a division in Lt. Gen. A. P. Stewart's corps. Warner, *Generals in Gray*, 12–13, 19, 46, 104, 325–26.

21. Rev. David Pise (pronounced "Pease") of New York, Rector of St. Peter's Church in Columbia from 1854 to 1868 and a supporter of CTQ in the reestablishment of the University of the South after the war. Jill K. Garrett, *Maury County, Tennessee, Historical Sketches* (Columbia, Tenn.: n.p., 1967), 86–87; Chitty, *Reconstruction at Sewanee*, 85.

General Cheatham and General Stewart crossed Duck River at sunrise; General Lee shortly afterwards.[22] There was considerable shelling of the town, and Colonel Beckham was wounded, but no lives were lost.[23] By Wednesday the enemy had all withdrawn, our forces had crossed over and the wagons were crossing. I crossed the river at two o'clock with Major John Green, of South Carolina, and Dr. Philips, of Hoxton's Artillery.[24] We met on the road several hundred prisoners going to the rear. At Spring Hill we heard that the Federal commanders were in a sad way. General Stanley had been heard to say, "I can do nothing more; I must retreat."[25] Three trains of cars were burned by the Federals at this place. Very much has been said about the Confederates' "lost opportunity," as it is called, at Spring Hill, and General Cheatham has been faulted for not doing something very brilliant there that would have changed the whole complexion of affairs. It is said that he failed to give battle when the "enemy was marching along the road almost under the camp fires of the main body of our army."[26]

22. The three infantry corps of the Army of Tennessee were commanded by Maj. Gen. Benjamin Franklin Cheatham, Lt. Gen. Alexander Peter Stewart, and Lt. Gen. Stephen Dill Lee. Hood's plan was to "go through the woods" with seven of his nine divisions under Cheatham and Stewart and fall on the line of the Federal retreat to Nashville at Spring Hill, about twelve miles from Columbia. See CTQ's diary entry for November 28, 1864.

23. Unfortunately, Virginia-born Col. Robert Franklin Beckham, Lee's chief of artillery, was mortally wounded when his skull was fractured by a stone fragmented by an exploding shell. OR 45(1):687; see Bryant Burroughs, "The Life and Death of Lieutenant Colonel Robert Beckham, CSA," Southern Partisan 17 (First Quarter 1998): 24–25; James W. Ratchford, Memoirs of a Confederate Staff Officer: From Bethel to Bentonville, ed. Evelyn Ratchford Sieburg and James E. Hanson II (Shippensburg, Pa.: White Mane Books, 1998), 61.

24. Maj. John W. Green was apparently in charge of the army's trains. See OR 45(2):729–31. Green, however, joined the army from Louisiana. John W. Green CSR, Confederate General and Staff Officers, RG 109, M-331, NA. N. D. Phillips was assistant surgeon of Hoxton's Artillery Battalion. N. D. Phillips CSR, ibid.

25. Maj. Gen. David Sloane Stanley (1828–1902) of Ohio, commander of the Federal 4th Corps.

26. Hood later termed this march as the "best move in my career as a soldier." John B. Hood, Advance and Retreat (New Orleans: Beauregard, 1879), 290. The failed attack at Spring Hill on November 29, 1864, remains a mystery and controversy to the present day, the debate hinging on who among the members of the Army of Tennessee's high command was to blame for the lost opportunity. Wiley Sword, The Confederacy's Last Hurrah: Spring Hill, Franklin, and Nashville (Lawrence: University Press of Kansas, 1992), 110–55. Two other good accounts are J. P. Young, "Hood's Failure at Spring Hill," Confederate Veteran 17 (January 1908), 26, and W. T. Crawford, "The Mystery of Spring Hill," Civil War History 1 (June 1955), 101.

During the war and after its close I was brought into such intimate association with General B. F. Cheatham, that I learned to appreciate his high character. He was a man of admirable presence. In manner he was free, without frivolity,—cheerful, kind-hearted and ever easy of access. He was a gentleman without pretensions and a politician without deceit; a faithful friend and a generous foe; strong in his attachments and rational in his resentments. He was clear in judgment, firm in purpose and courageous as a lion. He was fruitful in expedients, prompt in action and always ready for a fight. He won victory on many a well-contested field; but, best of all, he ruled his own spirit.[27]

He participated in the greater number of battles in the War with Mexico; and in the civil war he won distinction and promotion at Belmont, Shiloh, Perryville, Murfreesboro, Chickamauga, and on many fields besides, he exhibited the most perfect self-possession,—the utmost disregard of peril. He possessed in an eminent degree the indispensable quality of a soldier which enabled him to go wherever duty or necessity demanded his presence. He understood thoroughly that it was better that a leader should lose his life than his honor. I have every confidence in the statement he once made: "During my services as a soldier under the flag of my country in Mexico, and as an officer of the Confederate armies, I cannot recall an instance where I failed to obey and order literally, promptly and faithfully."

Major Saunders, of French's Division, has said: "The assumption that Schofield's army would have been destroyed at Spring Hill, and one of the most brilliant victories of the war achieved, had it not been for the misconduct of Cheatham, is one of the delusions that has survived the war. . . . No circumstance or incident that his strategy developed can be found that justifies [the] attacks [made] on the military reputation of General Cheatham."[28] My own opinion has always been that General Cheatham was in no way at fault in his conduct at Spring Hill. And this opinion has been strengthened by the letter from Governor Harris to Governor James D. Porter, dated May 20, 1877, and the brief letter from

27. CTQ discreetly fails to mention Cheatham's fondness for alcohol. In 1863, he told Gen. St. John Richardson Liddell that he observed Cheatham drunk on the field at Murfreesboro. Liddell, *Liddell's Record*, 119.

28. David Ward Sanders was assistant adjutant general on the staff of Maj. Gen. Samuel Gibbs French, who commanded a division in Stewart's Corps. Crute, *Confederate Staff Officers*, 65.

General Hood to Cheatham, dated December 13, 1864, both recently published in "Southern Historical Papers," vol. 9, p. 532.[29]

I baptized General Cheatham, confirmed him, officiated at his marriage, and it was my sad privilege to say the burial service over him. He died in Nashville, Tennessee, September 4th, 1886. His last words were: "Bring me my horse! I am going to the front!"[30]

Just before moving toward Franklin, General Strahl came to me and said: "I want to make you a present," and presented me with a splendid horse, named "The Lady Polk." I used the horse through the war and at its close sold her, and with the money erected in St. James' Church, Bolivar, Tennessee, a memorial window to General Strahl and his Adjutant, Lieutenant John Marsh, both of them killed in the fearful battle of Franklin. both of these men I had baptized but a few months previously, and both were confirmed by Bishop Elliott.

29. In "The Lost Opportunity at Spring Hill, Tenn.—General Cheatham's Reply to General Hood," SHSP 9 (1881): 525 ff., Cheatham replied to charges in Hood's autobiography (*Advance and Retreat,* 290) that Cheatham was largely responsible for the failure. Cheatham's article was supported in some particulars by letters of various witnesses and participants.

30. CTQ expressed his warm feelings toward Cheatham in a letter read at a Confederate veterans' reunion, which was later published in *Southern Historical Society Papers.* C. T. Quintard, "B. F. Cheatham, Major General C.S.A.: A Tribute to His Memory by Bishop C. T. Quintard," SHSP 16 (1888): 349.

CHAPTER XII

Personal Narrative — Franklin

The Battle of Franklin was fought on the 30th of November, 1864, and was one of the bloodiest of the war. On that dismal November day, our line of battle was formed at 4 o'clock in the afternoon and marched directly down through an open field toward the outer breastworks of the enemy. A sheet of fire was pouring into the very faces of our men. The command was: "Forward! Forward men!" Never on earth did men fight against greater odds, but they advanced towards the breastworks, — on and on, — and met death without flinching. The roar of battle was kept up until after midnight and then gradually died away, as the enemy abandoned their interior line of defences and rapidly retreated to Nashville.

We had about 23,000 men engaged. They fought with great gallantry, drove the enemy from their outer line of temporary works into their interior line, captured several stands of colors and about one thousand prisoners.[1] But our losses were about 4,500 brave men, and among them Major-General Pat Cleburne, Brigadier-General John Adams, Brigadier-General O. F. Strahl, Brigadier-General Gist, Brigadier-General Granberry and

---

1. The Army of Tennessee appears to have had about twenty thousand men engaged and to have suffered staggering casualties of over six thousand. Horn, *The Army of Tennessee* 403–4.

Brigadier-General John C. Carter was mortally wounded.[2] Among the wounded were Major-General John C. Brown, Brigadier-Generals Manigault, Quarles, Cockrill, Scott and George Gordon.[3]

General John Adams, on reaching the vicinity of Franklin, had immediately formed his line of battle near the residence of Colonel John McGavock and led his troops into the fight. A more gallant set of officers and men never faced a foe. General Adams was calm, cool and self-possessed and vigilantly watched and directed the movements of his men and led them on for victory or for death. He was severely wounded early in the action and was urged to leave the field. He calmly replied: "No, I will not! I will see my men through!" and at the same time gave an order to Captain Thomas Gibson, his aid-de-camp and Brigade Inspector. When he fell he was in the act of leaping his horse, "Old Charlie," over the outer works. Both horse and his rider were instantly killed,—the General falling within our lines, while old Charlie lay astride the works. The General received two wounds in the right leg, four balls entered his body, one ball passed through his breast and one entered his right shoulder-blade. These wounds were all received simultaneously and his death was instantaneous.[4]

Major-General Cleburne's mare was dead on the works and the Gen-

2. Brig. Gen. John Adams (1825–1864) of Tennessee commanded a brigade in the division commanded by CTQ's friend W. W. Loring. Accounts of Adams' and Strahl's deaths are published in Ridley, *Battles and Sketches*, 417–20, 424–25. The others named who have not been identified previously were Brig. Gen. States Rights Gist (1831–1864) of South Carolina, commanding a brigade in John C. Brown's division; Brig. Gen. Hiram Bronson Granbury (1831–1864) of Mississippi and Texas, commanding a brigade of Cleburne's Division; and Brig. Gen. John Carpenter Carter (1837–1864) of Georgia and Tennessee, commanding a brigade of Brown's Division.

3. Brig. Gen. Francis Marion Cockrill (1834–1915) commanded the famed Missouri Brigade in Maj. Gen. Samuel G. French's division. Brig. Gen. Thomas Moore Scott (1829–1876) commanded an Alabama brigade in Loring's Division. Brig. Gen. George Washington Gordon (1836–1911) commanded a brigade in Brown's Division, and was both wounded and captured. Warner, *Generals in Gray*, 109–10.

4. The eyewitness accounts of two Federal officers indicate Adams survived a short time after he was mortally wounded. Adams' last words were reportedly, "It is the fate of a soldier to die for his country." Ridley, *Battles and Sketches*, 419–20. Thomas Gibson, Adams' cousin, had formerly been a captain in the 10th Tennessee Regiment, but as Adams' aide, was only a lieutenant. Subsequently, he was assigned to staff duty in Featherston's Brigade. T. Gibson CSR, Confederate General and Staff Officers, RG 109, M-331, NA; Ridley, *Battles and Sketches*, 417.

eral himself was pierced with no less than forty-nine bullets.[5] The bodies
of these two brave Generals were brought from the battlefield in an ambulance and taken to the residence of Colonel McGavock, whose house
and grounds were literally filled with the Confederate dead and wounded.
Mrs. McGavock rendered every assistance possible and her name deserves to be handed down to future generations as that of a woman of lofty
principle, exalted character and untiring devotion.[6]

Captain Gibson, General Adams' aid and Brigade Inspector, although
badly wounded, accompanied by Captain Blackwell, conveyed the body
of his commander to the residence of the General's brother, Major Nathan Adams, in Pulaski. I officiated at the funeral and his mortal remains
were placed in the cemetery by the side of his father and mother.[7]

As a soldier, General Adams was active, calm and self-possessed, brave
without rashness, quick to perceive and ever ready to seize the favorable
moment. He enjoyed the confidence of his superiors and the love and
respect of his soldiers and officers. In camp and on the march he looked
closely to the comfort of his soldiers, and often shared his horse on long
marches with his sick and broken-down men.

He was a member of the Episcopal Church and a sincere and humble
Christian. For a year or more before his death he engaged, morning, noon
and night in devotional exercises. He invariably fasted on Friday and
other days of abstinence appointed by the Book of Common Prayer. He
was guided in all his actions by a thoughtful and strict regard for truth,
right and duty. In all the relations of life he was upright, just and pure.
There is no shadow on his memory and he left to his children the heritage
of an unblemished name and to coming generations the sublime heroism
of a Southern Soldier.

5. Cleburne actually approached the Federal works on foot and was killed by a shot to
the chest. Irving A. Buck, *Cleburne and His Command* (1908; reprint Wilmington, N.C.:
Broadfoot Publishing, 1987) 292.

6. Reminders of the service of the McGavock house, "Carnton," as a hospital can be
seen today in the bloodstains on its floors. An account of Mrs. McGavock's exertions on
behalf of the wounded can be found in Ridley, *Battles and Sketches*, 411–12. Another sad
distinction of the house is the remarkable fact that the bodies of four Confederate generals,
Cleburne, Strahl, Granbury, and Adams (although there seems to be some dispute over
Adams), were laid out on its lower porch. Sword, *Confederacy's Last Hurrah*, 263.

7. Oddly, there is no account of this funeral in CTQ's diary. Captain Blackwell cannot
be positively identified. A Nicholas Blackwell, however, was captain of Company E, 43rd
Mississippi Infantry, of Adams' Brigade.

After the battle General Strahl's horse lay by the road-side and the General by his side,—both dead. All his staff were killed. General Strahl was a native of Ohio, but he had come to Tennessee in his youth, and was as thoroughly identified with the latter state as any of her sons. He gave to the Fourth Tennessee Regiment its drill and discipline and made it a noted regiment before he succeeded General A. P. Stewart in command of a brigade. He was just recovering from a dangerous wound received at Atlanta the previous July when he entered upon the Tennessee campaign, which ended for him fatally.[8]

General Gist, of South Carolina, was lying dead with his sword still grasped in his hand and reaching across the fatal breastworks. General Granberry of Texas, and his horse were seen on top of the breastworks,—horse and rider,—dead! I went back to Columbia, hired a negro to make some plain coffins, helped him to put them into a wagon, drove with him about sixteen miles, and buried these brave men,—Strahl, Gist and Granberry,—under the shadow of the ivy-mantled tower of St. John's Church, Ashwood,—with the services of the Church.[9] Then I returned to the field.

Major-General John C. Brown, General George Gordon, and General Carter were seriously wounded,—the last named, mortally. After ministering to these and many another, I returned to Columbia to the hospital in the Columbia Institute. Here I found Captain William Flournoy and Adjutant McKinney of the First Tennessee Regiment, both severely wounded. There were hundreds of wounded in the Institute.[10]

I buried Major-General Cleburne from the residence of Mrs. William Polk. A military escort was furnished by Captain Long and every token of respect was shown to the memory of the glorious dead. After the funeral,

8. Strahl was seriously wounded while passing loaded rifles to soldiers firing over the Federal ditch. While being carried to the rear, he was hit twice more, the final shot killing him instantly. Ridley, *Battles and Sketches*, 425.

9. CTQ's diary for December 2 and 3, 1864, varies with this account to a substantial degree. See diary entries below. St. John's Church was built by Leonidas Polk and his brothers in the early 1840s at Ashwood, Polk's Tennessee home southwest of Columbia. The diary does not mention Gist, who was temporarily buried at Franklin. CTQ diary, December 2, 3, 1864, U of S; Parks, *General Leonidas Polk*, 98–99; Warner, *Generals in Gray*, 107.

10. William C. Flournoy was elected captain of Company K, 1st Tennessee, in April, 1862. Lieutenant McKinney is possibly George McKinney, who ended the war serving as lieutenant of Company L. Lindsley, *Military Annals*, 159, 169. CTQ's diary entry for December 2, 1864, states Flourney was wounded in the groin, McKinney in the head.

I rode out to Hamilton Place with General Lucius Polk. I there found General Manigault wounded in the head and Major Prince, of Mobile, wounded in the foot.[11]

Returning to Columbia, I met Captain Stepleton and through him paid the burial expenses of my dear friend, John Marsh,—three hundred dollars. The dear fellow had given me a farewell kiss as he entered the battle.[12] I also gave the Rev. Dr. Pise one hundred dollars and left myself without funds. While in Columbia I sent wagons down to the Webster settlement to procure supplies for our wounded at Franklin.

Having visited the sick and wounded in the hospitals at Columbia, I went with Captain Stepleton towards Franklin. I reached the house of Mr. Harrison, about three miles from Franklin, at dark, and stopped to see my friends, General Carter, General Quarles, Captain Tom Henry, and Captain Matt Pilcher.[13] Captain Pilcher was shot in the side. Captain Henry was wounded slightly in the head. Both were doing well. General Quarles had his left arm shattered. General Carter was shot through the body and his wound was mortal. I knelt by the side of the wounded and commended them to God. I had prayers with the family before retiring. All that night we could hear the guns around Nashville very distinctly, but all I could learn in the morning was that our lines were within a mile and a half of the city.

The following day was the Second Sunday in Advent, December 4th.

11. Manigault has been identified previously. Major Prince was probably Thomas Mc-Carroll Prince, Jr., of the 22nd Alabama Infantry Regiment. Thomas McAdory Owen, *History of Alabama and Dictionary of Alabama Biography*, 4 vols. (Chicago: S. J. Clarke, 1921), 4:1392.

12. Captain T. B. Stepleton was one of Strahl's staff officers. Marsh was the young friend CTQ nursed after Chickamauga, "knit to [CTQ] by the tenderest ties of friendship." Ridley, *Battles and Sketches*, 422. A sketch of Marsh's service and a romanticized account of his death can be found in Lindsley, *Military Annals*, 793–94.

13. Built in 1848, the Harrison house was the home of William Harrison, "one time High Sheriff of Williamson County." According to tradition, early in the afternoon of November 30, 1864, Hood and Forrest had a confrontation on the front steps as to the proper means of dealing with the entrenched Federals at Franklin. Reid Smith, *Majestic Middle Tennessee* (Prattville, Ala.: Paddle Wheel Publications, 1975), 68–69. Capt. (later Maj.) Thomas F. Henry was assistant adjutant general on Maj. Gen. John C. Brown's staff. Crute, *Confederate Staff Officers*, 27. Capt. Matthew Barrow Pilcher was a member of CTQ's own Rock City Guards and was paymaster of Cheatham's (Brown's) Division. Wounded and captured at Perryville, he escaped death in a train wreck shortly after his exchange. He was again captured after CTQ's encounter with him and confined at Camp Chase, a Federal prison camp, until May 1865. Toney, *Privations of a Private*, 47–55; CMH, 10:672.

I rode to Franklin to see Dr. Buist, the Post Surgeon. All along the way were abundant marks of the terrific battle,—dead horses and burnt wagons,—but at the line of the breastworks near Mr. Carter's house, where the heaviest fighting was done, there was a great number of horses piled almost one upon another. Mr. Carter's son was shot within a few yards of his home.[14] Returning to Mr. Harrison's house with Dr. Buist, who went down to attend to the wounded, I visited them all and had prayers with them. The Doctor and myself returned to Franklin in the evening and William Clouston called and took me to his house for the night.[15]

There I found General Cockrill of Missouri, wounded in the legs and in the right arm but full of life and very cheerful. Lieutenant Anderson, one of his staff, who had lost a part of one foot at Vicksburg, was now wounded in the other. Captain John M. Hickey, in command of a company in a Missouri regiment, while charging the main lines of the works just in front of the cotton gin, was desperately wounded, his leg being shattered. He fell into the mud and while in this deplorable condition, his left arm was badly broken by a minnie ball and soon afterwards he was shot in the shoulder. With thousands of dead and wounded lying about him, he lay upon the field of battle for fifteen hours, without food, water or shelter, in the freezing cold, and half of that time exposed to the plunging shot and shell of both friend and foe.[16]

I devoted my time while in Franklin, to visiting the hospitals. In one room of Brown's Division hospital, in the Court House, I dressed a goodly number of wounds, after which I went to visit General Cockrill and

14. The bullet-pocked house and outbuildings of the home of Fountain Branch Carter are among the few remaining period landmarks on the Franklin battlefield. Carter's son, Capt. Theodrick "Tod" Carter, was mortally wounded a few yards from the family home. Lindsley, *Military Annals*, 385–86; see also Sword, *Confederacy's Last Hurrah*, 197–213, 233–34.

15. William G. Clouston was the son of Edward G. Clouston, a native of Scotland, who, in 1857 was listed as a druggist. Virginia McDaniel Bowman, *Historical Williamson County: Old Homes and Sites* (Nashville: Blue & Gray Press, 1971), 139; James A. Crutchfield and Robert Holliday, *Franklin: Tennessee's Handsomest Town* (Franklin, Tenn.: Hillsboro Press, 1999), 129.

16. Cockrill has been identified previously. His Missouri brigade made one of the most desperate assaults at Franklin. Lt. C. Samuel Anderson of the 6th Missouri Infantry was Cockrill's aide. Capt. John M. Hickey commanded a company of the 2nd and 6th Missouri Infantry (consolidated), one of Cockrill's regiments.

thence to army headquarters at the residence of John Overton.[17] I met with a most cordial welcome, not only from General Hood, but also from Mr. Overton's family and several ladies from Nashville.

On Wednesday, I rode with Governor Harris to Franklin and thence to Mr. Harrison's, to be with General John C. Carter who was nearing his end. I found General Quarles and Captain Pilcher both doing well. Major Dunlop was also improving. Lieutenant-Colonel Jones of the Twenty-fourth South Carolina, however, was not doing so well, having had a profuse hemorrhage.[18] On visiting General Carter, I read a short passage of Holy Scripture and had prayers with him for which he thanked me in the most earnest manner. In his lucid moments my conversation with him was exceedingly interesting. But his paroxysms of pain were frequent and intense and he craved for chloroform and it was freely administered to him.

He could not be convinced that he was going to die. "But," I said, "General, if you should die, what do you wish me to say to your wife?"

"Tell her," he replied, "that I have always loved her devotedly and regret leaving her more than I can express."

I had prayers with all the wounded and with the family of Mr. Harrison, and sat up with General Carter until half past twelve o'clock. Lieutenant-Colonel Jones died some time in the night. General Carter died the following Saturday. I wrote to the Rev. Dr. Pise at Columbia to attend his funeral as his body was to be taken there for temporary burial. It was bitterly cold and the roads were very slippery.

General Carter was a native of Georgia but a citizen of Tennessee. He had been advanced for merit from a lieutenant at the beginning of the war to the command of a brigade. He had a wonderful gentleness of manner coupled with dauntless courage. Every field officer of his brigade but one, was killed, wounded or captured on the enemy's works at the dreadful battle of Franklin.

17. Col. John Overton (1821–1895) was the son of Judge John Overton, a political ally of Andrew Jackson. Forced to leave their home, Traveller's Rest, during the Federal occupation, the Overton family returned with the advance of the Army of Tennessee. Henry Lee Swint, "Traveller's Rest: Home of Judge John Overton," *Tennessee Historical Quarterly* 26 (Summer, 1967): 119–32; James H. McNeilly, "Col. John Overton," *CV* 7(January 1899): 34–35.

18. Maj. S. J. C. Dunlop was wounded leading the 46th Georgia Infantry, and Lt. Col. Jesse S. Jones was wounded in front of the 24th South Carolina Infantry. Both regiments were in Gist's Brigade. OR 45(1):686; CMH 6:343.

The following Sunday, (Third Sunday in Advent), I celebrated the Holy Communion at army headquarters. That night General Forrest shared my bed with me. One of the men remarked: "It was the lion and the lamb lying down together."

The following day, in the Methodist Church at Brentwood, I united in the holy bonds of matrimony, Major William Clare and Miss Mary Hadley, of Nashville.[19] The Major's attendants were Dr. Foard, Medical Director, and Major Moore, Chief Commissary.[20] A large number of officers were present. After the marriage, the party returned to the residence of Mr. Overton where a sumptuous dinner was provided. My empty purse was replenished by a fee of two hundred dollars, besides which a friend sent me, the following morning, fifty dollars in greenbacks.

I left headquarters the following day in Dr. Foard's ambulance for Franklin and on the way picked up a couple of wounded men and carried them to the hospital. We met Governor Harris and Colonel Ray, Secretary of State. I spent the evening at Mrs. Carter's with my friends, Colonel Rice and Captain Tom Henry.[21] The next day I made efforts to purchase shoes for my family. The merchants had hidden their goods and were unwilling to dispose of them for Confederate money. But by offering to pay in greenbacks, I not only secured shoes but all sorts of goods.

Meeting Captain Kelly, of the Rock City Guard, then off duty in consequence of wounds received in the recent battle, I proposed to him to go to Georgia for clothing for the soldiers.[22] To this he agreed and we left for Columbia. While there I attended a meeting of the ladies, the object of which was to organize a Relief Association.

Distressing reports began to come in of a reverse to our arms at Nashville. At first I did not credit them, but later I met Colonel Harvie, the Inspector General, who not only confirmed the very worst of the reports, but expressed both indignation and disgust at the conduct of our troops.[23]

19. Clare was Hood's assistant inspector general. The couple was only able to spend three days together as a honeymoon. Ridley, *Battles and Sketches*, 412. A romanticized version of the couple's courtship and wedding can be found in Emma Cook Scott, "Major Clare and Mary Hadley," *CV* 16 (August 1908): 399–400.

20. As CTQ indicates, A. J. Foard was the Army of Tennessee's medical director. Maj. William E. Moore is discussed in more detail below.

21. CTQ's diary entry for January 24, 1865, identifies Rice as Col. Horace Rice of the 29th Tennessee Infantry, who was wounded in the charge of Vaughn's (Gordon's) Brigade at Franklin. Lindsley, *Military Annals*, 435.

22. W. D. Kelly, captain of Company A, 1st Tennessee.

23. Col. Edwin J. Harvie was Inspector-General of the Army of Tennessee. See *OR* 45(2):681, 787. While Hood and his staff may have expressed indignation and disgust, the

General Lucius Polk sent a buggy for me and I drove out to Hamilton Place and spent the night. The next day, (Fourth Sunday in Advent), I celebrated the Holy Communion in the parlor at Hamilton Place, and after administering to the company assembled there, carried the consecrated elements to the rooms of General Manigault and Major Prince, that they might also receive the Comfortable Sacrament. In the afternoon I drove back to Columbia and assisted the Rev. Dr. Pise at the marriage of Miss Hages to Major William E. Moore, Chief Commissary of the Army.[24] After this I rode to the residence of Mr. Vaught, where I found General Hood and his staff.[25]

I was glad to find the General bearing up well under the disaster to our arms. It was now a very serious question whether General Hood should hold the line of the Duck River, (even if it were possible for him to do so), or fall back across the Tennessee. One officer remarked to the General in my presence, that while God was on our side so manifestly that no man could question it, it was still very apparent that our people had not yet passed through all their sufferings.[26]

The General replied that the remark was a just one. He had been impressed with the fact at Spring Hill, where the enemy was completely within our grasp, and notwithstanding all his efforts to strike a decisive blow, he had failed. And now again at Nashville, after the day's fighting was well nigh over, when all had gone successfully until the evening, our troops had broken in confusion and fled.

Early the following morning, General Forrest reached headquarters and advised strongly that General Hood withdraw without delay south of the Tennessee. "If we are unable to hold the state, we should at once evacuate it," were the words of General Forrest. At nine o'clock in the morning,

---

Army of Tennessee, ruined at Franklin, had little capability to resist the much larger Federal force at Nashville when attacked on December 15 and 16, 1864.

24. "Miss Hages" is a misnomer. The diary records the bride's name as Maria Naomi Hays, who earlier penned a poem honoring Cleburne that she laid on the dead general's coffin. CTQ diary, December 15, 18, 1864.

25. The home of Nathan Vaught was a mile south of Columbia. Vaught was a prominent contractor and builder who was also something of an industrialist. Frank H. Smith, *Frank H. Smith's History of Maury County, Tennessee* (Columbia, Tenn.: Maury County Historical Society, 1969), 336–37; OR 45(1):673.

26. This officer is identified as "Lieutenant Colonel Johnston" in the CTQ diary entry for December 18, 1864. Lt. Col. J. P. Johnson was an officer in the department of General Samuel Cooper, adjutant and inspector general of the Confederate army. Johnson was with the Army of Tennessee until December 23. OR 45(1):676; OR 45(2): 757.

cannonading began at Rutherford Hill. After a couple of hours, word came from General Cheatham that he had repulsed the enemy, and the firing ceased. General Hood finally decided to fall back south of the Tennessee; and Governor Harris, in whose judgment I had great confidence, thought it the best we could do. Still it was a dark day to me, and the thought of leaving the state of Tennessee once more, greatly depressed me.

Tuesday, the 20th of December, was a day of gloominess. I felt in bidding farewell to Columbia, that I was parting with my dearest and most cherished hopes. I recalled the days of our march into Tennessee, so full of delightful intercourse with Strahl, and Marsh and other friends. After saying "good-bye," I rode on to Pulaski, thirty miles, where I was cordially received at the home of Mrs. Ballentine.[27] The next day I baptized six persons there, and later at the headquarters of General Hood, in the residence of the Honorable Thomas Jones, four of Mr. Jones' children.[28] After this baptism Mr. Jones joined us at prayers in General Hood's room. The General said, "I am afraid that I have been more wicked since I began this retreat than for a long time past. I had so set my heart upon success,— had prayed so earnestly for it,—had such a firm trust that I should succeed, that my heart has been very rebellious. But," he added, "let us go out of Tennessee, singing hymns of praise."

The weather was exceedingly inclement. So many of our poor boys were barefooted that there was very great suffering. The citizens of Pulaski did all they could to provide shoes. I dined on Wednesday with Governor Harris, at Major Nathan Adams' and spent the night with Colonel Rice. The General informed me the next day that the enemy effected a crossing of Duck River at Columbia at noon, and began shelling the town. But Forrest told them by flag, that if the shelling were not stopped, he would put their wounded directly under fire. The firing consequently ceased.

Our forces all moved on toward Bainbridge. General Hood left the following morning. I joined Governor Harris as he was not to be detained en route. We rode thirty miles to a little town called Lexington, where Colonel Rice, Captain Ballentine and myself obtained rough accommo-

27. The 1860 census for Giles County, Tennessee, lists Mary T. Ballentine, age 52, one of whose sons, Andrew J., age 23, is discussed below.

28. Thomas McKissick Jones (1816–1892) was a lawyer who had served a term in the Confederate Congress and was later imprisoned for a period by Andrew Johnson, Federal military governor of Tennessee. Joshua W. Caldwell, *Sketches of the Bench and Bar of Tennessee* (Knoxville: Ogden Brothers & Co., 1898), 286–89.

dations for the night.[29] The next day, we started for Lamb's Ferry, thinking to find a boat there, but learned that General Roddy had ordered it to Elk River to cross his command. I therefore had another journey of eighteen miles to make. Just at the close of the day I found my friend, Major-General Clayton, camped by the road-side, and not knowing General Hood's location, I decided to accept General Clayton's very cordial invitation to spend the night with him. It was Christmas eve. After supper the General called up all his staff and couriers and we had prayers.[30]

The next day, Christmas day and Sunday, was very sad and gloomy. I had prayers at General Clayton's headquarters, after which I rode down to the river and watched the work of putting down the pontoons. Some one brought me a Christmas gift of two five dollar gold pieces from Mrs. Thomas Jones of Pulaski.

The following day I crossed the river at nine o'clock. On crossing the river on our forward march, I had sung "Jubilate." Now I was chanting "De Profundis." I joined General Hood at Tuscumbia on the 27th and found the General feeling the disaster more since he reached Tuscumbia than at any time since the retreat began. And after various adventures, I reached Aberdeen on Saturday, the last day of 1864. Though an entire stranger in Aberdeen, I received a most cordial welcome at the home of Mr. Needham Whitfield, whose family were church people.[31] And thus ended the year 1864.

29. CTQ's diary provides the first name of Capt. Andrew Ballentine, doubtless the son of Mary T. Ballentine. Maj. A. J. Ballentine is listed as a staff officer to Brig. Gen. George Gordon. Crute, *Confederate Staff Officers*, 72.

30. Henry DeLamar Clayton (1827–1889) of Georgia and Alabama commanded a division of Lee's Corps.

31. The 1860 census for Monroe County, Mississippi, indicates that Whitfield, then age seventy-one, was a farmer of substantial property.

Personal Narrative—The Crumbling of the Confederacy

New Year's day fell on a Sunday in 1865. There being no resident priest in Aberdeen [Mississippi], the Vestry of St. John's Church requested me to officiate for them, which I did both morning and evening, having large congregations. And on the following Tuesday, I began holding daily services in the church, which were exceedingly well attended. At the first of these services, I preached on "Earnestness in the Christian Life."

I remained in Aberdeen until the 14th of January, holding daily services, visiting the members of the parish and performing such priestly offices as were desired. Then I left for Columbus, Mississippi, where I had a cordial welcome at the house of Mr. John C. Ramsey, a vestryman of St. Paul's Church.[1] The Bishop of the Diocese, Bishop Green, was making Columbus his home, but was absent at the time and expected to return on the following Monday.

I met the Rev. Mr. Schwrar, of Tennessee, at the Bishop's residence, and on the following Sunday I preached at St. Paul's Church, both morning and night, the services being taken by the Rev. Mr. Schwrar and the

---

1. John C. Ramsey is listed in the 1860 federal census for Lowndes County, Mississippi, as a merchant, then age thirty-nine.

THE CRUMBLING OF THE CONFEDERACY / 111

Rev. Mr. Bakewell of New Orleans.[2] I held services daily, morning and evening, during that week, at most of which I preached. At this time the minds of the people of the South were becoming impressed with the idea that the victory and independence of the Confederate States were no longer certain. On the 19th of January, General Hood was relieved of his command and Lieutenant-General Taylor took temporary command.[3] Both officers and privates were holding meetings in the army asking for the return of General Johnston. General Hood deserved well of his country for his bravery, for his devotion, for his energy and enterprise. But the troops longed for General Joseph E. Johnston, the country was crying out for him, and Congress of the Confederate States was demanding that the President restore him to the command of the army of the Tennessee. And I am satisfied that no other man, had he the genius of a Caesar or a Napoleon, could have commanded that army so well as General Johnston.

On Sunday the 22nd of January, the Rev. John M. Schwrar, Deacon, was advanced to the priesthood in St. Paul's Church, Columbus, by Bishop Green. I presented him for ordination and preached the sermon, from the text: "What shall one then answer the messengers of the nation?

2. Although this passage and CTQ's diary state that he "met" John Miller Schwrar at this point, in August 1863 a correspondent indicated that he was "sending" Schwrar to CTQ, mirthfully stating his was "a shameful name for a preacher." The same correspondent stated that Schwrar was "affable, sympathizing [and] affectionate." J. Thomas Pickett to CTQ, August 6, 1863, Quintard Papers, DU. Schwrar was the chaplain to the 4th Tennessee Infantry Regiment, where he was known as a man of "simplicity and worth." Lindsley, *Military Annals*, 188. Rev. Alexander Gordon Bakewell (1822–1920) was a man of some substance who fought with the 5th Company of the Washington Artillery at Shiloh. Discharged from that unit in June 1862 as overaged, he was ordained a priest by Leonidas Polk and served as chaplain for the 28th Mississippi Infantry and the 8th Mississippi Battalion (consolidated). He purportedly read the Order of Morning Prayer to Polk a few days before the bishop was killed. Nathaniel C. Hughes, Jr., *The Pride of the Confederate Artillery: The Washington Artillery in the Army of Tennessee* (Baton Rouge: Louisiana State University Press, 1997), 288; Hodding Carter and Betty W. Carter, *So Great a Good: A History of the Episcopal Church in Louisiana and of Christ Church Cathedral, 1805–1955* (Sewanee, Tenn.: University Press, 1955), 107, 130.

3. Lt. Gen. Richard Taylor (1826–1879) of Kentucky and Louisiana. Taylor was an effective officer who was the son of President Zachary Taylor and, briefly, Jefferson Davis' brother-in-law. His command of the Army of Tennessee proved to be a temporary and empty honor, as its three tattered corps were shipped east to confront Sherman in the Carolinas.

That the Lord hath founded Zion and the poor of His people shall trust in it." Isaiah xiv, 32.

It saddened me to think that, because of the death of Bishop Otey of Tennessee, Mr. Schwrar had need to be ordained outside of the Diocese to which he belonged canonically. But after the close of the war and I had become Bishop Otey's successor, Mr. Schwrar was one of my most faithful and beloved clergymen, was for several years secretary of the Diocese of Tennessee and missionary in charge of several important places near Memphis. In the epidemic of yellow fever in 1878, he remained bravely at his post and died of the fever.[4]

A few days after the ordination, I met at General Elzy's, Colonel Baskerville, Captain Hudson, James D. B. de Bow and others and we discussed the policy of putting the negroes into the army as our soldiers, and we all agreed to the wisdom of so doing.[5] We also discussed the rumors then current of the readiness of the foreign powers to recognize us on the basis of gradual emancipation. And Mr. de Bow, who was the editor of the "Southern Quarterly Review," stated that Governor Aiken of South Carolina, the owner of over a thousand slaves, had spoken to him more than two years previously in favor of emancipation to secure recognition, and had urged him to employ his pen to bring the subject before the people of the Confederate States.

It was at this time reported that Commissioners had gone from the Confederacy to Washington on a peace mission.[6] I spent Wednesday, the

4. Schwrar was serving as rector at St. Thomas' in Somerville, Tennessee, at the time of his death in the epidemic. John H. Davis, *St. Mary's Cathedral, 1858–1958* (Memphis: Chapter of St. Mary's Cathedral, 1958), 42.

5. Maj. Gen. Arnold Elzey (1816–1871) of Maryland commanded the artillery of the skeletal Army of Tennessee. See OR 45(2):753. Charles Baskerville may have commanded a Confederate cavalry unit in the first year of the war (see OR 10[1]:15–16), but he is known to have been a merchant residing at Columbus who worked with De Bow in disposing of government cotton. OR 24(1):296; OR 39(2):572–73. James Dunwoody Brownson DeBow (1820–1867) was the widely known and influential publisher of the violently partisan *DeBow's Review* and was the government's chief agent for the purchase and sale of cotton. *Dictionary of American Biography*, s.v. "DeBow, James Dunwoody Brownson." Capt. E. M. Hudson was aide-de-camp on Elzey's staff. E. M. Hudson CSR, Confederate General and Staff Officers, RG 109, M-331, NA.

6. On February 3, 1865, Confederate Vice President Alexander H. Stephens, Senator Robert M. T. Hunter, and Judge John M. Campbell met with President Abraham Lincoln and Secretary of State William H. Seward aboard the steamer *River Queen* at Hampton Roads, Virginia (not Washington), in a failed effort to end the war. Charles M. Hubbard, *The Burden of Confederate Diplomacy* (Knoxville: University of Tennessee Press, 1998), 173–75.

1st of February, with Colonel Baskerville and with Mr. de Bow, who was of the opinion that we should have peace on the 1st of May. The thought of peace almost made me hold my breath, but I feared that the time was not yet. At the same time the President of the Confederate States appointed a day of fasting, humiliation and prayer.

Lieutenant-Colonel Llewellyn Hoxton, whom I had presented to Bishop Elliott for confirmation at Shelbyville in 1863, spent a night with me. He belonged to an old Virginia family from Alexandria where he was carefully nurtured in the Church and had instilled into his mind and heart the principles of virtue and religion by the quiet and steady influences of a Christian home. He graduated at West Point, in 1861, just at the time of the breaking out of the war. After reaching Washington, he resigned his commission in the United States army in order that he might go with his state. His resignation was not accepted, but his name was stricken from the roll. He crossed over to Virginia and was ordered by the Secretary of War of the Confederacy, to report to General Polk. He was a most faithful soldier and on many a battlefield displayed conspicuous gallantry.[7]

I was unable to get transportation from Columbus before the 7th of February, and before leaving, Bishop Green handed me an envelope containing two hundred dollars, an offering from a member of St. Paul's Parish. After many annoyances, owing to the crowded state of the trains, I arrived in Meridian. Here I found Captain Frierson of Tennessee.[8] Dr. Foster, the Post Surgeon, met me at the railway station and I accepted an invitation to be his guest during his [sic] detention at that place.[9] At his quarters, I found a number of Nashville friends—General Maney, Captain Alexander Porter, Captain Rice, Major Vaulx, Captain Kelly and others.[10]

7. At this point in the war, Hoxton commanded the artillery of Lt. Gen. Stephen D. Lee's corps. OR 45(1):683–84, 691–92.

8. CTQ's diary entry for February 7, 1865, identifies this officer as Capt. A. A. Frierson, assistant inspector general of Strahl's Brigade.

9. Possibly R. C. Foster, a Tennessean described by Confederate nurse Kate Cumming as "a high-toned, cultivated gentleman." Cumming, *Journal*, 278. See *CMH*, 10:268; OR 30(4):738.

10. After his experience in Virginia, Maney commanded a brigade in Cheatham's Division until he was mysteriously replaced during the Atlanta campaign. Christopher Losson, *Tennessee's Forgotten Warriors: Frank Cheatham and His Confederate Division* (Knoxville: University of Tennessee Press, 1989), 190–99. From May 28, 1863 to at least December 21, 1864, Capt. Alexander J. Porter was assistant adjutant general of Maney's Brigade. He was paroled on April 26, 1865, as assistant inspector general of Brown's Divi-

I visited Colonel Hurt who was commanding Maney's brigade.[11] The brigade was smaller than my old regiment at the beginning of the war. Of all the thousand and more who come out in the First Tennessee Regiment in May, 1861, I found but fifty men remaining. Many had been killed in battle, others had sickened and died, some were "in the house of bondage," and, worst of all, some had deserted their colors.

I left Meridian on Thursday, the 9th of February, for Demopolis, Alabama, where I arrived at three o'clock in the evening. My visit to Demopolis was a pleasant one. While there the report of the Peace Commission was made public. The failure of the commission was used to rally the spirits of the people, who were told that every avenue to peace was closed, excepting that which might be carved out with the sword. But this attempt to raise the drooping spirits of the South failed. The feeble flare of excitement produced by the fiasco of the Peace Commission was soon totally extinguished.

Leaving Demopolis, I accompanied the Rev. Mr. Beckwith to Greensboro, Alabama, to see Bishop Wilmer.[12] During this visit the Bishop held a Confirmation service at which I preached and the offerings, amounting to $530, were given to me for army missions. After the service a gentleman took me to one side and stated that several gentlemen of the congregation desired to present me with a slight token of their regard and presented me with $700. It took me greatly by surprise.

Accompanied by Frank Dunnington, I went to Selma. We put up for the night at a hotel. In the morning I paid for lodging and breakfast $13.

---

sion. A. J. Porter CSR, Confederate General and Staff Officers, RG 109, M-331, NA. Maj. Joseph Vaulx, Jr., was assistant inspector general of Brown's Division and the only member of the division staff to escape unwounded at Franklin. OR 38(3):711; CTQ diary, December 1, 1864. Captain Kelly was probably the previously identified W. D. Kelly of the 1st Tennessee. From the context of his presence with the other Tennesseans named in this passage, Captain Rice was probably James Love Rice (1824–1898), a Nashville Episcopalian, lawyer, and Democrat who began the war as captain of Company C, 20th Tennessee Regiment. He left the regiment after an unsuccessful election for its colonelcy to serve in various staff positions and, after the war, was elected to the Tennessee General Assembly. McBride and Robison, *Biographical Directory of the Tennessee General Assembly*, 2:763–64.

11. Charles Stuart Hurt was colonel of the 9th Tennessee and actually commanded Brown's Division for an interval after the slaughter at Franklin. Lindsley, *Military Annals*, 267–280; *CMH*, 10:158; see OR 45(1):667.

12. Reverend John W. Beckwith, originally of Washington County, Mississippi, eventually became bishop of Georgia. Carter and Carter, *So Great a Good*, 155, 162. Rt. Rev. Richard Hooker Wilmer was bishop of Alabama.

I declined the breakfast. The following day I had the great pleasure of meeting my friend Colonel Harry Yeatman. That morning I visited the Naval Works, and spent some time with Captain Ap Catesby Jones.[13] We had much pleasant chat about our Virginia friends. It seemed strange to find a naval establishment in an inland town or upon the banks of a small river. But the truth is, the Confederate government had learned the wisdom of selecting such places for the manufacture of gunboats and naval ordnance in order that they might be the better protected from the raids of the Federals.

Captain Catesby Jones had accomplished a vast amount of work at this place. He had some four hundred workmen employed, only ninety of whom were white. He had up to the time I visited him, turned out one hundred and ninety guns, besides doing a vast amount of other work for the government. He went through the works with me and showed me the different steps, from the melting of the ore to the drilling of the guns. He was casting the Brooks gun almost exclusively and said that it combined more good points than any other.

While in the office at the Naval Works, Mr. Phillips, of North Carolina, came in to take a look at the works.[14] He was just from Richmond having travelled with Vice-President Alexander H. Stephens as far as Atlanta. He told a story which illustrated Mr. Lincoln's wit, and as we all thought at that time, lack of dignity and perhaps also lack of sympathy with those who were interested in the war on the Southern side.

Mr. Hunter, one of the Commissioners from the South, suggested, during a four hours' interview with Mr. Lincoln and Mr. Seward, many instances in history in which governments had treated with insurgents, and mentioned one in the time of Charles I of England. Mr. Lincoln replied: "Seward may know all about the history of that time. All I know is, that Charles I lost his head."[15]

13. Yeatman and Jones have been identified previously. The "Naval Works" CTQ mentions is the Naval Iron Works, which made cannon, built gunboats, and fabricated steamboat boilers. James Pickett Jones, *Yankee Blitzkrieg: Wilson's Raid through Alabama and Georgia* (Athens: University of Georgia Press, 1976), 128.

14. Possibly Samuel Field Phillips (1824–1903), at this point an official of the North Carolina state government. William S. Powell, ed., *Dictionary of North Carolina Biography*, (Chapel Hill: University of North Carolina Press, 1994), s.v. "Phillips, Samuel Field."

15. Alexander H. Stephens did not take such a dim view of this comment: "This was the familiar manner in which Mr. Lincoln, throughout the conversation, spoke of and to Mr. Seward. In the same manner he addressed me throughout, as was his custom with all his intimate acquaintances when in Congress." Alexander H. Stephens, *A Constitutional*

I reached Montgomery by steamer too late Saturday night for the train to Columbus, Georgia. I was therefore obliged to spend Sunday in Montgomery. My expenses on the steamer, exclusive of fare, were twenty-five dollars, to wit: three cups of coffee furnished by one of the servants, fifteen dollars; and "tip" to the boy for waiting on me and caring for my traps, ten dollars.

With the Rev. Mr. Mitchell, I went that night to a meeting of the citizens of Montgomery, called to consider the condition of affairs then existing.[16] The theater in which the meeting was held, was crowded to excess. When we arrived, Governor Watts was addressing the assembled multitude.[17] We could scarcely get standing room. The Governor spoke for more than an hour, made many good points, defended President Davis, and altogether his speech was an able one, practical and thoroughly patriotic. He referred to the different spirit displayed by the people at home from that of the soldiers in the field. He was followed by other speakers and a series of patriotic resolutions was adopted by the people present.

I spent Sunday in Montgomery, preached morning and evening and baptized the son of Lieutenant-General Albert J. Smith.[18] Leaving Montgomery the next morning, I arrived at Columbus, Georgia, at five o'clock in the evening, after an absence of more than three months. I was glad to find my family well.

I took up my work of assisting the Rev. Mr. Hawks as before my departure for Tennessee. The 1st of March was Ash Wednesday and it rained incessantly. I said Morning Prayer and preached for the rector of the parish, who though able to attend the service, was looking very badly. His active labors were evidently at an end. Three weeks later, my former classmate, Dr. Frank Stanford, put him under the influence of chloroform, and operated upon him with a knife, removing a cancer. He bore the operation well, and was present to give his blessing, when on the 5th of April, at the rectory, I united in the bonds of matrimony, Captain John S. Smith, aid-de-camp to General Hood, and Sallie C. Hawks, the reverend

View of the Late War Between the States, 2 vols. (Philadelphia: National Publishing, 1870), 2:613.

16. Rev. J. M. Mitchell was rector of St. John's Church in Montgomery.

17. Thomas Hill Watts (1819–1892) had also served in the Confederate army and as the Confederate attorney general.

18. CTQ's diary indicates Smith was a lieutenant colonel. Smith served on the staffs of Albert Sidney Johnston, P. G. T. Beauregard, Braxton Bragg, and in 1865, Joseph E. Johnston. Crute, *Confederate Staff Officers*, 16, 22, 102, 105.

gentleman's daughter.[19] And his health continued reasonably good so long as I remained in Columbus.

During the season of Lent I officiated every Sunday for Mr. Hawks and delivered a course of lectures on "Confirmation." On the 10th of March, Friday and the day appointed by President Davis as a day of fasting, humiliation and prayer, I preached to a crowded congregation from Isaiah iv, 12. I attended to funerals, baptisms and other parochial duties for Mr. Hawks. Among the baptisms, was that of General Warner, chief engineer of the Naval Works at Columbus.[20] Another was that of Captain Rodolph Morerod, of the Thirty-third Tennessee, Strahl's brigade.[21] He was of Swiss parentage, a native of Indiana and a practicing physician before the war.

Major-General John C. Brown spent an evening with me just before he left to join his command, having recovered sufficiently from the wound received at the Battle of Franklin. He made a full statement to me of his movements at Spring Hill, which satisfied me that his skirts were clear of even a shadow of blame for the neglect of a great opportunity, as is sometimes said.[22] I had always believed it, for he was at once one of the noblest of men and most accomplished of soldiers. I had united him in the bonds of matrimony with Miss Bettie Childress, a little more than a year previously, at Griffin, Georgia, under somewhat romantic circumstances. Invitations had been issued for the wedding to take place at nine o'clock, in the evening of the 23rd of February, (1864). The groom, accompanied by nine officers of his staff, arrived in Griffin on the 22nd. But the following morning he received a telegram from General Joseph E. Johnston, ordering him to report at once at Rome, Georgia. The officers who were with him were likewise recalled.

19. John S. Smith was appointed Hood's aide on May 26, 1864. OR 38(4):743.

20. James H. Warner of Ohio and Virginia ranked as an engineer in the Confederate navy from October 1862, having had prewar experience in the production of steamship components at Gosport Navy Yard at Norfolk. It is unknown why CTQ calls him "General"; his rank was major. Warner was killed immediately after the war when he was shot on a Columbus street by "negro occupation troops." Diffee William Standard, *Columbus, Georgia in the Confederacy: The Social and Industrial Life of the Chattahoochee River Port* (New York: William-Frederick, 1954), 42–44, 69, n. 20.

21. The only mention of Morerod in OR is that a 2nd Lt. E. R. Morerod, acting commissary of the 33rd Tennessee, was wounded on April 7, 1862, at Shiloh. OR 10(1):436.

22. Brown's failure to attack at Spring Hill because of a small force on his flank has been styled by one historian of the affair as "the tactical cornerstone of the Confederate fiasco." Sword, *Confederacy's Last Hurrah*, 154.

General Brown at once sought Miss Childress and laid the case before her.

"You will have to return to your command," she said.

"But not before you are my wife," he replied.

I was in attendance at the hospitals in Griffin at the time and was sent for and married them at one o'clock in the afternoon in the presence of a few friends. The groom said "good by" to his bride and went to the seat of war. Two weeks later he had a leave of absence and with his bride took a wedding journey.

I baptized the children of this marriage, confirmed all but one, performed the ceremony at the marriage of the eldest daughter and officiated at her funeral a year later. I was with the heart-broken father at the deathbed of a second daughter and stood with him at her grave.

Thus I knew General Brown in peace and war, in joy and sorrow, in sunshine and beneath the clouds, and I always knew him to be a true man—faithful in all the relations of life, broad-minded and generous, an enterprising citizen, a lawyer, a statesman,—a man always to be depended upon. He had the good judgment, the force and decision of character, the methodical habit and the fidelity and integrity of purpose which compelled confidence and made success easy. After I became Bishop of Tennessee and especially during his term as Governor of Tennessee, we were warm friends. His death on the 17th of August, 1889, was sudden and unexpected. I was apprised thereof by telegram and hastened to the funeral at Pulaski, Tennessee, where I laid him to rest with the solemn and impressive services of the Church.

At another time we had as our guests Lieutenant-Colonel Dawson of the 154th Tennessee, and Brigadier-General Felix H. Robertson, both nearly recovered from their wounds.[23]

But I received the most distressing news of the death of Mr. Jacob K. Sass, President of the Bank of Charleston and Treasurer of the Council of the Church in the Confederate States of America. He had just escaped from Columbia, South Carolina, before its fall, and died at Unionville. He was one of the noblest laymen of the Church, of large heart and mind,

23. Lt. Col. John W. Dawson was a veteran of many of the Army of Tennessee's battles, wounded while commanding a special battalion of sharpshooters at Chickamauga. See OR 30(2):115. Felix Hutson Robertson (1839–1928) of Texas had commanded artillery and then a division in Wheeler's Cavalry and was severely wounded in November 1864. He was nominated, but never confirmed, as a brigadier general. Warner, *Generals in Gray*, 260–61.

full of love for Christ and the Church,—abundant in labors, earnest-minded and pure-hearted.[24]

Mr. Rhodes Brown one day handed me a brief and pointed note, to the following effect: "To the Rev. Dr. Quintard, for his private use, from a few friends." The note contained $2500 and was no doubt given to enable me to purchase theological books and I think Mr. Brown was the sole donor.

On Palm Sunday, (April 9th) I brought before the Church people at the services, the importance of establishing an Orphanage and Church Home in Columbus, and gave notice that the offerings on the following Sunday (Easter) would be for that purpose.

On Good Friday it was with great delight that I received into the Church by baptism, my old friend General Washington Barrow, of Nashville. He was one of my earliest friends in that city and always commanded my highest and warmest regard. He had received a classical education, studied law and was admitted to the bar. He was American Charge-d'Affaires in Portugal from 1841 to 1844, served in Congress as a Whig from Tennessee, was State Senator in 1860 and 1861, and a member of the Commission that negotiated a Military League between the Southern States on the 4th of May, 1861. He was arrested in March, 1862, by Governor Johnson, of Tennessee, on charge of disloyalty and was imprisoned in the penitentiary at Nashville, but was released the following week by order of President Lincoln. He died in St. Louis, in October, 1866.

Before Easter came, Charleston,—the City by the Sea,—after as gallant a defence as the records of history, ancient or modern, furnish,—had fallen. Columbia had suffered severely from a visit of the Federal forces. Selma, Alabama, had been taken and the larger part of it burned. Finally the rumors that had reached us from time to time, that Richmond had fallen, were confirmed. General Howell Cobb wrote to the Mayor of Columbus, urging him to do all in his power to arouse the citizens to a sense of their duty, to oppose the arming of the negroes, and to promise from the military authorities all the assistance that could be rendered.

But from the address of President Davis upon the occasion of the fall of Richmond, and from the proclamation of the Governor of Alabama to

24. As noted above, Sass was instrumental in publishing *The Confederate Soldier's Pocket Manual of Devotions* and *Balm for the Weary and Wounded*. See Albert Sidney Thomas, *A Historical Account of the Protestant Episcopal Church in South Carolina, 1820–1957* (Columbia: R. L. Bryan, 1957), 56.

the people of his state when it was threatened with an invasion of Federal troops, it was evident that hope was dying out in the hearts of the people and that the end of the Confederacy was not far off.

Easter Eve the enemy was in Montgomery and that city was surrendered by the Mayor without an effort at defence. Everything in Columbus was in commotion. The tranquillity of the place was not in the least served by the distressing news that was received of the assassination of President Lincoln. Absurd preparations were made for the defence of the city, but it was an insignificant force that could be gathered there.

Thus Easter dawned. The first service of the day was at half-past five in morning when I celebrated the Holy Communion. There was a very large attendance at this service. Many men were present. It was most solemn and impressive. All hearts were filled with forebodings of what was to come. The enemy was close at hand.

At the second service at half-past ten, I said the Litany and celebrated the Holy Communion. I did not preach, feeling that it was a time for prayer and supplication only. The offerings as previously announced, were for the Church Home and Orphanage. They amounted to $33,000.

I stood at the altar for a considerable time administering the sacrament to officers and soldiers who came to receive before going to the field. Among these I recognized General Finley, of Florida, and Lieutenant Green, son of the Bishop of Mississippi.[25] I was deeply touched by seeing an officer who was very devout, kneel at the chancel rail, and then hasten away, equipped for battle, clasping his wife by the hand as he tore himself from her.

At noon the Federal artillery began firing upon the city. The fight for the defence of Columbus was quite a brisk affair. Major-General Howell Cobb was chief in command, his second being Colonel Leon Von Zinken, Commander of the post.[26] Our whole force was less than 4,000,

25. Brig. Gen. Jesse Johnson Finley (1812–1904) of Tennessee and Florida had commanded the Army of Tennessee's Florida Brigade until the second of his two wounds in the Atlanta campaign disabled him. Kept from rejoining the Army of Tennessee in North Carolina by Federal troop movements, Finley reported for duty in the defense of Columbus. CMH, 11:201. Duncan Cameron Green was the son of the Rt. Rev. William Mercer Green and later became an Episcopal priest himself. Like Schwrar, he died in the yellow fever epidemic of 1878.

26. Leon Von Zinken was colonel of the 13th and 20th Louisiana Regiment (consolidated). He was retired from active duty after being wounded in the Atlanta campaign and assigned the command of the post at Columbus. Arthur W. Bergeron, Jr., *Guide to Louisiana Military Units* (Baton Rouge: Louisiana State University Press, 1989), 105; Andrew B.

while that of the Federals amounted to some 12,000 or 15,000, under Major-General James H. Wilson.[27] The enemy not only greatly outnumbered our force but was splendidly equipped.

The enemy was twice repulsed, but of course our troops had, before very long, to give way before such superiority of numbers and equipment. About ten and a half o'clock on Monday morning, our troops fell back across the river into the city and beat a hasty retreat on the road to Macon, numbers of them passing by my house.

I had made but little preparation for the coming of the enemy. I had in my possession the money collected at the offertory at the Sunday morning service. This I wrapped up in a piece of rubber cloth and friend put it in the top of a tall pine tree for me. It may be there yet for aught I know. I had at my house a considerable amount of silver ware. This was rapidly gathered up, put in a sack and lowered into a well. About mid-night we retired to rest thinking we might be disturbed at any moment.

But it was not until eight o'clock on Tuesday morning that any of the Federal soldiers put in an appearance. The first man who rode into my front yard was a sergeant of the Tenth Missouri Cavalry. He asked if I had seen any Confederates about there, to which I replied: "Not since last night."

"Which way were they going?" he next inquired.

"Towards Macon."

"Can we get something to eat?"

"Yes, breakfast will soon be ready. Will you walk in?"

He rode off and called a Lieutenant, who rode up, hitched his horse in the front yard, taking the precaution to throw the front gates wide open. As he went up the steps of the porch, I asked him his name. He then gave it as Jones, but after breakfast he told me his name was Freese, which it evidently was.

I had with me a guest, Mr. Samuel Noble, a very dear friend who had arrived from Selma on Sunday morning.[28] He was a Pennsylvanian, who

---

Booth, *Records of Louisiana Confederate Soldiers and Louisiana Confederate Commands*, Vol. III, Book 2 (1920; reprint, Reprint Co., 1984) 946.

27. Brig. (brevet Maj.) Gen. James Harrison Wilson of Illinois (1837–1925) commanded the cavalry corps of the Military Division of the Mississippi. Warner, *Generals in Blue*, 566–67.

28. Samuel Noble (1834–1888) was originally from Pennsylvania but doubtless became acquainted with CTQ in Rome, where Noble's family owned a rolling mill and foundry. Because of his southern connections, it is interesting that Noble had a commission from the Federal government to secure cotton. Later, Noble founded the city of Anniston, Alabama. *Dictionary of American Biography*, s.v. "Noble, Samuel."

had been sent South by the Federal government to secure cotton and prevent its being destroyed by the Confederates. At Selma he had fallen under the suspicion of the Federals and after being released by them, was taken up as a spy by our soldiers. He was asked with whom he was acquainted and gave me as his reference. He was accordingly sent to Columbus in charge of a Lieutenant, who instantly released him upon my recognizing him. He was of great service to me in the emergencies which now arose.

Lieutenant Freese seemed a gentlemanly fellow enough and gave me the following paper for my protection:

I have paid a visit to the house of the Rev. C. T. Quintard, (where Samuel Noble of Pennsylvania is a guest,) for the protection of his person and property. All soldiers will leave everything unmolested until General Wilson can send out a guard as applied for. This property must remain unmolested.

Henry H. Freese
1st Lieut. Co. D. 10th Mo. Cavalry, Volunteer U.S.A.

Armed with this document, Mr. Noble determined to keep out all intruders. Several friends took shelter at my house. Infamous outrages were committed in the presence of ladies at my nearest neighbor's; and in his effort to protect us, Mr. Noble was twice put in imminent danger, pistols being placed at his head with threats that he would be shot.

So I went to headquarters to secure a guard. A neighbor went with me and a soldier agreed to protect my premises until my return. I called first on General Winslow, with a note from Mr. Noble addressed to both General Winslow and Captain Hodge, his Acting Adjutant-General.[29] Captain Hodge not only treated me with great courtesy, but accompanied me to the office of the Provost Marshal. Not finding the latter as I desired, I determined to call upon General Wilson.

29. Twenty-eight-year-old Bvt. Brig. Gen. Edward F. Winslow led the 1st Brigade of Wilson's 4th Division. Warner, *Generals in Blue*, 595; Jones, *Yankee Blitzkrieg*, 32. On June 19, 1865, Winslow recommended that Capt. Ambrose Hodge, Company K, 4th Iowa Veteran Cavalry, be promoted to "major by brevet." The honor was "for long and valuable services as acting assistant adjutant general, and for gallantry in [the] presence of the enemy at Big Blue, Mo.; Oxford and Tupelo, Miss; Selma, Ala.; and Columbus, Ga." OR 49(1):488–89.

I wrote out a statement of what had transpired at my neighbor's house and sent it in to the General with my card. The General himself came to the door, shook hands with me very cordially and invited me into his room where he introduced me to General McCook.[30]

I asked General McCook to read the statement I had written and he did so. Then rising from his seat and pacing the floor, he said with great warmth: "Doctor, if you could identify these me who have committed this outrage, I would hang them in a minute if I could put my hands on them."

He immediately gave orders to his Adjutant who in turn gave the necessary orders to the Provost Marshal. By this means I secured a guard for my own house and for three of my neighbors. It was to the great relief of my family that I finally returned home, for they feared from my long absence that some mishap had befallen me.

We had a quiet night and I had the good fortune the next morning to save both of my horses. On leaving the breakfast table, I walked out on the front porch, and saw two Federal soldiers putting their saddles on my horses. I called to the Lieutenant in command of the guard, to know if I must give them both up. He came out immediately, buckled on his sword, went to the men, gave them a sound thumping with his sword and ordered them to unsaddle and give up the horses. They at once obeyed and I put the horses in the basement of my house. When an hour later four other soldiers came dashing up expecting to secure my horses, they failed to find them, and Mr. Noble went out and put the intruders off the premises.[31]

A few days later the guards were all called in, the troops having been ordered forward on the road to Macon. A number of stragglers came to the house from time to time and made efforts to enter it, but without success.

One night the torch was applied to the government property, factories, etc., in Columbus. The heavens were brilliantly lighted up and at intervals there were tremendous explosions. The loudest was at one o'clock,

30. Brig. Gen. Edward Moody McCook of Ohio (1833–1909), one of the "Fighting Mc-Cooks," commanded Wilson's 1st Division. Warner, *Generals in Blue*, 296.

31. Among CTQ's papers is a note from Captain Hodge to Noble, apologizing for "the untoward circumstances which have prevented your northward journey." Noble endorsed the document: "Officers and men will protect Dr. Quintard in person & Property. During my absence in town. his dwelling being my head quarters." Hodge to Noble, April 17, 1865, with endorsement by Noble, Quintard Papers, U of S.

when the magazine was fired. It shattered the glass in houses two miles away. All along the river, the enemy left a scene of desolation and ruin. All the bridges were destroyed. The factories, naval works, nitre works, and cotton houses, were all burned. The shops in the town were all pillaged chiefly by the poor of the town. The destruction is said to have involved about fifteen millions of dollars.[32]

32. "Before leaving Columbus General Winslow destroyed the rebel ram *Jackson*, nearly ready for sea, mounting six 7-inch guns, burned 15 locomotives, 250 cars, the railroad bridge and foot bridges, 155,000 bales of cotton, 4 cotton factories, the navy-yard, foundry, armory, sword and pistol factory, accouterment shops, 3 paper-mills, over 100,000 rounds of artillery ammunition, besides immense stores of which no account could be taken." OR 49(1):365. As CTQ notes, some of the destruction may have been caused by civilian mobs. Jones, *Yankee Blitzkrieg*, 142.

CHAPTER XIV

Personal Narrative — The Close of the War

From Columbus I made my way as best I could with my family, to Atlanta, where I was the guest of my friend Mr. Richard Peters.[1] The affairs of the Confederacy, its armies, its political organization, had all come to naught. General Thomas and his army had effected a junction with General Grant.[2] Cavalry, infantry and artillery completely surrounded the Confederate forces, whose supply of ammunition was nearly exhausted. Overwhelming circumstances compelled the capitulation of General Lee at Appomattox Court House, on Sunday April 9th, 1865. A few days later occurred the assassination of President Lincoln and that event was followed by the proclamation offering a reward for the apprehension of Jefferson Davis and certain other persons, — not as the chief actors in the recent war, — but as *particeps criminis* in that atrocious crime.

In my stay at Atlanta I was brought somewhat in touch with the march

1. Originally from Pennsylvania, Richard Peters (1810–1889) was a multitalented individual who was said to have given Atlanta its name in 1847. CTQ probably became acquainted with Peters through the Battey family of Rome. CTQ's closeness to the family is reflected in the name of their son, Charles Quintard Peters, born July 15, 1866. Coleman and Gurr, *Dictionary of Georgia Biography*, s.v. "Peters, Richard"; Elliott diary, undated note, GDAH.

2. This is incorrect. Thomas stayed in Tennessee. See OR 49(1):342–48.

of events. On the 20th of May the Honorable Ben Hill was brought to Atlanta.[3] He had been an intimate friend of President Davis and was a man of fine intellect. He bore himself nobly in the then depressing state of affairs. I had a long and most interesting conversation with him. Mr. Mallory, who had been Secretary of the Confederate Navy, seemed to take a pessimistic view of the situation, and told me that his greatest regret was that he had spent four years of his life in working for a people unfit for independence.[4]

Major-General Howell Cobb, although a paroled prisoner of war, was brought into Atlanta under guard, probably to accompany Mr. Hill and Mr. Mallory to Washington.[5] I had half an hour's conversation with him. He told me that he had no regrets for the past so far as his own conduct was concerned; that he was willing to let his record stand without the dotting of an *i* or the crossing of a *t*; that he felt that the future had nothing in store for him; that he was willing to submit to the United States laws; and that he had no desire to escape from the United States officers.

"Indeed," said he, "were there now two paths before me, one leading to the woods and the other to the gallows, I would rather take the latter than compromise my self-respect by attempting to escape."

On Sunday, the 21st of May, I officiated in the Central Presbyterian Church, Atlanta. There was an immense congregation present. It was made up of about an equal number of Federals and Confederates. Before beginning the service, I made I brief address in which I expressed my views as to the duties of all true men in the then present condition of the country. I said that every man should do his utmost to heal the wounds and to hide the seams and scars of the fratricidal war that had just closed. I told the congregation that I would not use the prayer for the President of the United States at that service, simply because it had not yet been authorized by the Bishop of the Diocese whose ecclesiastical jurisdiction in the matter I recognized. I then proceeded with the service.

3. Benjamin Harvey Hill of Georgia (1823–1882) served in both of the regular Congresses of the Confederate States. When CTQ encountered him in Atlanta, Hill was on his way north, destined to be imprisoned at Ft. Lafayette in New York for three months. At the time of his death, Hill served in the United States Senate.

4. Born in Trinidad, Stephen Russell Mallory (1813–1873) of Florida was en route to Ft. Lafayette as well, where he would be imprisoned for ten months.

5. Cobb surrendered to Federal Maj. Gen. James Wilson at Macon on April 20 and was paroled on April 25, 1864. Secretary of War Edwin V. Stanton ordered that Cobb be sent north with Hill and Mallory, but Cobb was released when it was determined he was properly paroled. OR 49(2):429, 462, 515, 839, 883–84, 922.

A few evenings later, Major E. B. Beaumont, Adjutant-General on Major-General Wilson's staff, took tea with us. He was from Wilkesbarre, Pennsylvania, and an intimate friend of Mr. Peters' relatives in that state.[6] As soon as he reached Macon, he wrote to Mr. Peters requesting him to call on him for any assistance he might be able to render. He was then on his way home on thirty days' leave.

He was a graduate of West Point, and,—like all from that institution with whom I was ever brought in contact,—a gentleman. From him I heard the Federal side of the story of the Columbus fight. I appreciated more than ever how utterly absurd was the attempt on the part of the Confederates to defend the place! We had but a handful of untrained militia and a squad of veterans from the hospitals, against 13,000 of the best disciplined and best equipped troops of the Federal army!

From Atlanta I started for Nashville, accompanied by my family and my friend Mr. Peters, who was most anxious to get to Philadelphia. The railroad between Atlanta and Chattanooga had been destroyed but had been re-built as far south as Kingston, Georgia. I found an old friend, the engineer in charge of the work of construction, who gladly received us into his coach and provided us with abounding hospitality.

As there was considerable difficulty in getting through Chattanooga, I called upon the Federal Commander at Kingston, and asked him if he would kindly facilitate my movements. I handed him my passport upon which he endorsed his name and asked me to hand it to an officer in an adjoining room. The latter, to my surprise, provided me with free passes to Nashville. Arrived at Nashville, I was very cordially received at the residence of my friend, Colonel Harry Yeatman. This was on a Friday. The next day, the Rev. W. D. Harlow, then in charge of Christ Church, called upon me.[7] I said to him in the course of our conversation: "I shall be glad to take part with you in the services tomorrow." For the hall, used by my congregation previous to the war, had been taken by the military, in 1862, and converted into barracks, and my congregation was scattered.

6. Wilson recommended Beaumont for a brevet appointment to lieutenant colonel "for faithful and intelligent discharge of his duties and for gallantry in action on the West Harpeth River on December 17, 1864, during the pursuit of Hood, and at the battle of Selma, April 2, 1864" OR 49(1):400.

7. Rev. William D. Harlow filled in at a number of Nashville churches before the war and helped keep Christ Church open during the war. On November 18, 1865, the Christ Church vestry voted Harlow a donation of $600 in gratitude. Anne Rankin, ed., *Christ Church Nashville: 1829–1929* (Nashville: Marshall & Bruce, 1929), 113.

"Perhaps you better not," he said.

"And pray, why not?" I asked.

"The authorities might not like it," he replied.

"Very well," I rejoined, "if they do not like it, let them come and arrest me. I shall not object in the least."

I learned subsequently that he had called upon General Parkhurst of Michigan, then Provost Marshal of Nashville, informed him of my arrival and asked him if I would be permitted to officiate.[8]

"Ah," replied the General, "has the Doctor returned? Where does he officiate? I shall be glad to attend his services."

Later I was called upon to visit the General's wife in sickness and I found myself very busily engaged in visiting the sick and wounded of the Federal forces at Nashville and in burying their dead. For weeks I was in constant attendance in the hospitals and in camp. Gradually I began to realize that I had been unconsciously converted from a Confederate to a Federal Chaplain. When I decided to take my family to New York, I was waited upon by a committee of Federal officers, the chairman of which made a touching address and asked me to accept a purse of gold in token of the high appreciation in which my services had been held by the Federal officers in Nashville. I need hardly say that I was both surprised and gratified.

In those days the railways were in charge of military conductors, the coaches were greatly crowded and it was difficult to obtain seats. But General Parkhurst came to my assistance, sent his adjutant to the railway station to secure seats for me and my family, and placed a guard over them. Thus my family made a very comfortable journey.

On reaching New York, I was most cordially received by my friend the Rev. Dr. Morgan, Rector of St. Thomas' Church, and invited to preach for him the following Sunday. His was therefor the first church in the North in which I preached or held service of any kind after the war.[9]

I returned to Tennessee on the 1st of September, 1865, and on the 6th of that month, a special convention of the Diocese met in pursuance of the call of the Standing Committee, to elect a Bishop to succeed Bishop Otey, who had died in April, 1863. The convention met in Christ Church,

8. Brevet Brig. Gen. John G. Parkhurst was provost-marshal general of the Federal Department of the Cumberland.

9. William F. Morgan was rector of St. Thomas from 1857 to 1868. St. Thomas Church (New York: n.p., 1965), xii.

Nashville. On the second day, the convention proceeded to the election. And in the afternoon of that day, the President of the Convention, the Rev. Dr. Pise, announced that the clergy, by an almost unanimous vote, had nominated me for that high office.

The laity retired to consider the nomination and soon returned and reported that they had ratified the same. The President thereupon announced that I had been duly elected Bishop of the Diocese of Tennessee. With my consecration in St. Luke's Church, Philadelphia, in the presence of the General Convention of the Protestant Episcopal Church in the United States of America, on Wednesday, the 11th of October, 1865, I felt that the war between the states was indeed over.[10]

10. A month later, CTQ wrote: "While the recollections of the last of the last four years are very sad, they are very sacred. I have carried the consolations of a blessed Gospel to the fields of carnage, and into the noisome hospitals. I have attended rigidly to my duties as a priest of the Church, ministering alike to friend and foe.

"I have now but one object in life, and that is to forward, as much as lieth in me, charity, peace, and good will among all men. I have taken the oath to support the Government of the United States. I have kept back no part of the price. I shall abide by my oath heartily and cheerfully, God being my helper." *Memphis Appeal*, November 17, 1865.

CHAPTER XV

A Long Episcopate

The consecration of Dr. Quintard to the Episcopate of Tennessee was of peculiar significance to the history of the Church in the United States. The consecration took place at the first meeting of the General Convention after the close of the war. At that convention all doubts as to the mutual relations of the Northern and Southern Dioceses were dispelled. The latter had never been dropped from the roll of the General Convention, notwithstanding the fact that pending the war they had been forced by the exigencies of the case, to withdraw from the Northern Dioceses and organize the "Protestant Episcopal Church in the Confederate States of America." They were still regarded as constituent members of the American National Church. Each day of the convention meeting in 1862, the Southern Dioceses had been called in their proper turn, beginning with Alabama; and though absent, their right to be present was never questioned. Still the question must have risen in the minds of many of the Southern Churchmen as to how far this feeling might extend among the Church people of the North.

With the General Convention meeting in Philadelphia in October came the opportunity for the Church and the Church people of the North to express clearly their feeling towards their Southern brethren; and this they did, first, by the cordial welcome extended to the two southern Bishops present, and to the clerical and lay deputies in attendance from three Southern Dioceses; secondly, by the ratification of the consecration of the Rt. Rev. Dr. Wilmer to the Episcopate of Alabama, which had taken place in 1862, at the hands of Southern Bishops acting wholly independently of the Church of the North; and thirdly, by the almost unanimous vote upon the report made to the House of Deputies on the Consecration of the Bishop-elect of Tennessee, wholly ignoring the especially conspicuous official position he had held in the Confederate army and the prominent part he had taken in the affairs of the Church in the Confederate States. His consecration, therefore, furnished a very significant act by which to crown the work of reunion of the Northern and Southern Dicoceses.

The service of Consecration was, in dignity of ritual, quite in advance of the times. Dr. Quintard prepared himself therefor, by a vigil held in the Church of St. James-the-Less. The Consecrator was the Rt. Rev. Dr. Hopkins, Bishop of Vermont and Presiding Bishop of the Church in the United States. Five other Bishops of the Northern Dioceses united in the act of Consecration, as did also the Rt. Rev. Francis Fulford, D.D., Bishop of Montreal and Metropolitan of Canada, whose presence "contributed to a growing sense of the unity of the Church throughout the whole American continent."

In the history of the Diocese of Tennessee, the consecration of a second Bishop marked, of course, a distinct and important epoch. That Diocese had met with other losses than that of her ante-bellum Bishop. The war had swept away to a large extent, the results of his work and that of his clergy. All the horrors of the war had been visited upon the State and Diocese. Churches had been mutilated and destroyed and congregations had been scattered. The effects of the war were very deeply impressed upon the mind of the new and young Bishop in the first series of visitations made by him in his Diocese,—a sad and laborious journey beginning in November, 1865. The evidences of devastation were fresh and visible on every side. In some places, where before there were promising parishes and missions, there was no fit building left standing in which services could be held. Only three churches in the whole Diocese were uninjured and very few were fit for occupation. Many were in ruins. The returns from two of the parishes showed similarly severe inroads upon congregations. In one of these there remained 63 out of 147 communicants reported before the war. In the other, ten only remained out of 65 previously reported.

The Bishop never faltered as he confronted conditions which foretold the anxious care, the exhausting labors, the weary journeys, the disappointments, the fears and the griefs the coming years were to bring. It was with the utmost cheerfulness that he took up the burdens of the Episcopate, and in gathering up the *disjecta membra* of the Church in Tennessee and in strengthening the things that remained, Bishop Quintard was a marvel. In labors, in journeyings and in "the care of all the churches," he was truly an Apostle,—not a step behind any of the heroes of the American Missionary Episcopate. His jurisdiction, though nominally a Diocese, was virtually a Missionary District in all respects save that it never received its due proportion of the Church's funds devoted to Missionary enterprises.

With far-sighted statesmanship, Dr. Quintard perceived in 1865, that the Church's effectiveness could be enhanced by the Division of the Diocese of Tennessee and the establishment of the See Episcopate in the three chief cities,—Memphis, Nashville and Knoxville. And from that time on, a division of the Diocese that would increase the efficiency of the work of the Church therein, was kept constantly before the minds of the people. But strange to say, the very arguments used in support of the plea for the relief needed, were made the excuse for not granting it. "It is impossible for the Church to grow in such a large territory under the supervision of a single bishop, let him work never so hard nor so wisely," constantly pleaded the Diocese of Tennessee. "The Church is not growing fast enough in the Diocese of Tennessee to warrant a division of that Diocese and an increase of Episcopal supervision therein," was the invariable reply. And so it was not until five years before the Bishop's death,— not until after he had worn himself out by his efforts to perform single-handed the work of three Bishops in his diocese,—not until after repeated illness had warned him that he must have relief,—that a Coadjutor was elected and consecrated for him.

The wide-spread popularity of Dr. Quintard, his personal magnetism and the large-hearted charity he had manifested in time of war, were not without their effect for a time upon the work he had undertaken. Wherever he appeared there flocked to meet him his old friends of the camp and battle-field. They felt that the religion he preached, having stood the test of adversity in war-time, was a good religion for times of peace,—a good religion to rule the every-day business of life. They readily yielded in large numbers to his persistent appeals to them to confess Christ before men. In his record of official acts published in the Diocesan Journal from year to year, he noted such gratifying incidents as the baptism and confirmation at his hands of some of the officers and men with whom his acquaintance had begun on the battle-field or in camp. In the few months that elapsed between his consecration and the meeting of his first Diocesan Convention, 314 persons were confirmed by him in Tennessee, and that number was a good yearly average of his confirmations for nearly thirty-three years; and his 470 confirmations, 152 sermons and 112 addresses, reported to the convention in 1867, for the first full year of his Episcopate, were a sample of the pace he set for himself at the beginning of his Episcopate.

But as before the war, Bishop Otey in an Episcopate of little less than twenty-nine years, discovered that there was a remarkable tendency among churchmen to move away from Tennessee, so it was after the war, as Bishop Quintard was to find. Bishop Otey confirmed more than 6,000 persons in Tennessee, yet the Diocese never numbered more than 3,500 communicants before the war arrested its development. Many of those whom the ante-bellum bishop confirmed took their way, like the Star of Empire, westward, and began to colonize the Dioceses of Missouri, Texas and California. Bishop Quintard, by actual count, confirmed more than 12,000 persons, and yet his Diocese was never, to the day of his death, able to count 6,000 communicants.

Despite the difficulties of the field in which it was given him to labor for the upbuilding of the Church, the Bishop was in the forefront of every movement which went on in the Church in the latter part of the nineteenth century. He was a pioneer in the adoption of the Cathedral system in the American Church. He was among the first to utilize the work of the Sisterhoods in the administration of Diocesan charitable institutions. With his refined and cultivated tastes, it was natural that he should give attention to the improvement of ecclesiastical architecture in his Diocese. And he was a leader in the work of the Church for the negro. In 1883, a conference of bishops, presbyters and laymen was held in Sewanee, to consider the relations of the Church to the colored people of the South. A canon was proposed for the organization of work among colored people, which, when it came before the General Convention, was known as "the Sewanee Canon." It was never adopted by the General Convention but the work among the negroes in Tennessee was organized in accordance with its suggestions.

In the list of the American Episcopate, Bishop Quintard's name is the seventy-fifth. It is an unusual name, especially conspicuous by beginning with an unusual letter. These may seem trivial circumstances to receive

mention here, but the fact is that they seem significant of the striking position which the Bishop held among his brethren, of the peculiarities of
his personality, and of the attention he attracted to himself throughout
the country. He was, as has been seen, a link between the ante-bellum
and the post-bellum Bishop. He was likewise a link between the clergymen of the old school and those of the new. It is curious to those who
knew him later than 1870, to see him represented in the portraits taken
soon after his elevation to the Episcopate, wearing the "bands,"—the surviving fragment of the broad collar worn in Milton's time. He probably
gave them up about the time of his first visit to England in 1867. He must
have been among the first in America to wear his college hood when of-
ficiating. For it is related that after he had officiated on one occasion in a
Church in Connecticut, a lady was heard to exclaim in great indignation,
"The idea of that Southern Bishop coming to this church and wearing a
Rebel flag on his back!"

In sympathy with the Oxford movement in the Church of England, he
was a leader in that movement as it affected the Church in America, and
so was called a "High Churchman," at a time when that term was of
somewhat different application from what it is now. And he was then
called a "Ritualist," and was regarded as an extremist though at the present day he would be considered a very moderate ritualist.

He was always a welcome visitor in all parts of the country and people
not only delighted to hear him preach but especially enjoyed social intercourse with him. His conversation was extremely entertaining, partly because of the breadth of his experiences in times of war and in times of
peace;—as a traveller in England and as the hard-working Bishop of a
Southern Diocese, but also because his talk scintillated with wit and
quick repartee.

When some one in New York asked him why he had named a Church
at Sewanee, "St. Paul's-on-the-Mountain," he answered: "Sewanee is
Cherokee Indian for 'Mother Mountain,' and you know St. Paul
preached on *Mars* Hill." On another occasion a man was attempting to
argue with him in regard to what he chose to call "the use of forms" in
the Church. "Well," said the Bishop, "you know that when the earth was
without form, it was void; and that is the way with many Christians."

The Bishop enjoyed a reputation as a pulpit orator that became wider
than national. His voice was "as musical as the lute and resonant as a
bugle." The Southern newspapers between 1868 and 1875 praised his eloquence and noted the fact that, in spite of his belonging to a school of

thought not altogether popular in the South at that time, people of all shades of opinion thronged the churches to hear him preach. He was a ready extemporaneous speaker, yet his sermons were for the most part carefully prepared and written out and delivered form the manuscript. Some of them became widely known through many repetitions, and not a few became famous. One of these had a history the Bishop was as fond of telling as he was of repeating the sermon.

It was known as the "Bishop's Samson Sermon," and was from the text, "I will go out as at other times and shake myself." (Judges xvi, 20.) When first delivered in one of the parishes of Tennessee, the Bishop was informed by a disgusted hearer that it was "positively indecent," and not fit to be preached before any congregation. Consequently the sermon was "retired" until it was almost forgotten. Some time afterward, however, it was by accident included among sermons provided for use on one of the Bishop's series of visitations; and when discovered with his homiletic ammunition, the Bishop read it over carefully but without finding anything in it that could be characterized as indecent. So he determined to "try it again." It made a deep and wholesome impression upon the minds of those who then heard it.

He preached it one Sunday night in Christ Church, St. Louis, and after the service a gentleman said to him, "Bishop, if you will preach that sermon here tomorrow night, I will have this church full of men to hear you." The sermon was accordingly preached the following night and the gentleman kept his promise.

The sermon was preached at Trinity College, Port Hope, Canada; at West Point, before a congregation of cadets; at Sewanee, Tennessee, before successive classes of students of The University of the South;—it was preached everywhere the Bishop went,—usually at some one's request who had heard it before and who wanted the impression made on his mind at the first hearing, renewed. Numberless were the letters received by the Bishop telling him of hearing that sermon and of good resulting from it.

In his repeated visits to England, Bishop Quintard enjoyed a distinction never before, and rarely since, accorded to any member of the American Episcopate. The first of these visits was made in 1867 in order that he might be present at, and participate in, the meeting of the first Pan-Anglican or Lambeth Conference. He attended subsequent conferences up to 1897, a few months before his death. At each of these visits he was the recipient of an unusual amount of attention from English Bishops and from the English people of every rank and he revolutionized the opinions of the Englishmen of that day as to America and Americans. The English newspapers were captivated by his powers in the pulpit. One of the Liverpool daily papers said that "the Bishop of Tennessee speaks English better than an Englishman and preaches with the fire and clearness of Lacordaire."

One of the leading London papers devoted two editorial columns to a description of him and said; "The Bishop of Tennessee is the first American we ever heard whose speech did not betray him." "His exterior is impressive." "His voice strong and searching and his enunciation deliberate." "His well-turned sentences are like solid carved mahogany." "He is a type of the highest average of the American public man." "His sermon was in every sense sufficient, strong, well-knit and balanced, and adequately emotional, while never falling short of the full dignity of the preacher's office and evident character. If the Church in America has many such Bishops it is indeed a living, efflorescent, healing branch of the great tree, which according to Dr. Quintard, has never withered a day in England since the epoch of the Apostles."

He was a guest of the Bishop of London at Fulham Palace; was present at his ordination examinations and took part with him in the ordination of twenty-five priests and nineteen deacons in the famous Chapel Royal, Whitehall; at the invitation of the Bishop of London, he preached the first sermon at the special evening services in St. Paul's Cathedral; he officiated at the service at the laying of the corner stone of the church of St. Paul, Old Brentford,—the stone being laid by H.R.H. Mary Adelaide, Princess of Teck; he laid the foundation stone of St. Chad's Church, Haggeston, London; he was present with Bishops from the far-away South Sea Islands, from Canada, and elsewhere, at the laying of the foundation stone of Keble Memorial College, Oxford; he reopened the restored parish church of Garstag; he assisted the Archbishop of York and preached the sermon at the consecration of the Church of St. Michael, Sheffield; he assisted the Archbishop of York at the parish church, Sheffield, where a class, numbering six hundred, was confirmed; he administered the Apostolic rite for the Bishops of London and Winchester; and on the invitation of the Bishops of Oxford and Ely, took part in their Lenten Missions in 1868.

A second visit was made in 1875–6. His reception by the Most Rev. the Archbishops, the Rt. Rev. the Bishops, the clergy and the laity of the English Church was all that could be asked. On two occasions he administered the Apostolic rite of Confirmation for the Lord Bishop of London and on two occasions held confirmations at the request of the Archbishop of Canterbury. He assisted the Archbishop of York also at the confirmation of more than 500 candidates presented in one class.

By the invitation of the Archbishop of Canterbury, he participated in the opening services of the Convocation of Canterbury and was the first Bishop of the Church, not a member of the Convocation, to be admitted to that service. The service was held in the Chapel of Henry VII in Westminster Abbey.

He assisted at the opening service of Keble College, Oxford, the laying of the foundation stone of which he had witnessed eight years before. He united, with Bishops of the Anglican Communion from England and Africa, in the consecration, in St. Paul's Cathedral, of a Bishop for Asia,— the Rt. Rev., Dr. Mylne, Bishop of Bombay.

He visited the continent also and Scotland; attended the Church Congress at Stoke-upon-Trent; and assisted at the Consecration of the Cathedral of Cummbrae, in the Diocese of Argyle and the Isles. Returning to England he was again present at the opening of the Convocation of Canterbury. The degree of Doctor of Laws was conferred upon him by the University of Cambridge on the occasion of this visit.

He was again in England in 1881 and attended, by invitation, the funeral of Dean Stanley, (July 25th). On the invitation of the Queen's Domestic Chaplain, the Hon. and Rev. Dr. Wellesley, he preached in the Chapel Royal, Windsor, on Sunday, August 14th. No American had ever previously been invited to preach in this chapel. He took for his text on that occasion: "If thou has run with the footmen and they have wearied thee, then how canst thou contend with horses? and if in the land of peace, wherein thou trustedst they wearied thee, then how wilt thou do in the swelling of Jordan?" (Jeremiah xii: 5.)

In these three visits, therefore, the Bishop performed every service appertaining to the Episcopal office. Such experiences were absolutely unique for an American Bishop at that time. It had often been asserted that Bishops and clergy of the Church in America were not permitted to officiate in the Church of England. These visits of the Bishop not only gave him an extended acquaintance among the Bishops and clergy and prominent laity of the English Church, but changed the relations between them and the American Church, so that the latter has since been held in higher regard by the Church of England. How much this was influential in leading up to the present amicable relations existing between England and America, it is not necessary for us to inquire, though doubtless such an influence might be taken into account in tracing up the history of the present Anglo-American alliance.

In 1887 the Bishop was in England and was present by invitation of the Dean of Westminster, in the Abbey at the Queen's Jubilee. He assisted at an anniversary service of the Order of St. John of Jerusalem, in the Chapel Royal, Savoy. As a Chaplain of the Order, he attended a meeting in the Chapter House, Clerkenwell Gate. The following year, as Chaplain of the Order, he assisted at the Installation of H.R.H. the Prince of Wales, (now Edward VII), as Grand Prior of the Order of St. John, in succession to the Duke of Manchester, who for twenty-five years had held the office.

He was also in attendance, in 1888, at the Lambeth Conference, was the guest of the Archbishop at Lambeth Palace, and assisted at the consecration of two Bishops. With the Lord Bishop of Peterborough, he was presenter of one of them,—the Rev. Dr. Thicknesse, consecrated Bishop Suffragan of Leicester, in the Diocese of Peterborough.

CHAPTER XVI

Bishop Quintard and Sewanee

The enthusiasm with which Bishop Quintard, immediately after his consecration, took up and pushed forward whatever promised to be of spiritual benefit to the people of the South, was characteristic of the man. Especially attractive to him was the scheme set forth in the address by Bishop Polk to the Bishops of the Southern Dioceses, published in 1856, emphasizing the importance of building up an educational institution upon broad foundations, for the promotion of social order, civil justice, and Christian truth; to be centrally located in the Southern States. The scheme had been formulated and developed by its projector and originator, Bishop Polk; and "The University of the South" was duly organized in 1857. A liberal charter was secured from the State of Tennessee; title was acquired to a domain of nearly ten thousand acres of land upon the top of Sewanee Mountain; the corner-stone of a main college building was laid; and pledges of an endowment amounting to half a million of dollars were obtained before the war broke out.

In the fall of 1865, before his election to the Episcopate, Dr. Quintard met upon a train between Nashville and Columbia, the Rev. David Pise, a prominent presbyter of the Diocese of Tennessee, and Secretary of the Board of Trustees of The University of the South as it was organized before the war. On the same train was Major George R. Fairbanks, of Florida, a lay Trustee on said Board. The conversation of these three gentlemen was upon the proposed University. The magnificent domain secured for that institution, it was asserted, would revert to its donors unless the proposed University were in operation within ten years of the date of the donation, that is, in 1868. Dr. Quintard pledged himself not only to save the domain, but to revive the scheme for the University and to establish such an institution of learning as Bishop Polk, Bishop Otey, and others had in view when the University of the South was organized in 1857.

The day that he took his seat for the first time in the House of Bishops, Dr. Quintard entered into correspondence with the Rev. John Austin Merrick, D.D., a "man of godly and sound learning," and offered to meet him in Winchester, Tennessee, on a specified day; to go with him to Sewanee and see what might be done toward carrying out the educational enterprise which was intended to mean so much to the Southern people, and which meant all the more to them in the condition in which the war had left them.

The way for such a movement had been prepared at the special convention of the Diocese of Tennessee at which Dr. Quintard had been elected Bishop. Reviving a measure that had evidently been adopted in 1861, at the last convention over which Bishop Otey had presided, (the journal of this convention was lost in the printing office to which it was committed for publication), the special convention of 1865 appointed a committee to take measures for establishing, (with the concurrence of the Executive Committee of the Board of Trustees for the University), a Diocesan Training and Theological School upon the University Domain. Dr. Quintard, as Bishop-elect, had made sure that the war had not impaired the charter, nor up to that time, the title to the domain; even thought it had swept away the endowment, and though soldiers of both armies, marching over the mountain and encamping about the spot, had amused themselves by blowing up the corner-stone laid in 1860, and making out of the fragments trinkets for their sweet-hearts.

In the course of his first series of visitations throughout his immense Diocese, in March 1866, Bishop Quintard arrived in Winchester, and there met the Rev. Dr. Merrick, the Rev. Thomas A. Morris, rector of the church in Winchester, and Major George R. Fairbanks. Accompanied by these gentlemen he ascended the mountain, visited "University Place," (Sewanee), and found shelter and a most cordial hospitality in a log cabin occupied by Mr. William Tomlinson. He selected locations for buildings for the Diocesan Training School and a site for a chapel. In the evening he erected a rustic cross about twelve feet in height, upon the latter site, which is the exact spot whereon now stands the oratory of St. Luke's Hall. Gathered around the cross with the Bishop and his companions, were members of Mr. Tomlinson's household, a few mountaineers and some negro workmen. The Nicene Creed was recited and the Bishop knelt down and prayed God to give to those who were then engaging in a great enterprise, "grace both to perceive and know what things they ought to do, and strength faithfully to fulfill the same." The woods rang with the strains of "Gloria in Excelsis." It was a scene worthy of association with those of the sixteenth century, where discoverers and Conquistadors pre-empted new lands by planting a cross and claiming the territory for their king and for the Church. Thus was the domain at Sewanee reclaimed for the King of Kings and for the cause of Christian education.

The site selected for the University in ante-bellum times was ideal for the purpose to which it was consecrated. Sewanee is on a spur of the Cumberland Mountains,—a plateau some two thousand feet above the level of the sea and about one thousand feet above the surrounding val-leys. The scenery is of unparalleled grandeur with many points of pictur-esque beauty,—primeval forests, cliffs, ravines and caves,—immediately at hand. The climate is of such a character as to exempt the residents from malarial or pulmonary troubles. It is especially adapted to the re-quirements of a school whose terms were to be held in the summer months and with mid-winter vacations, to suit the convenience of a south-ern population whose home life was more or less likely to be broken up in the summer.

The conception of a grand landed domain as an important feature in the planning and planting of an institution of learning, was at that time quite unusual in America. Colleges and universities had previously looked to populous centers and environment to build them up and sus-tain them. The University of the South deliberately chose to go out into the wilderness and create therein its own environment. The site had been carefully studied by Bishop Hopkins, who was an accomplished architect and landscape gardener, and who had it mapped, and had a tentative scheme of buildings designed for it upon the models of the English Uni-versities.

In furtherance of the enterprise, Bishop Quintard accepted the tender of a lease, for educational purposes, of a school property in Winchester, twelve miles from Sewanee, at the foot of the mountains; and there estab-lished "Sewanee College," with Major Fairbanks as President of the

Board of Trustees, and with Rev. F. L. Knight, D.D., and a competent faculty in charge. Although this Collegiate Institute was formally opened and remained in operation for a time, the Bishop found it too expensive for him to maintain; and so, as the University developed, he gave up the lease of the Winchester property and concentrated his efforts upon the work at Sewanee.

He made immediate efforts to collect funds to advance the work of building up the Diocesan Training School. He recorded with deep gratitude the gift of $1000 and of a handsome communion service from Mrs. Barnum of Baltimore. The following May, out of funds thus early collected, a building was erected and called "Otey Hall." That summer the Bishop and Major Fairbanks erected residences near Otey Hall and removed their families to Sewanee.

The Episcopal residence at Sewanee was at first a log dwelling-house. This was improved and added to until it assumed the character of what the Bishop was wont to call "the cucumber-vine style of architecture," and acquired the name of Fulford Hall, in commemoration of the Canadian Metropolitan who had participated in the Bishop's consecration. Memphis had been made the residence of Bishop Otey in the latter part of his Episcopate, and as the work at Sewanee increased and that place became widely known and its importance recognized, the Memphians regarded it with some jealousy and sought to secure the person of the Bishop by providing a residence for him in that city on the western borders of the Diocese. The Bishop accordingly adopted Memphis as his winter residence. But his work at Sewanee was too dear to his heart to permit his abandoning his home there,—as much as a Bishop could be said to have a home anywhere. And so while Memphis became officially the ecclesiastical capital of his Diocese, he strove earnestly to make Sewanee the scholastic, and, to some extent, the ecclesiastical capital of all the Southern Dioceses, and in great measure he succeeded.

It would be impossible to estimate the value of the Bishop's thus fixing his residence at Sewanee, not only to the work of building up the University, but in its influence upon the cause of Christian education. For The University of the South "has been built up upon men, not upon things." The faith, the enthusiasm and the personal magnetism of Bishop Quintard drew around him at Sewanee a band of high-minded and consecrated clergymen and laymen of fine scholarship and noble aims. Thus was realized the idea of Bishop Polk, who, when on one occasion he was asked in reference to the apparently isolated location of the University, "Where will you get your society?" replied, "We will make it; and not only so, but we will surround our University with such a society as is nowhere else possible in this land."

The tone, the temper, the social and religious atmosphere of Sewanee came from Bishop Quintard more than from anyone else. For the first twenty years of the University's existence at least, it could almost be said that Bishop Quintard was Sewanee and that Sewanee was Bishop Quintard; and throughout that period Fulford Hall was the visible center of Sewanee life. Into it the Bishop gathered the spolia of his travels, rich art treasures, rare and valuable books and autographs, and made it a most interesting place to visit. When the building was destroyed by fire in June, 1889, most of its interior attractions were saved from the flames through the energetic efforts of the students of the University, and the elegant building which replaced it, retains the name of Fulford Hall. Therein the Bishop passed the last years of his life. It is still the residence of the Vice-Chancellor of the University.

Bishop Elliott of Georgia, the senior Bishop of the Southern Dioceses, was likewise deeply interested in the University and was ex-officio Chancellor. At the suggestion of Bishop Quintard, he called a meeting of the Board of Trustees to be held at "University Place" in October, 1866. It was attended by the Bishops of Georgia, Mississippi, Arkansas and Tennessee, respectively, together with several clerical and lay members of the Board who unanimously resolved that the work of establishing the University be prosecuted. Bishop Quintard was appointed a Commissioner to solicit funds for the erection of plain but substantial buildings, in order that the University might begin its work at the earliest possible date. He accordingly made a trip to New Orleans where he held services in all the churches and made an earnest appeal at every service to the church people of that city to carry on the work in which the first Bishop of Louisiana had been so deeply interested.

He was able to report the results of his visit to New Orleans, at a meeting of the Board of Trustees held at a private residence in Montgomery, Alabama, in February, 1867. Bishop Elliott had died in December, 1866, and Bishop Green, of Mississippi, had succeeded him in the Chancellorship of the University. Bishop Quintard's report to the Board was of such a character that the Board proceeded to the reorganization of the University forthwith. The Bishop offered Otey Hall, at Sewanee, which was capable of accommodating a goodly number of students, as part of the property of the University, on condition that the Board adopt the Diocesan Training

School (for which the building had been intended), as the Theological Department of the University, and the offer was accepted. The actual establishment of the Theological Department was delayed, however, for nearly ten years and until more favorable opportunities offered.

The deliberations of the Board upon the question of the most feasible plan for beginning work, resulted in the recommendation that a Vice-Chancellor be elected, and this officer be charged with the duty of soliciting subscriptions and otherwise advancing the interests of the University. Bishop Quintard was thereupon elected Vice-Chancellor and Major Fairbanks was appointed Commissioner of Lands and Buildings to act as General Agent and Business Manager; to be associated with the Bishop in the work of soliciting subscriptions; to reside at the University site; and, under the direction of the Executive Committee, to have charge of all the business affairs of the University.

No more efficient officers could have been selected, and with this action of the Board, the University scheme might be said to have been fairly launched. Of the trials and antagonisms the Bishop was to meet with in his work, there is no need to speak now. It was no easy matter to solicit funds for this project at that time. Not only had the South been impoverished by the war, but the Southern people had not become fully acquainted with the changed condition of their affairs, and did not fully appreciate the value of a plan to educate their sons and make the best citizens of them.

In June, 1867, at the request of the Trustees, the Bishop made an attempt to raise funds for the erection of additional buildings, confining his efforts to the state and Diocese of Georgia. Early in August the cornerstone of St. Augustine's Chapel was laid by Bishop Green, in the presence of a concourse of clergy and laity. The occasion was signalized by a dignity of ceremonial befitting the prospective magnitude of the undertaking. The function began with a celebration of the Holy Communion in the portion of Otey Hall then used as a chapel. The Bishops and clergy moved in solemn procession to the spot selected. The Doctors wore hoods expressive of their degrees. A scholastic as well as an ecclesiastical tone was thereby given to the function, and from that time forward The University of the South conformed in the details of its regulations to the models set by the English Universities. In 1871, the University, then in full working order, adopted the cap and gown for the distinctive uniform of its advanced students, divided the Academic Department into Juniors and Gownsmen, and provided rich robes for the Chancellor and Vice-Chancellor. In these respects it was quite in advance of other institutions of learning in America, though its customs have since grown in favor with other and older universities. Still it was possible for some one who attended the commencement in 1891, to write:—"Probably nowhere else in America is there any such formal and stately collegiate ceremony as at Sewanee."

In 1867, the Bishop being in England, he consented at the earnest solicitation of his friends, to spend the winter there, and do what he could to promote the cause of the University. The influential friends he made in England took up with enthusiasm a movement which resulted in such liberal offerings that the University was enabled to start afresh with most encouraging prospects of final and complete success.

The Rev. Frederick W. Tremlett, of St. Peter's Church, Belsize Park, London, inaugurated the movement and a committee was appointed which issued a circular inviting subscriptions. The committee consisted of the Archbishop of York, the Earl of Carnarvon, Viscount Cranbourne, (afterwards Lord Salisbury,) the Lord Bishop of Oxford, Earl Nelson, Lord John Manners, the Rt. Hon. W. E. Gladstone and others. The Archbishop of Canterbury, the Most Rev. Campbell Tait, in a letter, expressed his deepest interest in the project and subscribed twenty-five pounds toward it. The Archbishop of York, and Bishops of the Anglican Communion from all part of Her Majesty's realms, expressed a like sympathy. Among the subscribers were names of great distinction both in state and church. Considerably more than ten thousand dollars was thereby raised, and with this sum the Bishop returned to America. Much needed buildings were erected in Sewanee, and on the 18th of September, 1868, as Vice-Chancellor, the Bishop formally opened the Junior Department of the University of the South. Thus after twelve years of labor and anxiety, of disappointment and sorrow,—after the death of Bishops Polk, Otey, Elliott, Rutledge and Cobbs,—all of them actively interested in the project for building a Church University of the first class in the South that would in some degree do for our country what the Universities of Oxford and Cambridge have so well done for England and the civilized world,—The University of the South began its work for God and our land. That day has since been annually observed at Sewanee as "Foundation Day."

Among the men who were early attracted to the work at Sewanee, were Brigadier-General Josiah Gorgas, (who had been head of the Confederate Ordnance Department, and became at first head-master of the Junior Academic Department of the University, and was afterward made Vice-

Chancellor); Brigadier-General F. A. Shoup, (who was now the Rev. Professor Shoup, acting-chaplain and Professor of Mathematics); General E. Kirby-Smith; and Colonel F. T. Sevier, the Bishop's old friend of the First Tennessee Regiment, who became Commandant of Cadets and headmaster of the Grammar School. For it was but natural that the military feature of the school should commend itself to men who had just passed through war and had seen the benefit of military discipline upon life and character. These men felt that a higher duty awaited them at the close of the war, than trying to make money,—that the training of the youths of the land as Christian citizens was of paramount importance,—and they gave themselves up to that educational work.

The splendid sacrifice of these and others set high the standard of the University and invested it with a poetic beauty and a sacredness that dwells there still. "Nowhere in the South," said Charles Dudley Warner, in 1889, "and I might say, nowhere in the Republic, have I found anything so hopeful as The University of the South." "Of the wisdom of founding this University," said a visitor who spent the summer of 1878 at Sewanee, "no one would question after a single visit here. Its highest development is yet to be obtained. Its present standard is equal to the best, but its aims are to reach the highest and best culture obtainable. It is slowly and surely reaching forward and satisfactorily filling the measure of its allotted work. . . . It is difficult to explain to one who has had not opportunity for a personal observation, how many excellent formative influences are here combined. . . . Everything here promotes a feeling of reverence and respect for sacred things. The presence and influence of men of high standard in Church and state, whose example is potent for good. . . . The book of nature is always open here to the investigations of the geologist, the botanist, and the student of natural history. . . . The physical education goes on with that of the intellect; an invigorating atmosphere strengthens the capacity. . . . The various gymnastic and military exercises give a clear complexion, an elastic step and a noble carriage, and then mind and body, acting in healthy unison, fill out the measure of a well rounded man."

Bishop Quintard's ideals regarding the University to the upbuilding of which he was giving the most valuable years of his life, were shadowed forth in his words to the Convention of his Diocese in 1874, in referring to the meeting of the Board of Trustees which he had attended the previous year. "It is the aim and purpose of any true system of education to draw out, to strengthen and to exhibit in active working, certain powers which exist in man,—planted, indeed, by God, but latent in man until they shall have been so drawn out. Education is not the filling of a mind with so much knowledge, though, of course, it includes the imparting of knowledge. As education is the drawing out of the dormant powers of the whole man, it must in its highest sense be commensurate with the whole man. The body must be trained by healthful exercise, the mind or thinking power, must be drawn out and strengthened, and finally a heart must be sanctified and a will subdued. It is the aim and object of The University of the South to give to its students every advantage,—physical, mental and moral; to develop a harmonious and symmetrical character; to fit and prepare men for every vocation in the life that now is, where we are strangers and sojourners; and to teach all those things which a Christian ought to know and believe to his soul's health. The momentous and concerning truth that intellectual power unrestrained and unregulated by sound moral and religious principle tends only to mischief and misery in our race, has been in the educational systems of the age, almost overlooked."

The heroic struggle the University was making, began to attract admiring attention. Gifts began to flow into it,—small as compared with those that have been given to the cause of education in these later days, but large when the impoverished condition of the South form which many of them came, is taken into consideration. And not only was the continued existence of the University guaranteed, but its ultimate success was assured.

The responsibility and work devolving upon the Vice-Chancellor of a University, even in its nascent stages, were too great a burden when added to the cares of a large and exacting Diocese, and Bishop Quintard resigned the office of Vice-Chancellor in 1868 in order that some one else might be elected to fill that position. An effort to secure the valuable services of General Robert E. Lee, for the University, resulted in the following letter:—

WASHINGTON COLLEGE, LEXINGTON, VA., 23 Sept., 1868

RT. REV'D AND DEAR SIR—Absence from Lexington has prevented me until to-day from replying to your kind interesting letter of the 20th of August last. I have followed with deep interest the progress of The University of the South from its origin, and my wishes for its success have been as earnest as my veneration for its founders and respect for its object have been sincere. Its prosperity will always be to me a source of pleasure, and I trust that in the Providence of God its career may be one of eminent benefit to our country. That it has survived the adverse circumstances with which it has been surrounded and has surmounted the difficulties with which it has had to contend, is cause of great rejoicing to me, and I am glad to learn that it has so fair a prospect of advancement and usefulness.

I need not, then, assure you that I feel highly honored that its Board of Trustees has thought of me for the office of Vice-Chancellor, and I beg that you will present to them my most fervent thanks for their favorable consideration. They have, however, been misinformed as to my feelings concerning my present position, and even were they as represented, I could not now resign it with propriety unless I saw it would be for the benefit of the college. I must therefore respectfully decline your proposition, and ask you to accept my grateful thanks for the frank and courteous manner in which it has been tendered, as well as for the considerate measures you proposed to promote my convenience and comfort.

I am, with great respect and highest regard, your friend and obt. servt.,   R. E. LEE

Rt. Rev'd WM. M. GREEN, D.D., Chancellor of the University of the South.

Commodore Matthew Fontaine Maury was then elected by the Board, and when Commodore Maury declined, the Bishop withdrew his resignation and continued his work. In various parts of the South, in the North and in England, he represented the needs of the University.

A trip made to New Orleans and Galveston in 1870 was in some respects characteristic of the Bishop's appeals and of the breadth of scope of the University as presented by him. In Galveston, the first person who responded to his appeal was a Hebrew; one of the most active helpers was a Presbyterian, and these two with a Churchman composed a committee to work for The University of the South.

In 1871 the Academic Department was formally organized by the election of five professors. In 1872, the Bishop once again resigned the Vice-Chancellorship and General Gorgas was elected to succeed him. General Gorgas was in time succeeded by the Rev. Dr. Telfair Hodgson, and he in turn by the Rev. Dr. Thomas F. Gailor. In 1893 the last named was succeeded by Bishop Quintard's son-in-law, Dr. B. Lawton Wiggins, an alumnus of The University of the South, and the preserver of what his father-in-law had founded.

But the Bishop's interest in the University was not relaxed. Wherever he went he represented the needs of the University as well as those of his Diocese. In 1876, he attended a "matinee" at the London residence of Lord Shrewsbury. Cards of invitation had been issued by the Earl and Countess of Shrewsbury and about three hundred guests assembled. The Lord Bishop of Winchester presided at this meeting, which was organized in the interests of The University of the South—not so much to collect money for the University but to make known in England the work the University was doing. The Church in Scotland was represented by the Primus and by the Bishop of Edinburgh; the Irish Church by the Bishop of Derry and Raphoe and by the Bishop of Moray and Ross. A large number of prominent clergymen were present. Addresses were made by the Bishops, by Lord Shrewsbury, A. J. Beresford-Hope, M.P., and others.

In 1887 Bishop Green died and was succeeded in the Chancellorship by Bishop Gregg of Texas. When the latter died in 1893, his logical successor was Bishop Quintard, who, however, felt unfitted for the office by reason of his infirmity of deafness which had come to him in his later years. He accordingly stood aside and favored the election of the Rt. Rev. Dr. Dudley, Bishop of Kentucky.

Bishop Quintard had seen buildings of permanent character grow up and upon the University domain,—built of Sewanee sand-stone, unsurpassed either in quality or appearance as a building material. He had seen the Theological Department opened in 1878, the Medical Department opened in 1892, and the Law Department in 1893. He had acted as consecrator at the elevation of an alumnus of the University to the Episcopate of Louisiana.* He had consecrated as his own coadjutor one whose life had been closely connected with Sewanee and the University. He had ordained to the priesthood many alumni. He had seen degrees conferred upon many men who were to go out into the world and carry the influence of the noble work the Bishop himself had done so much toward establishing. And in many ways he had seen in the Church University, whose broad foundations had been wisely laid by godly men who inaugurated the enterprise, a visible advance made toward the ideals set for it by its founders and re-founder.

*Five other alumni have been elevated to the episcopate since the Bishop's death. [A. H. N.]

The last Convention at which the Bishop presided, was held in Sewanee in 1897. The Bishop, shortly afterward, went to England to be present at the Lambeth Conference held that year. He returned to Sewanee somewhat refreshed in body and resumed the work of his Diocese. But further rest became necessary and he went to Dairen, Georgia, in search thereof. There the end came on the 15th of February, 1898. His body was brought back to Sewanee, lay for a time in the Otey Memorial Church, watched by the clergy and the Sisters of St. Mary, and was thence taken to St. Augustine's Chapel, where the service was said over it by the Bishops in attendance. The University was not in session at the time, but the University town was filled with sorrowing friends, representing the Army of the late Confederate States, the clergy and laity of the Diocese, the House of Bishops, and the alumni of the University. The Coadjutor Bishop of Tennessee, now Bishop Quintard's successor, committed his body to the ground in the Sewanee cemetery.

A movement was begun soon after the Bishop's death to endow a professorship in the Theological Department of the University as a memorial of him. Very fittingly, the new Grammar School Dormitory, erected on the University domain in 1901, was named the "Quintard Memorial." But the greatest monument and the most lasting one, to the second Bishop of Tennessee, is and will be the University which he re-founded and did much to build up.

THE END

Charles Todd Quintard as a young man
Courtesy University of the South

Quintard with survivors of the Rock City Guard, 1865. From left, standing:
Alex Allison, Alex Fall, William Foster, Dr. J. R. Buist, Maj. Joseph Vaulx,
Joe Mason; seated: Col. R. B. Snowden, Quintard, Dr. R. Foster,
Jack Wheeless, Maj. W. D. Kelly.
Reprinted from Confederate Veteran

William Wing Loring
Library of Congress

Leonidas Polk
Library of Congress

Braxton Bragg
Library of Congress

John H. Marsh
Reprinted from Confederate Veteran

Otho F. Strahl
Library of Congress

John Bell Hood
*Massachusetts Commandery, Military Order of
the Loyal Legion, United States Army Military
History Institute*

Bishop Quintard in 1868
*Coutesy Michael
Hammerson*

Bishop Quintard in later life
Courtesy University of the South

Appendix

The following is a copy of the petition, with signatures attached, of the Rock City Guard, which induced Dr. Quintard to suspend his parochial work in Nashville, and enter the military service of the Confederacy.

We the undersigned members of the "Battalion of Rock City Guard" do hereby respectfully invite the Rev. C. T. Quintard to accompany us throughout the campaign as our friend and spiritual adviser, and we herby pledge ourselves to sustain him and attend regularly whatever service he may institute, being willing to be guided by him.

F. J. Reamer, C. H. Stockell, John Gee Haily, W. Willis, E. C. Leonhard, John B. Johnson, Robt. Gordon, B. M. Franklin, Nat Hampton, jr., Jno. M. Pearl, Robert Swan, John W. McWhirter, John W. Branch, D. W. Sumner, M. N. Brown, Joseph Freeman, J. C. March, R. J. Howse, Jas. McManus, R. S. Bugg, E. W. Fariss, Douglas Lee, Sam Robinson, F. I. Loiseau, V. L. Benton, Wm. T. Hefferman, James P. Shockly, Wm. Morrow, Berry Morgan, Rowe Foote, R. R. Hightower, H. B. Finn, Joseph A. Carney, D. J. Roberts, J. H. Hough, A. W. Harris, I. M. Cockrill, R. A. Withers, R. W. Gillespie, J. H. Bankston, Harry Ross, R. Darrington, T. J. Gattright, John K. Sloan, B. J. McCarty, L. H. McLemore, A. J. Phillips, W. A. Mayo, R. H. Fiser, James T. Gunn, Wm. A. Ellis, T. H. Atkeison, R. B. Rozell, R. Cheatham, W. N. Johns, J. P. Shane, J. L. Cooke, Geo. A. Diggons, T. O. Harris, Victor Vallette, D. G. Carter, J. W. Thomas, J. Clarke, F. M. Geary, W. B. Ross, Wm. Baxter, J. T. Henderson, John W. Barnes, James P. Kirkman, H. N. Stothart, D. K. Sanford, R. W. Burke, James Carrigan, T. H. Griffin, W. P. Prichard, J. H. Allen, P. Bartola, G. T. Hampton, F. H. Morgan, Wm. R. Elliston, jr., Wm. H. Everett, T. B. Lanier, I. L. Smith, T. C. Lucas, W. P. Wadlington, Jas. W. Nichol, Wm. B. Maney, John A. Murkin, jr., J. Walker Coleman, Jo H. Sewell, G. E. Valette, Geo. M. Mace, Mason Vannoy.

The Diary of
Rev. Dr. Charles Todd Quintard,
October 1864–May 1865

Introduction to the Diary

The surviving portion of Quintard's wartime diary begins on October 15, 1864. It is kept in two volumes in the Archives of the University of the South. The first volume covers the period from October 15, 1864, to January 31, 1865. The second volume includes the period from February 1, 1865, to May 26, 1865. As will be seen, there are few entries after the Federal occupation of Columbus, Georgia, on Easter Sunday, April 16, 1865.

At various points in the diary, Quintard pasted or loosely kept newspaper articles or other materials that he found to be of interest. In the first volume of the diary, before the narrative begins on October 15, 1864, after some items of family history, there are several matters of interest. These include a prayer prescribed for a Fast Day on June 13, 1861, and a "Prayer to be used During the Continuance of the War," both by Bishop Elliott of Georgia. There is also a prayer written into the diary in different handwriting than Quintard's, ascribed to his friend, Rev. David Pise. Additionally, Quintard quoted an inspirational poem attributed to Bishop Doane, entitled "St. Ignatius to St. Polycarp" with the theme "stand like an anvil," as well as other verses Quintard apparently found of some spiritual use.

More interesting for the historical reader is Quintard's setting the stage for the diary with several newspaper excerpts from September and October 1864. The first undated and unattributed piece relates to speeches made on October 5, 1864, during President Davis' visit to Augusta, Georgia. Davis *avowed that "[h]e had never felt more confidence in the success of our cause than now." Other newspaper articles relate to destruction of crops, mills, and other property of use to the rebellion in the Shenandoah Valley, a piece from the* La Grange Reporter *in support of General John B. Hood's strategy, a general order from Hood on straggling issued on September 13, 1864, and two pieces relating to the Battle of Allatoona on October 5, 1864. There are also two obituary pieces relating to soldiers of the 1st Tennessee— William G. Graham, killed at Zion Church on July 4, 1864, and James Brandon, killed at Kennesaw Mountain on June 27, 1864. Both were members of the famous Company H of that regiment. Also relating to the 1st Tennessee is a piece in which Quintard is quoted refuting a rumor that Colonel Feild of the 1st Tennessee had deserted and taken the oath of allegiance to the Federal government. Finally, there is a piece relating to the funeral of Brig. Gen. Preston Smith and Capt. John M. Donelson, killed at Chickamauga. Quintard is reported to have conducted their funeral service at a private residence.*

My Face Towards Tennessee
October 15 to November 30, 1864

OCTOBER 15, SATURDAY, COLUMBUS, GEORGIA
After sundry vexatious delays, have at length succeeded in securing a car in Macon for the transportation of our furniture. Today got possession of a house rented from Mr. J. R. Banks, two miles from town. Have rented a place to the 1st of June, 1865 for $2,500.[1]

OCTOBER 16TH, SUNDAY
Read Prayers in the morning. Sermon by the Rev. Mr. Ellis of Tallahassee, Fla.[2] In the afternoon I preached. Offertory for the poor, $1,000.

OCTOBER 17TH, MONDAY
The kindness of my excellent friend, J. Rhodes Brown, enabled me to get all the furniture out to the house without difficulty. He sent men and drays and has placed me under lasting obligations by real, hearty kindness. Have had a hard day's work. This frequent moving is exceedingly disagreeable, and though we have very much to be thankful for, I long very much for peace that we may be once more in a settled home. It may be that God has not so great a blessing in store for us and I trust we may have grace to be content with whatever His loving providence may appoint, but I cannot help praying earnestly for my old home and my dear flock.

I have been sadly disappointed in not being able to return to the Army. I was extremely anxious to accompany General Hood in the present campaign. The spirit of our Army has been greatly improved by this forward movement. It is indeed astonishing to see our noble fellows, who in all the retrograde movement from Dalton to Jonesboro have maintained their morale to so great an extent. Their devotion to the cause which they

1. The 1860 federal census for Muscogee County, Georgia, does not list a J. R. Banks as such but does list John Banks, age sixty, a man with a large family and real and personal property worth $43,000.
2. The 1860 federal census for Leon County, Florida, lists W. J. Ellis, an Episcopal minister born in New York, age forty-two.

have espoused is unrivaled in the annals of history. Never have a soldiery stood up more nobly, or battled more bravely than ours. Through hardships almost past endurance, through toils that would make the stoutest heart quake to anticipate, they have stood up with unflinching resolution. The sufferings endured by the little band who followed Washington to Valley Forge and spent with him that memorable winter, half famished, were not more poignant than the sufferings of those who are now enlisted under the Southern Cross. In wind and rain, beneath the summer sun, and on the snows of winter, they have stood at their posts manfully. Every hope they may have indulged, every ambition they may have fostered is swallowed up in one great ambition of having a free country. And our noble women too—how wonderful their endurance and their sacrifices. In the history of the war, none of its pages will be brighter than those which record their services.

OCTOBER 18TH, TUESDAY
Arranging household affairs and purchasing provisions. This being the Festival of St. Luke, morning service was at 10 o'clock.

OCTOBER 19TH, WEDNESDAY
This is the 16th anniversary of my marriage. As I look back over the whole period, I feel that I have great reason to be thankful to God for all the blessings he has vouchsafed me with—the best of wives. I have enjoyed more happiness than falls to the lot of most men. Mrs. Shorter, Miss Theresa, Miss Bailey and Miss Sally Green spent the day with us.[3] I rode into town in the morning. No Army news.

OCTOBER 20TH, THURSDAY
Though suffering from a severe attack of influenza, I rode with Mrs. Carter and her sisters, Mrs. Woolfolk and Ticknor to call upon the family of

3. The 1860 federal census for Muscogee County, Georgia, lists R. C. Shorter, then living in Columbus and age forty, occupation listed as "none"; Mary M. Shorter, then age twenty-eight; and five younger members of the household. "Miss Teresa" is apparently Teresa Shorter, identified in the entry for October 28. Since the R. C. Shorter family did not, on the face of the census, list a Teresa, the Shorters cannot be identified with certainty. The 1860 federal census suggests Miss Bailey was one of the four daughters, in 1864 ranging in age from sixteen to twenty-seven, of Francis Bailey. Miss Sally Green was possibly Sarah G. Green, age thirteen, or Sarah Green, age twenty-five.

General Bethune, our nearest neighbor.[4] Most of the family happened to be away from home, but I had the pleasure of seeing one very important member of the household—no less a personage than the celebrated Negro pianist, "Blind Tom," who belongs to General Bethune. On hearing my voice, Tom came into the parlor in the most uncouth way and paid his respects to the ladies and myself. He was not as much in the humor for playing as usual for he had already spent four hours at the piano for the amusement of some cavalrymen who had visited him. He, however, sat down to the instrument and gave us some very delightful music. His playing is most wonderful, nor can it be accounted for by any natural laws. To me it seems an inspiration. He has improved since I heard him in Richmond in 1862. He sang a French song in which his power of mimicry was wonderfully displayed. He is now a well grown boy of 15 years of age. His musical talent was exhibited in earliest childhood. From General Bethune's we rode a mile further to visit Mrs. Judge Tarpley and her family, refugees from Mississippi.[5] Mrs. Tarpley was originally from Nashville and was very familiar with the history of the substantial families of the city.

OCTOBER 21ST, FRIDAY
Too unwell to leave my room. Have had a large lot of wood hauled. From the following it appears that there are some of the North who realize the true nature of "the situation" and whose brains are not completely befogged.[6] It is reported, and no doubt correct, that Hood has captured the Yankee garrison at Dalton, consisting of 800 Negro soldiers and 250 Whites. What is to be the result of General Hood's grand movement is impossible to imagine. The gravity of the situation and the uncertainty is

4. From the 1860 federal census for Muscogee County, Georgia, it appears Mrs. Carter was Mrs. Robert Carter, vice president of the Ladies' Soldiers' Friend Society in Columbus. Mrs. Woolfolk was probably Manah B. Woolfolk, the wife of William G. Woolfolk, a farmer. Mrs. Ticknor was probably Rosa Lee Ticknor, wife of Francis Orray Ticknor (d. 1874), although CTQ elsewhere tended to style the wives of doctors "Mrs. Dr." Dr. Ticknor lived at "Torch Hill," and served as a surgeon in one of Columbus' military hospitals. His celebrated poem, "Little Giffen of Tennessee" memorialized Ticknor's care for a wounded soldier. Telfair, *History of Columbus*, 122–23.
5. Mrs. Judge Tarpley cannot be identified.
6. As was his frequent practice, here CTQ pastes an undated newspaper clipping, "The Progress of Subjugation" from the *New York Daily News*, which paints a gloomy view of Federal prospects in the fall of 1864.

at least sufficient to repress exultations that might prove premature. We have much, however, to encourage and cheer us.

Have occupied my time today in reading Dr. Samuel Johnson's "Lives of the Poets." His life [of] Richard Savage is most remarkable. He was born January 10, 1697—being the natural son of Earl Rivers by Anne, Countess of Macclesfield. Born with a legal claim to honor and affluence, he was in two months illegitimated by the Parliament and disowned by his mother, doomed to poverty and obscurity, and launched upon the ocean of life, only that he might be swallowed by its quicksands or dashed upon its rocks. His mother pursued him through life with unrelenting cruelty, having first endeavored to starve him, then to transport him, and afterwards to hang him. While writing his masterpiece, "The Wanderer" he was compelled to consort with beggars and thieves, spending his nights in cellars among the riot and filth of the meanest and most profligate of the rabble. Without money for the most limited comforts he frequently walked the streets till he was weary and exhausted. Such was the lot of a man who, as Dr. Johnson observes, possessed "exalted sentiments, extensive views, and curious observations; a man whose remarks on life might have assisted the statesman, whose ideas of virtue might have enlightened a moralist, whose eloquence might have influenced senates and whose delicacy might have polished courts."

Having been arrested for a debt of £8, he was confined in Newgate prison where after six months confinement, he died on the 1st of August, 1743. At once remarkable for his misfortunes, his weaknesses and his ability, the moral to be drawn from his life warns all men of a necessity of prudence without which whatever a man's capacity or attainments, the end must be misery and disappointment—and further that negligence and irregularity long continued "make knowledge useless and ridiculous and genius contemptible."

OCTOBER 23RD, 22ND SUNDAY AFTER TRINITY
Being too unwell to go to church, I assembled my family, servants and all, in my bedroom and read the full morning service. It was a delightful refreshment. I do not know how those who profess to call themselves Christians, and yet who live without the Church, can hold a faith as once delivered to the Saints, without prescript forms of Prayer. And I believe it is a fact of universal application to all such that they have not only drifted a long way from their own standards and platforms, but also from the simplicity of the truth.

As for the Methodist sect and the Baptist heresy, they have rioted in false doctrine. The Presbyterian Establishment of Scotland well nigh rejects the "Apostles Creed." It makes no part of the Westminster Confession of Faith; but was subsequently inserted at the end of the Shorter Catechism with this apology: "Albeit the substance of the doctrine comprised in that abridgment commonly called *The Apostles Creed* be fully set forth in each of the Catechisms so as there is no necessity of inserting the Creed itself; yet it is here annexed, not as though it were composed by the Apostles, or ought to be esteemed canonical Scripture, as the Ten Commandments and the Lord's Prayer (much less a prayer as ignorant people have been apt to make both it and the Decologue) but because it is a brief sum of the Christian faith, agreeable to the word of God and anciently received in the Churches of Christ." So too with the Seraphic Hymn and Gloria Patri which is at once the Christian's Hymn of Glory and his shorter Creed—for the mystery of the Holy Trinity in the unity of the Lord Jehovah is the sum of his faith—this hymn was sung in Scotland in the time of John Knox but after Melville introduced Presbyterianism and extemporary praying it was prohibited; and on one occasion in a country parish the clerk was beginning to sing it as usual when the minister suddenly called out to him from the pulpit, "Stop, Stop, no more glory to the Father; the Assembly has forbidden it." Look at the Presbyterianism of today and what do we behold but schism added to schism—its standard is neglected or forgotten—and a miserable looseness of both doctrine and discipline—in striking contrast to all which is our own glorious branch of the one living and true vine. She is as a city at unity with herself and one great cause is the grand conservatism of her Liturgy—"It is not," says Mr. Taylor "for its antiquity alone that I respect and venerate the public worship of the Church. I am struck with its excellence. I admire the beauty, the order, the fitness of the whole service; and to me it appears to bear internal marks of its divine original; for it approaches nearest to a sublime simplicity and inspiration of scripture. I know not any human composition which in chastity, in grandeur, in energy, in sublimity of thought, and simplicity of expression can be compared to the established Liturgy of our National Church. There is in the prayers of it such a chastised and sober dignity, such unaffected humility, such a sanctity befitting the temple of God, such fire of devotion, such inspiration of faith, hope and charity; such conciseness and yet such fullness that nothing short of inspiration has attained to so near a resemblance of the perfect form of prayer which our Divine Master has left us for our use and for our pattern."

Read service again for my household in the evening.

OCTOBER 25TH, TUESDAY

Dr. Anderson arrived from Macon. Much to my regret the Polk Hospital to which he is attached, is ordered to Selma, Alabama. It is reported that Hood has crossed the Tennessee. Dined with Mr. Rhodes Brown where I met Rev. Mr. Hawks, Mr. Spencer and Dr. Douglass, Post Surgeon.[7] The dinner was very sumptuous. At the table there was port, sherry and Madeira wines and champagne. Such a thing I have not met since the war began. After dinner Mr. Brown drove me out home.

OCTOBER 26TH, WEDNESDAY

Kate sick with headache and so we failed in having company at dinner. I went to town and purchased cloth for George, Eddie and the servants.[8] My family is now very comfortably settled and I am feeling very anxious to rejoin the Army. The report of the crossing of the Tennessee by our army is continually repeated but nothing satisfactory. General Beauregard published an address to his army at the same date of this order.[9] It was in excellent taste and tone, promising a forward movement and caused great enthusiasm. He is very popular with the troops and his name is a tower of strength.

OCTOBER 27TH, THURSDAY

Heavy rain this morning which cleared away about 11 o'clock when Dr. Anderson and I rode to town. I visited the Carnes Hospital—dined with Dr. Douglass, Post Surgeon and the surgeons of the Hospital and promised to hold service for them on Saturday.

7. The 1860 federal census for Muscogee County, Georgia, identifies two Spencers—L. Spencer, a clerk, and Perry Spencer, a merchant. George B. Douglas (see CTQ entry for October 29, 1864) was originally mustered in as surgeon of the 1st Regiment, Georgia Regulars. Henderson, *Confederate Soldiers of Georgia*, 1:306.

8. George and Eddie (Edward) were CTQ's two sons.

9. At this point is pasted a newspaper clipping of Beauregard's General Orders No. 1, relative to his assumption of command of the Military Division of the West, which can be found at OR 39(2):824. For a discussion of the rationale of Beauregard's new appointment, see Connelly, *Autumn of Glory*, 472–76.

OCTOBER 28TH, FRIDAY

Festival of Saints Simon and Jude. Rode to town with Mrs. Carter and breakfasted with Mrs. Shorter. Service at 10½. I said morning prayer. Hawks read Ante-Communion and I made an address on the importance of earnestness in the Christian life. At dinner today had the delightful society of my excellent friend, Rhodes Brown and family, Dr. Robert Battey and Miss Theresa Shorter.[10] Dr. Battey is en route to Selma with his hospital which is now at the depot in transit to Selma where it is to be established.

OCTOBER 29TH, SATURDAY

Had service at the Carnes Hospital at 11 A.M.—A good congregation of surgeons and convalescents with a number of ladies from town. During the service I baptized Hugh Archer, aged 3 months—Parents, John R. and Mary B. Gregory—Sponsors, Dr. George B. Douglass and Georgia Lawton.[11]

I gave an extemporary discourse on repentance in which the congregation seemed very much interested and gave me their undivided attention. Rhodes Brown gave me another $1,000 for "Army Reading." He also presented me with a pair of blankets for my own use. His kindness is very great and I am abundantly thankful to the good Lord for giving me such a generous friend.

OCTOBER 30TH, 23RD SUNDAY AFTER TRINITY

The Rev. Mr. Hawks having gone to fulfill an appointment some thirty miles from town, I was left in charge of the parish. The Rev. Frank Starr read the morning Prayer, I taking the Ante-Communion.[12] At morning

10. Dr. Robert Battey (1828–1895) of Rome, Georgia, was a pioneer gynecologist and surgeon, and, at this time, in charge of the Polk Hospital. CTQ was very probably acquainted with Battey through Catherine's connections in Rome. H. H. Cunningham, *Doctors in Gray: The Confederate Medical Service* (1958; reprint, Baton Rouge: Louisiana State University Press, 1993), 188; Coleman and Gurr, *Dictionary of Georgia Biography*, s.v. "Battey, Robert."

11. The 1870 federal census for Chatham County, Georgia, lists as living in Savannah John R. Gregory, a druggist, then age thirty-three; his wife, Mary, then age thirty; and their son, Hugh, then age six. Georgia Lawton cannot be identified.

12. Bishop Elliott's diary for May 8, 1864, indicates he anointed the Rev. Francis R. Starr to the Holy Order of Priest that day. Elliott diary, May 8, 1864, GDAH. The 1860 federal census for Muscogee County, Georgia, lists Frank R. Starr, then age twenty-one, living in the home of his father, Edward W. Starr, a physician.

service I preached again on the nature and character of repentance. In the afternoon I was all alone. Preached from the text, "I speak concerning Christ and the Church" showing that to preach Christ was to preach the Church, and to preach the Church was to preach Christ—Full congregations. Dined at Mr. Brown's. I did not return home until after evening service. To my great joy Dr. Anderson has received orders to report for duty in the Lee Hospital in this city.

OCTOBER 31ST, MONDAY
Went with Dr. Nth. M. Cooke to his residence some two or three miles out from Columbus across the river in Alabama. I found the family in great distress in consequence of the recent death of the second son, Henry, a noble young fellow who fell in his country's cause near Petersburg. I was very glad to find Mrs. Cooke receiving the stroke as from a Father's hand. I baptized their youngest child, Nathaniel Minturn, born 13 August, 1864, parents N. M. and Harriet M. Cooke, sponsors, parents and Miss Sarah Green. The little one was baptized for the dead. Returning to town, my old classmate, Dr. Bemiss of Kentucky, assistant Medical Director of Hospitals, rode out home and dined with us.[13]

NOVEMBER 1ST, TUESDAY
Festival of All Saints—Angels and living Saints and dead——but one communion make. Those who have passed beyond the vail are at rest waiting the perfect consummation and bliss. They cannot be disappointed of their crown; their expectation cannot be cut off. Through much tribulation they have passed to that land where there is no more death, neither sorrow nor crying, but where they sing the song of Moses, the servant of God, and the song of the Lamb, saying, "Great and marvelous are Thy works, Lord, God, Almighty. Just and true are Thy ways, Thou King of Saints."
How different their state from the saints in the Church Militant who

13. Except for the fact of their marriage on May 1, 1839, in Chatham County, Georgia, neither Dr. Cooke nor his wife, Harriet M. Schroder, nor their sons can be identified. "Some South Carolina Marriages in Georgia," *South Carolina Magazine of Ancestral Research* 20 (Winter 1992): 9. Dr. Samuel Merrifield Bemiss (1821–1884) was assistant medical director of the hospitals of the Army of Tennessee. Glenna R. Schroeder-Lein, *Confederate Hospitals on the Move: Samuel H. Stout and the Army of Tennessee* (Columbia: University of South Carolina Press, 1994), 187.

are warring against principalities and powers and spiritual wickedness in high places—who are brought into bondage through the temptations without and the confusion within—who are subject to a thousand forms of grief and pain and fear—the one serene, calm, rejoicing in their security and the other, often perplexed, timid and cast down. It is not any good for us, but it is a blessed privilege for us to remember those who have gone before us for though separated we still have fellowship with one another. We speak of them as dead, but it is not the true way of speaking— they are removed to a higher life than we can enjoy in the body and there is a mystical sympathy of soul between them and ourselves.

The service this morning was full of refreshment although I sadly missed the Holy Communion, in which office more than in any other act of worship, is the communion of Saints made a living reality—"for who of the faithful" says St. Gregory, "can doubt, that, in the very moment of offering, the heavens are laid open at the words of the Priest; that in that mystery of Jesus Christ, the choirs of Angels are present—the highest are associated with the lowest, earthly things are joined with heavenly, and things visible and invisible are made one." "At a time" says St. Chrysostom, "that the sacrifice is performed, angels are standing by, and the priest and a whole host of celestial powers crieth aloud; and the space about the altar is filled with choirs of angels in honor of Him who is present—a thing we may most readily believe from the nature of the sacrifice there offered."

Today Mr. Brown exceeded all his former magnificence by presenting me three hundred yards of excellent factory cloth for clothing my Regiment. He added buttons, thread and lining. He gave me also three hundred pairs of socks—cloth valued at $15.50 per yard. The liberal soul shall be made fat.

NOVEMBER 2ND, WEDNESDAY
Mrs. Richard Peters writes me that her son, Richard, has run the blockade and sailed for Liverpool. He is a noble boy and I am glad that he will be at school in glorious old England.[14]

Miss Mary Bethune having called and invited all the family to spend the day, we all went over to General Bethune's accompanied by our good

14. Richard Peters (1810–1889), previously identified, was said to have given Atlanta its name. Coleman and Gurr, *Dictionary of Georgia Biography*, s.v. "Peters, Richard."

neighbor, Mrs. Carter. The family is a very pleasant one. I was particularly
pleased by the younger son, Joe.

Blind Tom played for two or three hours. His imitations on the piano
are marvelous. He played some selections from Traviata, Trovatore and
other operas. He wound up with his own composition, "The Battle of
Manassas." The visit was most agreeable.

NOVEMBER 6TH, 24TH SUNDAY AFTER TRINITY

Walked to town—Hawks led morning prayer—I taking the Ante-Communion and preaching a Communion Sermon of the Love of God which
passeth knowledge. Mrs. Ellis informed me of the death of Matt Myers. I
had known him well in Nashville while he was at the University. He was
a young disciple, pure-hearted and full of earnestness in the Christian life.
He died in Florida—another martyr of this fearful war. A lady in the congregation handed me $100.00 for the soldiers.

Dined with Mr. Adams, the Cashier of Bank of Columbus. Himself
and wife in great affliction for the loss of their only child, a noble Christian who fell in Virginia. Met Lieutenant Moses at 3:00 P.M. for appointment to talk with him on the ministry. He has resolved to devote himself
to the service of the Altar. I did not attend the Evening Service but spent
the time with Col. Bransford (of Nashville) who is fast repining for God's
Paradise. I had prayers with him and he expressed a wish to receive Confirmation. Mr. Brown very kindly sent his carriage to convey me home. I
hope this day has been profitable to my soul and to the souls of those to
whom I have ministered. God give me grace to work while it is day—God
give me more energy—more love for souls—more strength—more life.
Wrote to Mrs. Myers.[15]

15. The 1860 federal census for Muscogee County identifies David Adams as the cashier of the Bank of Columbus, age fifty-seven in 1860; his wife, Anna, age forty-one; and
their son, Frederick G. Adams, then age 12. Not only did Matt Myers die in Florida, but
the entry for December 19 indicates that he was from Florida. Records show that 1st Sgt.
Mathew Rawdon Myers (1844–1864) of the 2nd Florida Cavalry died November 4, 1864.
David W. Hartman and David Coles comps., *Biographical Rosters of Florida's Confederate
and Union Soldiers, 1861–1865*, 6 vols. (Wilmington, N.C.: Broadfoot Publishing, 1995),
4:1409. Lt. William Q. Moses of Tennessee originally served in the artillery. The last record
relating to Moses is an order from General Hood dated September 29, 1864, requiring
Moses to report to an engineering officer in Macon, Georgia. William Q. Moses CSR,
Confederate General and Staff Officers, RG 109, M-331, NA. The obituary of Col. Thomas
L. Bransford is pasted in the second volume of the diary at the entry for March 21, 1865.
The obituary reports Bransford died on February 26, 1865, of "pulmonary consumption."

NOVEMBER 7TH, MONDAY

Major Baylor, Lieutenant McLaughlin of the Navy and Mrs. McLaughlin at dinner today. During the afternoon Miss De Launey called bringing with her a basket of beautiful flowers. Mrs. Meigs and Lieutenant Blanche, C.S.N. also called. Lieut. B. is the grandson of the late Samuel J. Peters, Esq. of New Orleans and I was greatly rejoiced to see him at Holy Communion yesterday. No news from the Army.[16]

Have written a little story for the Children's Department of the Church Intelligencer entitled "Nellie Peters' Pocket Handkerchief and What it Saw." Have prepared a new edition of my Tract "Preparation for Confirmation."[17]

NOVEMBER 8TH, TUESDAY

Dr. Frank Hawthorne of the Academy Hospital having been ordered to "Iuka" sent me a very fine cow to winter for him.[18] Captain Wickham informed me that he wanted to start in the morning and I have been very busy arranging my affairs for my departure.

NOVEMBER 9TH, WEDNESDAY

Up early. My dear wife driving to town to see me off. It is a very sad leave-taking, but the path of duty is the path of happiness and I know God will

---

A businessman, Bransford was "expelled" from his home in Nashville, apparently because of Confederate sympathies.

16. Maj. Eugene W. Baylor of Kentucky had served in the artillery and as a quartermaster. Originally quartermaster of Strahl's Brigade, in July 1864 he was assigned as quartermaster of Pettus' Brigade. Baylor appears to have been in Columbus on sick leave at this time. E. W. Baylor CSR, Confederate General and Staff Officers, RG 109, M-331, NA. Mrs. Meigs was probably the wife of the William Meigs identified in the entry for March 10, 1865. Miss De Launey cannot be identified. Lt. Augustus McLaughlin of Maryland commanded the Confederate Naval Station at Columbus. "Lieutenant Blanche," almost certainly Samuel P. Blanc, listed as a "Passed Midshipman" earlier in 1864, was the executive officer of the CSS *Chattahoochee*. Naval War Records Office, *Register of Officers*, 16, 124; ORN, Series 1, 17:874. The 1850 federal census for Orleans Parish, Louisiana, lists Samuel J. Peters, Sr., then age forty-eight, a banker and owner of real estate worth $201,000, and Samuel J. Peters, Jr., then age twenty-six, a merchant.

17. *Nellie Peters' Pocket Handkerchief and What It Saw: A Story of the War* was published as a little book in 1907.

18. Dr. Frank Hawthorn (1835–1876) of Alabama was moving the Academy Hospital to Iuka in the wake of the advancing Army of Tennessee. Soon afterward, he suffered a physical breakdown and had to be relieved. Schroeder-Lien, *Confederate Hospitals on the Move*, 190–91.

give His Angels charge concerning them.[19] I have so much to be thankful for—so many blessings that shove me into a living faith and stir me up to do my Master's work while it is still day. As I look back over my stay in Columbus, I have the hope that my labors have not been in vain for the Lord. Today I forwarded to Bishop Elliott testimonials required by Canon for admission of Lt. William Q. Moses as a Candidate for Holy Orders. I received a letter from Capt. Charles Shorter, now in the Army of General Early, announcing his intention, if his life is spared, of devoting himself to the service of God in the holy ministry of the Altar.[20]

Leaving Columbus on the freight train, in a miserable box car with fellow passengers of the most disagreeable character, the way seemed very long, and the hours very weary. A boy three years old last May was puffing a full sized cigar with great apparent gusto, and I was not at all surprised later in the day to hear him curse his mother. We reached Montgomery in a drenching rain and had to walk to the hotel where we found accommodations or what passed for accommodations in the topmost story.

NOVEMBER 10TH, THURSDAY
Up early and called on my excellent friend the Rev. Mr. Mitchell with whom I took breakfast. Mrs. Mitchell being ill, I did not have the pleasure of meeting her. Major Banks placed a horse and buggy at my disposal and I made a number of calls, visited the Rev. Mr. Shepherd at the Hamner Hall, Mrs. General Brown at Mr. Gilmer's, and Judge Phelan at the Capitol. With Judge Phelan I spent a couple of hours in most agreeable conversation on the state of the country and the work of the Church. He is one of the noblest laymen in all of the Confederacy.[21]

19. At this point in the diary is an undated newspaper excerpt attributed to the *Chicago Times* mocking Union Maj. Gen. Philip H. Sheridan's inability to "settle" matters with Confederate Lt. Gen. Jubal Early in the Shenandoah Valley.

20. Charles S. Shorter was captain of Company A, 31st Georgia Infantry Regiment, until his transfer on October 14, 1864, to the Engineering Corps. He was captured April 2, 1865. Henderson, *Roster of the Confederate Soldiers of Georgia*, 3:598.

21. Major Banks was probably Edwin A. Banks, who had served on the staffs of Generals Mansfield Lovell, John C. Pemberton, and William W. Loring. He was transferred in September 1864 to the post of assistant inspector general of field transportation, headquartered at Montgomery. E. A. Banks, CSR, Confederate General and Staff Officers, RG 109, M-331, NA. Rev. Mr. Shepherd was probably the Rev. J. Avery Shepherd, referenced in the diary entry for February 26, 1865. Shepherd was the rector of Hamner Hall in Montgomery. Clebsch, *Journals*, III-215. Mr. Gilmer was probably Francis Meriwether Gilmer (1810–1892), a Montgomery businessman with railroad, mercantile, and banking interests. At or

Dined at Dr. Scott's in company with several Tennessee friends, among whom were Colonel Battle late the gallant commander of the 20th Tennessee Regiment, now State Treasurer, Colonel Ray, Secretary of State, General Dunlap, Comptroller Gen., Henry Watterson and Albert Roberts, now editing the Montgomery Mail. After leaving the house some distance, Col. Battle came up with me and calling me to one side, handed me a roll of bills which he begged me to accept from Colonel Ray, General Dunlap and himself to assist in paying my expenses. I thanked him most kindly and it came very opportunely as I had not five dollars in my pocket. The amount was $150.00. Took a steamboat for Selma at 4 P.M. It was crowded to excess in the cabins, on deck and all about the guards.

NOVEMBER 11TH, FRIDAY
Had a much pleasanter night than I anticipated in the floor of the cabin. I arrived at Selma a little before day. Called on the Rev. Mr. Ticknor who handed me a letter from my dear friend, Bishop Wilmer, containing a check for $500.00 which he begs me to use for my own comfort. Verily my funds are increasing. Taking the cars at 8:00 A.M. I started for Demopolis in company with Captain Wickham and my good friend, Major Thomas Peters, formerly of General Polk's Staff. He secured seats for us in the mail car and our ride was very pleasant. At Demopolis I enjoyed the great pleasure of seeing the Rev. John Beckwith who remained with me all the while I was in Demopolis. Taking a boat at about 12:00 P.M., we sailed four miles down the Tombigbee River to the terminus of the sailing where taking the cars once more we started for Meridian. We had a most tedious trip being about 10 hours in making the 50 miles to Meridian. At Meridian, finding no room in the hotel, Wickham and myself rolled up in our blankets with our feet towards a good fire and so we passed the night comfortably enough.

NOVEMBER 12TH, SATURDAY
Cars crowded to excess. I stopped at Macon to visit Captain Yates and Wickham pressed on to Okolona to wait for me until Monday. Found a number of friends in Macon, among them Mrs. General Govan, Miss

---

near this time, Gilmer was the president of the Central Bank of Alabama. Judge John Dennis Phelan (1810–1879) was, at that time, a justice of the Alabama Supreme Court. After the war, he served as Professor of Law at the University of the South. Owen, *History of Alabama*, 3:656–59, 4:1356.

Otey and Lt. Otey and wife, Colonel Dupree, and Dr. Lyles, formerly General Polk's Medical Director.[22] I hired a conveyance for $15.00 and rode out to Captain Yates' plantation seven miles from the town. This was my first experience over prairie roads in winter and the mud and general character of the road made a *profound impression*. I met the heartiest of welcomes from Captain and Mrs. Yates who were taken completely by surprise. Found the Captain much improved and getting about a little on his crutches. His nephew, Robert Bracy, who lost a leg at Murfreesboro, was with him. I was very much pleased with his whole manner and bearing.[23]

NOVEMBER 13TH, 25TH SUNDAY AFTER TRINITY
Rode into town and held service for a good congregation in the Baptist meeting house which had been secured for me by Colonel Dupree and Major Cox. Had full service. Dined with Colonel Dupree at his father's. Afterwards called on Dr. Lyles, Mrs. Govan, and then rode out to the plantation of Captain Yates' mother, a mile distant from his own, where all the family had assembled. His mother thanked me with tears for my kindness to her son. After tea I talked to them for several hours on Christ and the Church. To my surprise I find that the Doctor's father had been a rigid Romanist and all his family have received baptisms at the hands of a Romish priest. His sister and niece, Miss Bracey, gave me their names for confirmation. After the ladies retired I spoke to the Captain on the Ministry and urged him to consider the matter of studying for Holy Orders. God put it into his heart![24]

22. Bishop Otey had nine children, including Mary Otey Govan, the wife of Brig. Gen. Daniel Chevilette Govan (1829–1911), of North Carolina and Arkansas; Lt. Mercer Otey; and three other surviving daughters, one of whom would have been the Miss Otey of this entry. Biographical File, James Hervey Otey Collection, U of S; William Mercer Green, *Memoir of Rt. Rev. James Hervey Otey, D.D., LL.D., the First Bishop of Tennessee* (New York: J. Pott & Co., 1885), 107. Col. Dupree cannot be positively identified, either in connection with the Polk clan or otherwise. The 1870 federal census for Noxubee County, Mississippi, lists Daniel Dupree, then age 67, who might have been the father referenced in the next entry or Colonel Dupree himself. Dr. William D. Lyles was Polk's medical director at the time of Shiloh. See *OR* 10(1):412–13.

23. The 1860 federal census for Noxubee County, Mississippi, lists Robert Bracy, age nineteen, as a farmer living in the household of Robert E. V. Yates. Pvt. Robert Bracy is listed as serving in White's Battery of the Horse Artillery. At the time of Murfreesboro, Capt. B. F. White, Jr.'s, battery was attached to the cavalry brigade of Brig. Gen. John A. Wharton and was engaged in a hot fight near Triune on the Nolensville Pike on December 27, 1862, where Bracy may have been wounded. See *OR* 20(1):896–98.

24. Maj. Robert M. Cox of Kentucky was inspector of the consolidated 2nd and 3rd Districts of Mississippi, stationed at Macon. On November 15, 1864, a citizen charged Cox

NOVEMBER 14TH, MONDAY

Started for town immediately after breakfast. Mrs. Yates had an abundant supply of provisions put up for us on our journey—two roasted turkeys, a boiled ham and all of the etc's. When the train came along, I found Major Winter of the Engineers in a car with his baggage and implements and as he invited me to a seat, I had a comfortable ride to Okolona which place we reached at 4:00 P.M. and found Captain Wickham waiting me at the station. Spent the evening at the quarters of Major Billups with Captain McIver and Captain Bradford and other friends.[25]

NOVEMBER 15TH, TUESDAY

Ye Rats! Ye Rats! For size and multitude the Okolona rats cannot be excelled. All the night long they played the most fantastic tricks in the room we occupied. Once I got up and lighted the fire to drive them off. It having been decided not to go forward until General Cheatham could be heard from, Captain Wickham, Bradford, Mayrant and myself took the cars at 7:00 A.M. for Columbus, where we arrived at 2:00 P.M. At Artesia, where we took the branch road—12 miles—to Columbus, I saw a number of Negroes captured at Dalton—some in the most distressing condition—evidently dying. They were brought on to Columbus.[26]

Nothing strikes me with more amazement than the immense fields of corn. From Selma to Demopolis, through the "cane-brake region" and from Meridian to Okolona, it is one vast corn field—a veritable Egypt. It is wonderful.

---

with being a "Reconstructionist" and with misappropriating supplies. By letter dated December 14, 1864, Cox denied the misappropriation charges, writing he had never stated he had favored reconstruction, only that he favored an honorable peace. There is no record as to the disposition of the charge, but Cox was paroled in his rank and position in May 1865. R. M. Cox CSR, Confederate General and Staff Officers, RG 109, M-331, NA. The 1860 federal census for Noxubee County lists Mrs. A. E. Yates, then age fifty-two, with real and personal property valued at $55,000. The same census shows that living in Robert E. V. Yates' household were Mrs. A. E. Bracy, then age thirty-two, Martha Bracy, then age fourteen, and Emma Bracy, then age eleven.

25. Maj. John M. Billups of Columbus, Mississippi, was originally captain of Company B, 43rd Mississippi. At this time, he was post quartermaster at Okolona. J. M. Billups CSR, Confederate General and Staff Officers, RG 109, M-331, NA. E. J. McIver started the war as assistant quartermaster of the 45th Alabama Regiment. At this time, he was captain and quartermaster of the Army of Tennessee's pontoon trains, attached to army headquarters. E. J. McIver CSR, ibid.

26. Approximately 600 black soldiers from the 44th United States Colored Infantry were surrendered to Hood at Dalton on October 13, 1864, along with miscellaneous white troops. OR 39(1):717–21, 801.

NOVEMBER 16TH, WEDNESDAY
Was delighted to find Bishop Green at home and from him I received a most cordial welcome. This day having been set apart by the President of the Confederate States as a day of supplication and prayer for God's blessing on our cause, I officiated in St. Paul's Church, preaching from the text "Think not I came to send peace on the earth. I came not to send peace but a sword." The day being rainy, there was but a small congregation. I trust, however, God heard our prayers and that He will give us His blessing. The Bishop was too unwell to venture out. General Cheatham has telegraphed us to go forward and we leave in the morning. I have given during my trip thus far $75.00 to Tennessee soldiers from the money handed me by Colonel Battle.

NOVEMBER 17TH, THURSDAY
A brighter day—the rain has ceased and only a few light clouds are draping the sky. I have asked Bishop Green to write his prayer for the country on the following page.[27]

A Prayer for Our Country
Oh Eternal God who rulest over the Kingdoms of men; Thou art the Great God of battles, and the Disposer of all events. By thy glorious wisdom, thy Almighty Power, and thy secret Providence, thou dost determine the issues of war, and the returns of Peace and Victory. Oh, let the light of thy countenance and the blessing of thy forgiveness be turned upon our land.

Thou seest the many evils we suffer from this cruel and unrighteous war. And although we acknowledge the justice of all that has come upon us, yet we beseech Thee to hear our supplications and bring to an end our present calamities. Let not our Counsels be defeated; nor the Defenders of a righteous cause be overthrown. Let thy Holy Religion be no longer hindered amongst us; nor our Institutions of Learning continue to be deserted.

Hear the sorrowful sighing of our imprisoned soldiers; and if it please Thee, put a speedy end to their captivity.

27. Attached at this point in the diary is a newspaper excerpt attributed to the *New Hampshire Democrat* entitled "Great Discoveries Made too Late," mocking the North's perceptions and war effort. As CTQ states, Bishop Green's prayer appears to have been written in the bishop's own hand.

May the sick and wounded be had in thy remembrance, be comforted with a sense of thy mercy, and in thy good time, find a happy deliverance out of all their troubles. Inspire with wisdom the counsels of our Military Leaders. In all their trials and dangers, support them with thy Heavenly aid. Let no unhallowed arm do them violence; and no devices of the enemy prevail against them.

Bless our Civil Rulers and all our people, and make us day by day more worthy of thy blessing.

Strengthen the hands and comfort the hearts of all engaged in our defence. Watch over them by thy Providence; and be Thou their shield in the day of battle.

Forgive our enemies, and turn their hearts, that they may depart from us, and no longer seek to destroy us.

And grant, Oh Gracious Lord, that we may soon become not only a separate and independent people, but a holy nation, a peculiar people, zealous of good works, and in all things devoted to thy service.

Grant this, oh King of Kings for *His* sake, through whom alone cometh every blessing, thy Son, Jesus Christ our Lord. AMEN.

NOVEMBER 18TH, FRIDAY
Reached Artesia at the regular hour. I had to wait until 4:00 P.M., then took cars for West Point where we spent the night. The miserable little hamlet was crowded. I found a place with Captain Mayrant at the house of an acquaintance of his, a Mr. Baptist, where we had *enough* to eat and a bed—but all about the place was slovenly. The others of our party spent the night in the car.[28]

NOVEMBER 19TH, SATURDAY
Left West Point at 7:00 A.M. in a car loaded with corn (in shuck). The party in our car consisted of Brig. General Quarles and Mr. Sterling

28. The 1860 federal census for Lowndes County, Mississippi, identifies J. G. Baptist, then age thirty-seven, who supported his large household with his position as Postmaster.

Cockrill, Esq. of Nashville, his wife and daughter, Captains Shute, Wickham, Bradford, Jones, Mayrant, and a Colonel Young of the 49th Tennessee Regiment who lost his right arm at Atlanta on the 28th of July. The day wore away pleasantly enough and about 8:00 P.M. we reached Corinth—transferred the ladies to a car where they would be comfortable. General Quarles and myself built a fire in the car and made some coffee. The Rev. Mr. Markham, a very excellent Presbyterian clergyman, shared my blankets with me.

NOVEMBER 19TH, SATURDAY[29]

A miserable night of rain storm without and a miserably uncomfortable bed within the car.

General Beauregard leaves this morning for Mobile. The report that Sherman is making his way to the seaboard seems credited. He is reported within 30 miles of Macon. Met Major Whitfield, Chief Quartermaster at Major Bucher's who said the Army of Tennessee would begin its advance today. We left in the train for Cherokee at 11:00 A.M. and reached the place of present terminus of the railway at 4:00 P.M. The Cockrills, who remain here for the present, found accommodations at Mr. Newsome's. Captain Wickham and myself were comfortably quartered at the Post Office. I was under great obligations to Mr. Clarke, from Army Headquarters, for attention to my comfort. Had prayers with my roommates before lying down.[30]

NOVEMBER 20TH, SUNDAY, NEXT BEFORE ADVENT

Started in wagon with the supply train—made five miles and stuck in mud. I walked on three or four miles while Wickham transferred the baggage to another wagon driven by a fine young fellow named Herman Peebles. We floundered along through the mud until we came to the residence of a Mr. Guy, six miles from Tuscumbia, where we found quar-

29. This is the second of two entries for November 19 in the diary.
30. Maj. George Whitfield was given the task of repairing the railroads in Mississippi to facilitate the Army of Tennessee's advance. OR 39(2):855, 902–3; OR 45(1):1212. Mr. Clarke was possibly Capt. William B. Clarke, a commissary officer. OR 39(2):784. Maj. Bucher cannot be identified. No Newsomes are listed in census records for Colbert County, Alabama, in which Cherokee, Alabama, was located. Three Newsoms are listed as residing at Cherokee in the 1870 census for Colbert County, but CTQ's host cannot be positively identified.

ters for the night. After prayers, we made down our bed and retired at 7:00 o'clock.[31]

NOVEMBER 21ST, MONDAY

Up and off at daylight. The weather wretched. It began to snow briskly after we had walked for an hour. I left the wagon and took it on foot to Tuscumbia. Had the pleasure of meeting Major Eustice and was greatly gratified at meeting the Hon. J. L. M. Currey of Alabama who went with me to Mrs. Dr. Newsome's, where I had two refreshing cups of tea.[32] Met Joe Martin and Captain Rufus Polk just as I was leaving Tuscumbia. Over indescribable roads, we made our way to Florence, where Captain Wickham and myself dined at 4:00 P.M. with the charming family of Mr. Simpson. Leaving Florence we spent the night at the home of a Mr. Andrews, a devout Methodist. Had prayers with the family, all my companions being present.[33]

NOVEMBER 22ND, TUESDAY

A bright beautiful day. Before starting once more had prayers with the family of Mr. Andrews who to my astonishment informed me that he had

31. Herman Peebles cannot be identified. Several men named Guy are listed in the 1870 federal census for Colbert County, Alabama, but none can be identified as CTQ's host.

32. Major Eustice may have been Maj. James B. Eustis, a member of Beauregard's staff at the time. Crute, *Confederate Staff Officers*, 14. Jabez Lamar Monroe Curry (1825–1903) of Georgia and Alabama served in the prewar United States Congress and was elected to a term in the Confederate Congress. At this point, he was serving as a lieutenant colonel of cavalry. Joel D. Treece, ed., *Biographical Directory of the American Congress, 1774–1996* (Alexandria, Va.: CQ Staff Directories, 1997), 894. The 1870 federal census for Colbert County lists B. F. Newsom, then age fifty-three, an M.D. The next oldest female in the household was Mary V., age twenty-three, occupation "keeping house."

33. Joe Martin may have been Lt. E. J. Martin, aide-de-camp to Maj. Gen. Edward Johnson. Although there were three members of the Polk clan named Rufus King, only Capt. Rufus King Polk (d. 1902), son of Leonidas' brother George Washington Polk, was living in 1864. He was listed in various sources as a lieutenant in the 10th Tennessee Infantry and as a captain on the staffs of Generals Lucius E. Polk, John Gregg, and Frank Armstrong. See Turner, *Maury County*, 247; "The Last Roll: Capt. R. K. Polk," *CV* 10 (December 1902): 561; CWCCT, *Tennesseans*, 2:325. Mr. Simpson cannot be identified, as numerous male Simpsons are listed as residing in Florence in the 1860 and 1870 federal censuses for Lauderdale County, Alabama. The 1860 federal census for Lauderdale County lists Robert L. Andrews, then age fifty-four, as a Methodist preacher and farmer with seven children.

been for thirty years an itinerant Methodist preacher. The enemy have taken all his Negroes and other property, even his provisions, and he is compelled to move to Mississippi to feed his household. He told me of his trials with a stout, brave heart. He has lost two sons in the war.[34] One of the mules being stolen last night delayed our starting. Peebles found it tied in a dense wood a quarter of a mile from our camp.

The ground is frozen hard and a sharp, cold wind is blowing, but as my face is towards Tennessee, I heed none of these things. God in mercy, grant us a successful campaign.

At 11:00 o'clock—clouded up and a driving snow storm—cleared off cold an hour or two later.

Crossed the line into Tennessee at 4½ P.M.[35]

Bless the Lord O my soul and all that is within me bless His Holy Name.

Walked seventeen or eighteen miles and spent the night uncomfortably enough, it being intensely cold. Two or three of the party were broken down.

NOVEMBER 23RD, WEDNESDAY

Got breakfast by daylight and started off by myself determined to overtake the Army. About half past ten came up with my friend General Strahl going to the rear with his brigade to help forward the supply train. A little further on, met my dear friend, John Marsh. Passing on I soon overtook Gist's Brigade. I was a long while passing it—there are in it at present 1100 muskets. Overtaking the General I had a long and pleasant chat with him. His aid, Lt. Trenhohn, loaned me his horse and I rode on to Strahl's ambulance train.[36] I concluded to spend the night with General Strahl as I was very tired. Had a pleasant evening and after prayers at Headquarters turned into a most comfortable bed.

NOVEMBER 24TH, THURSDAY

Prayers at Headquarters before sunrise. Command moved at daylight on the road to Waynesboro but took a right hand road seven miles south of

34. The 1860 federal census for Lauderdale County lists Andrews as having two sons of military age in 1864, Robert P., who was age twenty in 1860, and James A., age thirteen in 1860.

35. At this point, CTQ was in the very wake of the advancing Army of Tennessee, army headquarters having crossed into Tennessee on the same day. See OR 45(1):669.

36. Lt. Frank Trenhohn, who would accompany Gist into the maelstrom at Franklin just eight days later. OR 45(1):737.

there and reached the Mount Pleasant road just as Cleburne's Division was passing the point of intersection.[37] Met a number of old friends, Generals Cheatham, Cleburne, Govan, Colonel Gale, Whitthorne and etc. We marched on towards Mt. Pleasant making in all 22 miles today. Saw Major Hampton, and made arrangements for him to distribute the packages I brought. In the evening Colonel Hoxton and Capt. Jack Phelan came to Headquarters and were with us at Prayers. It is very delightful thus to mark each stage of our progress by prayer to God for his blessing.[38]

NOVEMBER 25TH, FRIDAY
Up and had prayers and breakfast long before day. Troops in motion at the earliest dawn. On the march passed forty Yankee prisoners going to the rear. Passed through Henryville on the road to Mt. Pleasant where I arrived about 3:00 P.M. and at once went to General Hood's Headquarters where I met a most cordial welcome. The General is in the best of health and spirits, and full of hope as to the results of the present movements. Met General Pillow at Headquarters. I was sorry to learn of the bad accident by which his arm was fractured. I concluded to go on to Gen. Lucius Polk's three and half miles toward Columbia. I therefore rode forward with General Pillow. Such a greeting! How I thank God for the friends He has given me. Was delighted to find Miss Jeannie Bell, Miss Betty and Miss Susy Wood from Nashville.[39] General Chalmers and Staff were the

37. According to one account, during his march with the army, CTQ encountered a "well-known Confederate General" who was "using terrible language" relative to an artillery train bogged down in the mud. CTQ purportedly "seized the General by the collar and shook his fist in his face, and commanded him to cease his blasphemy and respect his God." The general took it like a gentleman, apologized, and thanked CTQ for the rebuke. Gailor, *Some Memories*, 84.

38. Washington Curran Whitthorne (1825–1891) of Columbia, Tennessee, had served in President James K. Polk's administration and the Tennessee General Assembly. In 1861, he was appointed adjutant general of Tennessee, and during the war he served as a volunteer aide on the staffs of several general officers. McBride and Robison, *Biographical Directory of the Tennessee General Assembly*, 1:790–91. Capt. William D. Gale, previously on the staff of his late father-in-law, Leonidas Polk, was at this point serving on the staff of Lieutenant General Stewart. In January 1865, Gale wrote an interesting description of the events of the campaign in a letter to his wife. Ridley, *Battles and Sketches*, 408–15. Maj. Henry Hampton was a member of Cheatham's staff. Crute, *Confederate Staff Officers*, 35. Capt. John Phelan commanded an Alabama battery in Hoxton's Battalion. OR 38(3):643.

39. Brig. Gen. Gideon Johnson Pillow (1806–1878) of Tennessee was responsible for the Confederate conscript bureau in Tennessee. Miss Jeannie Bell was probably the Jenny Bell mentioned below. Neither she, Miss Betty, nor Susy Wood can be identified.

guests of General Polk. Met General Forrest and Governor Harris a mile or two from General Polk's residence and had a short chat with them. I find from the *Cincinnati Commercial* of the 19th of November that the enemy have destroyed a vast amount of property in Rome, Georgia among other things the Quintard Iron Works.

Jehovah jireh!

Had prayers with the family and offered a special thanksgiving to God for our return to our homes.

> Oh, for the peace which floweth like a river,
> Making life's desert places bloom and smile!
> Oh, for the faith to grasp Heaven's bright "forever,"
> Amid the shadows of earth's "little while."

NOVEMBER 26TH, SATURDAY

This has been, indeed, a day of real enjoyment. I have not moved out of the house—just rested. I realized that I was once more in Tennessee. How many happy meetings and greetings—and yet how many will be looked for who will never come again. All day long there has been a stream of visitors to the family. General Hood and Governor Harris came early in the day as did also General Cheatham. Then came Generals Brown and Bate, Gibson and handsome Frank Armstrong of the cavalry and Walthall, who with his staff spent the night with us. During the day a Louisiana band came to the house and gave us some fine music. On someone's remarking that this was the residence of a brother of the late Lt. General Polk, one of the musicians replied, "Yes, we looked upon him as the father of all Louisianans." Frank Armstrong reports the burning by the enemy of the fine residence of Mrs. Trotter where I have in days of peace passed some pleasant hours. The enemy have also burned the residences of Mr. Fleming [and the] Hon. James Thomas. Sent for my dear friend, Dr. Pise, by courier but by a note from his wife, learn that he is in Columbia. And there he must remain until the enemy walk out or we walk in. General Hood established Headquarters at Andrew J. Polk's.[40]

40. Mrs. Trotter may have been Mrs. M. A. Trotter, age forty-one in 1860, wife of John Trotter, a businessman and farmer. The diary entry for December 21, however, suggests that Mrs. Trotter more probably was Myra Bell Trotter. Mr. Fleming was probably W. S. Fleming, listed in 1860 as a lawyer, age forty-four. Sandra Wilson Thurman, comp., *Maury County, Tennessee, 1860 Census* (Columbia, Tenn.: P-Vine Press, 1981), 95, 134. James Houston Thomas (1808–1876) of North Carolina and Tennessee was a former United States Congressman and Attorney General of Tennessee. Treece, *Biographical Directory of the American Congress, 1774–1996*, 1936. Andrew Jackson Polk (1824–1867) was the younger

NOVEMBER 27TH, ADVENT SUNDAY
"Our glad Hosannas, *Prince of Peace.*
Thy welcome shall proclaim."

I find this striking thought in the "Pax Terris" of good Bishop Hall. "In that grief of heart which has fallen so generally upon all good men there is just this one consideration to console the minds of the pious in the depth of their distress, that these are but the signs of our Deliverer, the Lord Jesus Christ approaching, yea, standing as it were before the door. For so it is: the Son of God, Blessed forever, who at His first Advent— 'Burst the huge posts and iron gates of war' and chose not to descend upon earth till it was first brought into a state of peace under the sceptre of Augustus, has assigned the period of His sacred Advent to that age, when all things will be full of trouble and embarrassment to the end that, when the world is ready to sink under the fatigue of her lust and most miserable confusion, she may both more earnestly expect, and more gladly welcome, the arrival of the Prince of Peace, the Asserter of Truth and Justice, the Rewarder of the Patience of the Saints, and the Comforter of the Church."

Had full morning prayer at the residence of Lucius J. Polk—at which I baptized Caroline, daughter of George W. and Sally L. Polk—and Henry Yeatman, son of J. Minnick and Emily Polk Williams—a record of which I made in the Parish Register of St. John's, Maury County. This was my first full service in Tennessee since entering the state and my heart went up in gratitude to God for all his great goodness in delivering us from the snare of the fowler. The lessons for the day—the Psalms—were full of comfort and warmed my hope into a trusting faith.[41]

After service I started for Headquarters and stopped at General Pillow's to make a call. There I found Lieutenant General Lee and Maj. Gen. Edward Johnson. Found General Hood at the residence of Mrs. Warfield

---

brother of Leonidas Polk and early in the war served as captain of Company C, 1st Tennessee Cavalry Battalion. He reportedly made a fortune in blockade running during the war. Lindsley, *Military Annals*, 883; Turner, *Maury County*, 248.

41. George Washington Polk was the brother of Leonidas Polk, Andrew Jackson Polk, and Lucius Julius Polk and the husband of Sallie Hilliard Polk. Caroline was the youngest of their six children. J. Minick Williams had been a captain on Bishop Polk's staff and gave a statement in support of Polk's report on the controversial second day of the Battle of Chickamauga. His wife, Emily Donelson Polk Williams was the daughter of Lucius Julius Polk. Turner, *Maury County*, 247; OR 30(2):60.

on the Pulaski Pike.[42] During the evening had much pleasant conversation with him in which he expressed such an earnest trust in God and such deep religious feelings that I could plainly discern the Holy Spirit's work upon his heart. He detailed to me his plan of taking Nashville, calling for volunteers to storm the Key of the works about the city and etc. which I do not feel at liberty to write down just now—but 700 men will fill the graves of 700 heroes and receive the laurel crown.

Had evening prayers at which the ladies of the family were present with the ladies of the Hon. James H. Thomas' family who have been obliged to leave their home, as it is just on our line of skirmishers.

NOVEMBER 28TH, MONDAY
Enemy left Columbia at 6:00 P.M. last evening and our forces entered the town during the night. I rode in about 7:00 A.M. After prayers, I found the good people in a state of the wildest enthusiasm.[43] Almost the first person I met was my dear old friend, Pise. He went with me to Mrs. Dr. Polk's where I breakfasted, thence to Rector Smith's, thence to Mr. Martin's, Mr. Dale's, Mr. Dunnington's, etc.[44]

General Beauregard telegraphs General Hood that Sherman is making his way rapidly to the Atlantic Coast and urges him to press forward so as to relieve General Lee. He therefore will press forward with all possible speed and told me just now confidentially that he would either beat the enemy to Nashville or make him go there at a double quick. The enemy is still on the opposite side of the river tonight but it is thought he will

42. Mrs. Amos (Cornelia A.) Warfield lived at Beechlawn, in Maury County along the Pulaski Pike. Jill K. Garrett and Marise P. Lightfoot, *The Civil War in Maury County, Tennessee* (Columbia, Tenn.: n.p., 1966), 94, 172, 184.

43. The citizens of Columbia joyously awoke that morning to find the Federals gone and the troops of the Army of Tennessee in their streets. Ratchford, *Memoirs*, 60.

44. Mary Rebecca A. Long Polk was the widow of Dr. William Julius Polk (1793–1860), half brother of Leonidas Polk. Mrs. Polk was also the mother of Brig. Gen. Lucius E. Polk. Rev. Franklin Gillette Smith (d. 1866) was the founder of the Columbia Athenaeum, a nondenominational preparatory school. "Rector" appears to have been more a nickname than a title. Mr. Martin was probably Barclay Martin (1802–1890), a Columbia lawyer who had successively served in the Tennessee General Assembly and United States Congress in the 1840s. Mr. Dale was probably E. W. Dale, a Columbia businessman. It appears Mr. Dunnington was Francis ("Frank") Cobey Dunnington (1826–1875), a Middle Tennessee lawyer and newspaper publisher. Turner, *Maury County*, 133–34, 245–46, 276; McBride and Robison, *Biographical Directory of the Tennessee General Assembly*, 1:221, 500; Garrett, *Maury County Historical Sketches*, 149, 247.

withdraw before morning. At all events our forces cross at daylight, and, as the General says, will "go through the woods." God speed us on our way. As the General advises, I will go with the ambulance later in the day. Wrote my wife and sent the letter by Miss Jenny Bell.[45]

NOVEMBER 29TH, TUESDAY
The General up at 3 A.M.—so that with couriers, coffee which made me wakeful, and a very early hour—I did not get much rest. When the General came to tell me goodbye I prayed God's blessing, guidance and direction upon him. "Thank you, Doctor," he replied, "That is my hope and trust" and as he turned away, he remarked, "the enemy must give me fight, or I will be at Nashville before tomorrow night." Cheatham and Stewart crossed Duck River before sunrise. Lee being in Columbia and ready to cross so soon as the enemy withdraws from the opposite side of the river. Considerable shelling of the town but no lives lost and very little damage. Colonel Beckham wounded by the guns of the enemy. As there was no prospect of an early crossing, I walked out to Mrs. Brown's where Pise is boarding with his family and spent a very delightful evening with the family.[46]

NOVEMBER 30TH, WEDNESDAY
Walked in town with Pise—but very early, just after breakfast. Called to see a young man named Parker of Hardeman County belonging to Forrest's Cavalry who was shot through the lungs. I had sent him morphine the evening before which had had a very beneficial effect. Had prayers with him.[47]
   Reached town at 10:00 A.M. and found the enemy all gone. Our forces all crossed over and the wagons [were] crossing. Had the pleasure of meeting my excellent friends, the Websters.[48] Dined at Mrs. Polk's and left at 2:00 P.M. crossing the river with Major John Green of South Caro-

45. Miss Jenny (or Jeannie) Bell cannot be identified.
46. It is impossible to identify Mrs. Brown positively among the many Mrs. Browns in Maury County at that time.
47. Men from Hardeman County were in companies of three of Forrest's regiments on the campaign, one of which was known as "Forrest's Cavalry Regiment." Parker, however, cannot be identified with certainty.
48. If CTQ is referring to the Websters of Maury County who lived in Columbia, they may have been the couple listed in the 1860 federal census as Thomas, then age seventy-six, and Rhoda, then age sixty-eight, both originally from North Carolina.

lina and Dr. Phillips of Hoxton's Artillery. Met on the road several hundred prisoners going to the rear. I found on reaching Spring Hill that there had been some sharp skirmishing. Mr. Hardin's family, at whose hospitable house I found a hearty welcome, had been compelled to run during the cannonading. Mrs. Mallette tells me that the Yankee Generals, Stanley, Schofield, and Wagner were in a sad way. Stanley very nervous and weak-kneed, and Wagner mad. Stanley was overheard to say "I can do nothing more. I must retreat. I am sorry, but I can't help it." Three trains of cars were burned by the evening at this place. Heavy firing at Franklin.[49]

49. Mr. Hardin may have been the William Hardin who had charge of the Spring Hill Female Academy from 1865 to 1868. *Century Review, 1805–1905, Maury County, Tennessee* (1905; reprint, Columbia, Tenn: Maury County Historical Society, 1971), 126. Mrs. Mallette cannot be identified. Maj. Gen. John McAllister Schofield of New York (1831–1906) was overall commander of the Federal troops at Spring Hill, which consisted of the 4th and 23rd Corps. *OR* 45(1):339–44. Brig. Gen. George Day Wagner of Ohio and Indiana (1829–1869) commanded the 2nd Division of Stanley's 4th Corps. *OR* 45(1):229–34.

Darkest of All Decembers
December 1 to December 31, 1864

DECEMBER 1ST, THURSDAY
Visited the hospital before breakfast. Found one hundred and fifty patients in one. [*Sic.*] Saw a Yankee Captain who was shot through the
hips—his case, desperate. He will die. One of our own dear boys of the
33rd Alabama was vomiting profusely—bile, and I spoke a few words of
comfort and directed his mind to the Holy Saviour.

At 10:00 o'clock started in company of Lieutenant Morse of the Orleans Light Horse and James Hardin for Franklin.[1] After riding several
miles toward Franklin, I met Capt. Stepleton who was conveying the bodies of my beloved friends, General Strahl, Lt. John H. Marsh, and Capt.
James Johnston from the field of battle at Franklin. From him I learned
that Stewart and Cheatham attacked the enemy in his entrenchments at
4½ P.M. yesterday, the fight stretching far into the night. Our loss in general officers was terrible—Cleburne, Strahl, Granbury, Gist, being killed,
John C. Brown and all his staff except Major Vaulx wounded—General
Gordon seriously, and General Carter supposed mortally wounded—
General Quarles reported to have lost an arm—Colonel Young killed.
Our troops with the most determined gallantry charged and carried three
lines of entrenchments routing the enemy who fled this morning in confusion towards Nashville—Forrest being, when Captain Stepleton left, in
his rear.[2]

With General Strahl, fell his Adjutant, Captain James Johnston, and
his Inspector, Lieutenant Marsh. It is with profound satisfaction, and with
devout thanksgiving to Almighty God that I look back on my intercourse

1. Lt. Edward M. Morse's unit, the Orleans Light Horse, was the corps headquarters
guard for Stewart's Corps. Private James O. Hardin was a member of the Orleans Light
Horse. Andrew B. Booth, comp., *Records of Louisiana Confederate Soldiers and Louisiana
Confederate Commands*, 4 vols. (1920; reprint, Spartanburg, S.C.: Reprint Co., 1984), 3:184,
1067.
2. At approximately this point, loose in the diary, is a postwar newspaper sketch of Brig.
Gen. Alfred Jefferson Vaughan, Jr. (1830–1899), who fought with the Army of Tennessee
throughout the war until seriously wounded at Atlanta. See Warner, *Generals in Gray*,
315–16. Col. Robert B. Young commanded the 10th Texas Infantry.

with these men. General Strahl I baptized on the 20th of last April and presented him for confirmation to Bishop Elliott at the same service at Dalton. Lieutenant Marsh, I baptized in the Gilmer Hospital, Marietta, Georgia on the 22nd of February, 1864. He was confirmed by Bishop Elliott on the following day. [With] the both of them I have broken the bread which came down from Heaven—and night and morning on our march up while with them, we have all knelt in prayer. General Strahl was a native of the state of Ohio, Lieutenant Marsh from Bolivar, Tenn., and Captain Johnston from Tuscumbia, Alabama.

To John Marsh my soul was knit in all the tenderest ties of friendship and affection. His was a great and generous mind, and a braver place "in my Heart's love" had no man. His heart was warm, his hands pure, his doctrines and his life coincident, there was in him what Shaftsburg calls the "most natural beauty in the world"—honesty and moral truth. Honesty that was firm and upright, "He would not flatter Neptune for his trident or Jove for his power to thunder"—Truth whose halo was sincerity. My heart bleeds but I know that all his love is made immortal for me. He is another treasure in Paradise.

The three bodies were brought to Columbia and deposited in the house of Captain Johnston, brother of the Captain. Burial cases were procured and I pressed one kiss upon John's cold brow, the last on earth. How long, O Lord, how long!

A Prayer for My Return to My Flock

O Lord my God! I am not worthy that thou shouldest come under my roof, yet Thou has honored Thy servant with appointing him to stand in Thy house and to serve at Thy Altar. Bring me home O God, to my flock from which I have been so long separated. To thee and Thy service I have devoted myself, my soul and body with all their powers and faculties. In mercy restore me to my charge and cure that I may minister to my people doctrines and sacraments of Christ. And in to this day of Thy visitation, maintain and set forward quietness, peace, and love among all men. O God I am unworthy of the least of all Thy blessings but I ask this for the sake, and through the merits of Thy blessed Son Jesus Christ, the great shepherd and Bishop of souls. amen.

DECEMBER 2ND, FRIDAY
Went to the Institute Hospital to see Captain Flourney and Adjutant McKinney of the 1st Tennessee Regiment, the former wounded in the groin,

the latter in the head. One hundred wounded were brought in at 9:00 o'clock last night. Reports this morning place our forces far on the way to Nashville.

This has indeed been to me a day of darkness and distress. At 12:00 P.M. I officiated at the funeral of Brig. General Strahl, Capt. James Johnston and my dear friend, Lt. John H. Marsh.[3] At 3:00 P.M. I buried from the residence of Mrs. Dr. Polk, Major General Cleburne, Brig. General Granbury, and Colonel Young. Their bodies were all deposited in Rose Hill Cemetery. I regretted that they were not taken to Ashwood. Generals Cleburne and Strahl and Lieutenant Marsh were all baptized, confirmed, and communing members of the Church. General Cleburne was a vestryman in his parish in Helena, Arkansas. Captain Johnston had been brought up a Methodist but his heart was in the Church. Of General Granbury and Colonel Young, I have no knowledge as to their religious views. A military escort was furnished by Captain Long and every token of respect was shown to the memory of the glorious dead. Brig. Gen. John Adams of Pulaski, Tenn. who I had dined with at the Hon. James H. Thomas' the day before he left Columbia fell most gallantly. I wrote letters to Mrs. Marsh and Mrs. Johnston informing them of the death of their sons. It will be a crushing blow to them both.

Dined at 6:00 P.M. at Mrs. Polk's, and then rode out with Gen. Lucius Polk to Hamilton Place to spend the night. My excellent friend, General Manigault wounded in the head—Major Prince of Mobile wounded in the foot, and Willie Huger are at Hamilton Place. Will Polk rode my horse out.[4]

In my room found a book entitled "The Romance of Yachting" in which I find a passage so thoroughly in accordance with my views of the truth of history that I must transcribe it. The writer shows that the three great eras of the New York Colonization are:

1. Its first commercial planting by the Hollanders.
2. Its becoming the principal asylum of the Huguenots in America after the revocation of the Edict of Nantes.
3. The influx of cavalier and anti-Puritan English, after it became a province of the British Stuarts.

3. Throughout this entry, CTQ mistakenly left the *t* out of Johnston, which the editor has corrected to avoid confusion.

4. Will Polk was probably Major William Polk (Major was the young man's actual first name), a son of Lucius Julius Polk. Turner, *Maury County,* 247.

190 / DOCTOR QUINTARD, CHAPLAIN C.S.A.

He shows that the Puritans never imprinted their peculiarities nor their fanaticism upon New York and says: "Their religion was a ferocious fanaticism; their freedom a tyranny over conscience; an exclusion and a persecution, and their civilization (exemplified by their practices and their laws, by which a nation is always to be judged) the most brutal and barbarous invasion of the rights of their fellow men. Their schools in that entire century, instead of flourishing in healthy literature, were only the nurseries of the narrowest bigotry, and the most vehement intolerance. These things can no longer be covered up by our charitable forbearance, and never can be atoned. They place New England without the pale or recognition of civilization for the first century of her history and not only a century behind New York but a century behind every other American people as plantation of that early period. The rule of the Puritans was a blot upon the age in which they lived, and an iron heel set upon the growth of liberty." All this finds its verification in the present state of the country. The book is by Joseph C. Hart, 1849.

DECEMBER 3RD, SATURDAY
Left Hamilton Place at 10:00 A.M. and rode into Columbia where I met Captain Stepleton, and through him paid the expenses of the burial of my dear Marsh, $300.[5] I also gave Dr. Pise $100 and left myself without funds.

I could not content my mind with the resting place which had been chosen by the sexton for our gallant dead—in close proximity to the graves of soldiers, both white and black, of the federal army. I therefore made arrangements to have the bodies disinterred and removed to the Church yard at St. John's, Ashwood. The bodies removed are those of Major General Cleburne, Brig. Generals Strahl and Granbury, Colonel Young and Lt. John Marsh. I know that in the grave all earthly distinctions cease. These all are equal side by side, the poor man and the Son of Pride.

Lie calm and still—but it is only so *of the dead,* and it is becoming in the living to see that all honor is bestowed upon the earnest Christian and the devoted patriot. I wrote a note to General Polk requesting him to select the places of interment. As the body of Lieutenant General Polk will probably be placed in the yard of St. John's, it is in every way proper that

5. The books of Lamb and Boyd, the only undertakers in Columbia during that time, showed that Strahl and Marsh were buried in the most expensive coffins ever sold by that firm. Smith, *Smith's History of Maury County,* 251.

his companions in arms should rest in the same hallowed ground. Before leaving Columbia, I sent a wagon down to the Webster settlement to procure supplies for our wounded at Franklin.

Captain Stepleton and myself reached the house of Mr. Harrison—three miles from Franklin—about dark. I stopped there to see my friends, Generals Carter and Quarles, Capt. Tom Henry and Capt. Mat Pilcher. General Carter is shot through the body and is probably mortally wounded. General Quarles has his left arm shattered. Captain Pilcher is shot in the side and is doing well. Captain Henry wounded slightly in the head. Mat Pilcher is a thoroughly pious man. He said to me, "I have a great deal to live for, but it is all well." I said, "Matt, you can trust it all to *Him* whether for life or death." "Oh, yes," he replied, "I can leave all in his hands." I had prayers with him and also with the family before retiring. Mrs. Harrison seemed greatly gratified.

DECEMBER 4TH, 2ND SUNDAY IN ADVENT

All last night the cannonading at Nashville was heard very distinctly, but all I can learn is that our lines are within a mile and a half of the city. After breakfast I rode to Franklin to see Dr. Buist who is Post Surgeon. All along the way I found marks of the fight—dead horses, burnt wagons, etc., but at the line of breastworks at Mr. Carter's house where the heaviest fighting was done there was a great number of horses among which was poor John's white horse—within ten feet of the works. The horse of General Adams was further to the right just *on top* of the breastworks. Here the General had fallen, pierced by thirty or forty bullets. How little, I thought when we dined at Mrs. Thomas' on the 28th, and he was in such high glee, that he was soon to fall. His body was taken to Pulaski for interment.

I returned with Buist to Mr. Harrison's. Had prayers with Pilcher and then visited and had prayers with Colonel Watters of Georgia and Colonel Jones of the 24th South Carolina Regiment. Visited Wilkerson of the 1st Tennessee at Mrs. Johnson's two and a half miles further on the road to Spring Hill.[6] We then rode back to Franklin and dined with Dr. Wool-

6. Lt. Col. Zachariah L. Watters commanded the 8th Georgia Battalion in States Rights Gist's brigade, and, as of December 10, 1864, commanded the brigade itself, as a result of its severe casualties in officers at Franklin. OR 45(1):667. Wilkerson and Mrs. Johnson cannot be identified.

dridge.[7] In the evening Mr. Clouston called for me and took me to his house for the night. Found a number of wounded being cared for by the family, among them, Brig. General Cockrill of Missouri. He is wounded in both legs and in the right arm, but is full of life and very cheerful. Lieutenant Anderson of his Staff, who lost a part of one foot at Vicksburg, has now a ball in the other.

What a sad Sunday. This blessed season which breathes nothing but peace and good will to man — and ushers in the festival of the Nativity of the Prince of Peace, is, by the wickedness of man, filled with all the horrid sounds of war. The whole creation groaneth.

> O Lord send peace in our day.
> Deal not with us according to our sins
> Neither reward us according to our iniquities.

December 5th, Monday

Visited Cheatham's (Brown's) Division Hospital in the Court House, Franklin. Found all the wounded members of my Regiment in one room. Dressed a number of them. Thence to call on Mrs. Beech who I find has a son seven years old bearing my name.[8] Thence to say goodbye to the Cloustons and General Cockrill. I reached Army Headquarters just about dusk and had a warm welcome not only from the General but from Mr. Overton's family and several lady friends from Nashville.

December 6th, Tuesday

Capt. John Claiborne rode with me today to call upon my good friends and parishioners, the Edmundson family. I had a very hearty welcome.[9]

December 7th, Wednesday

Rode with Governor Harris to Franklin, thence to Mr. Harrison's to be with Brig. Gen. John C. Carter whose life is despaired of. Found him much worse than when I left.

7. Dr. Wooldridge was probably F. S. Woldridge, listed in an 1853 newspaper advertisement as a purveyor of "drugs, medicines, perfumery and dyestuffs." *Franklin (Tenn.) Review*, May 20, 1853. Woldridge was listed as a seller of dry goods in 1857. Crutchfield and Holliday, *Franklin: Tennessee's Handsomest Town*, 129.

8. The 1860 federal census for Williamson County, Tennessee, lists Edward Beech, then age thirty-two, a dentist; his wife, S. J. Beech; and three children, including their son Charles, then age two.

9. Capt. John Claiborne is the editor's best interpretation of a difficult name in the diary. He cannot be identified, nor can the Edmundsons.

DECEMBER 8TH, THURSDAY

Brig. General Quarles and Captain Pilcher are both doing well. Major Dunlop is also improving. Lieutenant Colonel Jones of the 24th South Carolina is not so well having had a profuse hemorrhage. Today I read a few verses to General Carter and had prayers with him for which he thanked me in the most earnest manner. In speaking with him on the subject of the atonement I said that our Saviour by the one oblation of Himself once offered—made a full, perfect, and sufficient sacrifice, oblation and satisfaction for the sins of the whole world. "Yes," he replied, "what a sublime thought—so sublime that our weak faith can hardly grasp it." He then exclaimed, "O God: Thou knowest that I love Thee—but to *know* Thee—to *know* Thee." "We can only know him through Christ," I said. "Yes, through Christ," he replied. "That simplifies it, and yet," he continued, "the proposition is made up of compounds, as thus—I have five senses and each and all of them at one point or another, in one way or another, brings me in contact with my God."

In his lucid moments my conversations with him were exceedingly interesting but his paroxysms of pain were frequent and intense. He could not be convinced that he was going to die. But I said, "General, if you should die what do you wish me to say to your wife?" "Tell her that I have always loved her devotedly and that I respect her more than I express." He craved chloroform and it was freely administered. I had no further opportunity of speaking to him on the subject of his soul's salvation. I have had prayers with the family, with Major D[unlop] in his room and with Captain Pilcher upstairs.

DECEMBER 9TH, FRIDAY

Bitterly cold and snowing hard. Had prayers with all the wounded. Lt. Colonel Jones died last night. Sat up with General Carter until 12½ on Thursday night.

DECEMBER 10TH, SATURDAY

General Carter died at 12 o'clock last night. Wrote to Dr. Pise at Columbia to attend his funeral as his body is to be taken there for temporary burial. Then rode to Franklin and as the roads are so slippery that I could not travel on horseback, I joined Dr. Brysacker and found pleasant company in his ambulance. My horse got along so badly tied behind the ambulance that I left him at Mrs. James Johnston's, six miles from Franklin. Reached headquarters at dark.[10]

10. Dr. A. L. Brysacker was medical director of Cheatham's (formerly Hardee's) Corps. Cunningham, *Doctors in Gray*, 284. Mrs. James Johnston may have been Sarah I. John-

DECEMBER 11TH, 3RD SUNDAY IN ADVENT

Litany and Holy Communion at Army Headquarters at 11½ o'clock A.M. Prayers at 8 P.M. This afternoon walked with Miss Correy to Mr. John Thompson's to see Miss Sue Clarke of Nashville where I had the pleasure of meeting General Clayton.[11] I called over to see my parishioners, the Platers, where I was warmly welcomed.[12] Met Generals Loring and Edward Johnson there. Tonight General Forrest shares my bed. Haggerty says, "It is the lion and the lamb lying down together." He is certainly an uncut diamond—of remarkably fine personal appearance and great native vigor of thought and expression.[13]

DECEMBER 12TH, MONDAY

Today in the Methodist meeting house at Brentwood, I united in the holy bonds of matrimony, Major William Clare, Inspector General, and Miss Mary Hadley of Nashville. The attendants of the Major were Dr. Foard, Medical Director and Major Moore, Chief of Commissary. Miss Hadley's attendants were Miss Allison of Nashville and Miss White May.[14] A large assemblage of officers was present. After the ceremony, the party retired to the residence of John Overton, Esq. where a grand dinner was given. My empty purse was replenished by a fee of $200, beside which my friend, Mr. Plater sent me this morning, $50 in greenbacks. Lieutenant Wigfall and myself walked to Brentwood but took a seat in Major Ayers' ambulance on our return.[15]

---

ston, listed in the 1860 federal census for Williamson County, Tennessee, as then age twenty-eight, who lived with James P. Johnston, a farmer, and their three small boys.

11. The 1860 federal census for Davidson County, Tennessee, indicates Miss Correy was either Susan Correy, then age twenty-five, or her sister Rebecca, then age twenty-two. The same census identifies the most likely "John Thompson," Jonathan Thompson, in 1860 age sixty-seven, a farmer of substantial property. Miss Sue Clarke cannot be identified.

12. The 1860 federal census for Davidson County, Tennessee, lists Thomas Plater, then age thirty-one; his wife, Sarah, then age thirty; and their three small daughters.

13. At this point in the diary appears the following, apparently in Forrest's handwriting: "I was born in Marshall County, Tennessee, on the 13th day of July, 1821. N. B. Forrest, Maj. Genl."

14. Miss Allison and Miss White May cannot be identified.

15. Major Ayers was very probably Major F. W. Ayer, the Army of Tennessee's chief quartermaster. See OR 39(2):865, 798; OR 47(2):1112. Lt. Francis Halsey Wigfall, son of Senator Louis T. Wigfall of Texas, was an aide-de-camp on Hood's staff. See Richard M. McMurry, *John Bell Hood and the War for Southern Independence* (Lexington: University Press of Kentucky, 1982), 177, 178.

I find in an old Review of last January an article entitled "The Beginning of the End" in which a writer takes the ground that the success of the Federal Army during the year of 1863, and particularly in the fall, had well nigh subdued the people of the South. He says: "We have deprived the enemy of extensive portions of territory in most of their states. Tennessee is rescued; Maryland, Kentucky and Missouri are placed beyond all danger of being taken by the Rebels; in Arkansas, Louisiana and Texas, we hold places of much political and military importance; Mississippi is practically ours; Alabama yields little to our foe; Georgia is invaded instead of remaining the basis of a grand attack on Tennessee and Kentucky; the Carolinas, greatly favored by geographical circumstances, are barely able to hold out against attacks that are not made in force and portions of their territory are ours; Virginia is exhausted, and there the enemy cannot long remain, even should they meet with no reverses in the field, and finally as General Grant's successes halved the Confederacy, so have his Chattanooga successes quartered it." From all this the sapient writer argues that the rebellion is on its last legs. It is to be hoped he will take another birds eye view this year. In Virginia he will find our Army stronger than ever—Richmond not yet taken and our Congress in session there. Mississippi is ours, and here, we are at the gates of Nashville with Tennessee rescued from the grasp of the invaders. The following article from the Chicago Times of the 5th of December puts the matter in such a light as ought to let the miserably deluded people see the South if they have eyes and brains.[16]

General Hood says that this campaign will change very greatly the movements of both armies. There will be no more great flanking operations—that the enemy will have to seek our armies and fight them where he can find them—that there will be more blood spilled in 1865 than in 1864—but that the losses will be on the side of the Federals.

DECEMBER 13TH, TUESDAY
Left headquarters at 11 A.M. in Dr. Foard's ambulance for Franklin. Roads very slippery. Took in a couple of wounded soldiers on the way to the Hospital and carried them to Franklin. Met Governor Harris and Colonel Ray, Secretary of State. The Governor gave me some letters and copies of

16. The one-column newspaper article "Hoping Against Reason" is pasted on two pages of the diary and presents a pessimistic view of the Federal military situation.

his excellent Proclamation. Spent the evening at Mrs. Carter's with my friends, Colonel Rice and Captain Tom Henry.[17]

DECEMBER 14TH, WEDNESDAY
Spent the day in ferreting out and purchasing shoes for my family. The people have hidden away their goods and seem unwilling to dispose of them for Confederate money. By promising to pay in greenback, I not only secured shoes, but the promise of dress goods, etc.

Called upon Mrs. Dr. Cliff, an old friend who has a son named after me. Dr. Cliff was, at the beginning of the war, a surgeon in our service, was at the battle of Fishing Creek with the 20th Tenn. Regt.[18] After the disaster at that place, he left the service and has been in Franklin ever since espousing the cause of our enemy. He is a man for whom I always entertained a very high regard both as a gentleman and a man of ability. He left for Nashville on the advance of our Army. Mrs. Cliff met me most cordially and although she expressed her sentiments very strongly, there was a hearty cordiality in her manner that made my visit very agreeable. Charley Quintard is a fine sprightly boy. Mrs. Cliff says that on one occasion General Rosecrans told her she had better change the boy's name— that "Quintard is a rebel," and that his own name would be much better. Before leaving she gave me a package for my wife containing a very elegant black dress and a handsome balmoral. I accepted these for the sake of auld lang syne, but when she added for myself a $50 greenback note—I was put to my trumps—not wishing to accept of such a favor, and fearful to decline lest she might attribute it to unkind motives. On the whole I thought it best to "pocket the insult."

Met Captain Kelly of the Rock City Guards who is in Franklin off duty in consequence of wounds received in the fight of the 30th. I proposed to

17. Mrs. Carter was probably Sarah Ann Ewing Carter, "a woman of great beauty and vivacity." General Hood stopped at her house as he advanced on and later retreated from Nashville. Bowman, *Historical Williamson County,* 127–28. Rice and Henry have been identified previously.

18. Dr. Daniel Bonaparte Cliff (or Cliffe) (1823–1913) was captured at Fishing Creek (or Mill Springs) Kentucky in February 1862 when he remained behind with the wounded after the Confederate retreat from the field. Cliff was later given permission by the Federal authorities to accompany the bodies of Confederate Brig. Gen. Felix K. Zollicoffer and Lt. Bailie Peyton, Jr., to Nashville for burial. Disillusioned by the Rebel cause, he became a Unionist, but often intervened with the occupying Federal troops on behalf of his fellow citizens. See OR 7:109, 565; Bowman, *Historical Williamson County,* 106.

him to go to Alabama for the box of clothing and as he agreed to do so I gave him a note to Captain Smith, General Hood's A.D.C., and he went up to Headquarters and had all papers arranged for a trip to Georgia. Colonel Cox, Commander of the Post, sent a courier for my horse.[19]

DECEMBER 15TH, THURSDAY
Captain Kelly and myself took the cars for Columbia where we arrived at 2 P.M. and dined at Mrs. Dr. Polk's. All the way down the road there are pleasant evidences the enemy left in hot haste. The bridges were all left standing except the one at Franklin. Even the bridge across Duck River was left, only the two ends being slightly injured. Captain Kelly, Dr. Stout, Dr. Pise and myself took supper at Mr. Frank Dunnington's. Pise spent the night with me at Mrs. Polk's. When General Cleburne's body was brought to Mrs. Polk's, Miss Naomi Hays placed upon the coffin the following verses:

Fare thee well departed chieftain
Erins land sends forth a wail
And O my country sad laments thee
Passed so late through Death's dark vale

Blow, ye breezes softly o'er him
Fan his brow with gentle breath
Disturb ye not the peaceful slumb'rer
Cleburne sleeps the sleep of death

Rest thee, Cleburne! Tears of sadness
Flow from hearts thou'st nobly won
Memr'y ne'er will cease to cherish
Deeds of glory thou hast done

Columbia Tenn. 2d December, 1864

19. Capt. John S. Smith was Hood's aide-de-camp. See OR 38(3):743; OR 38(5):913; OR 45(2):733. Colonel Cox may have been Nicholas Nichols Cox (1837–1912), a lawyer born in Bedford County, Tennessee who, at the time, commanded the 10th Tennessee Cavalry. Cox settled in Franklin after the war, and eventually served five terms in the United States Congress. CMH 10:434; Joint Committee on Printing, *Biographical Directory of the United States Congress, 1774–1989* (Washington: U.S. Government Printing Office, 1989), 836.

DECEMBER 16TH, FRIDAY
Attended a meeting of the ladies at Mrs. James Walker's, the object of which was to organize a Relief Organization.[20]

DECEMBER 17TH, SATURDAY
Most disturbing reports came in this morning of a reverse to our arms. I did not at first credit them, but about 1 P.M. I met Colonel Harvie, the Inspector General, who confirmed the very worst. He expressed both indignation and disgust at the conduct of our troops. Bate's Division gave way and the whole army seems to have fled like a pack of whipt hounds. I do not let this cast me down, my sure trust is in the Lord of Hosts. General Lucius Polk having sent a buggy for me I drove out to Hamilton Place to spend the night. I found the family in great distress. Captain Minnick Williams reached home a few moments before my arrival and from him I learned all the particulars.

DECEMBER 18TH, 4TH SUNDAY IN ADVENT
Full services and Holy Communion at General Polk's house. I rejoice today at the ingathering of two precious souls into the ark of Christ's Church, Major Prince and Captain Williams—Major Prince was wounded at the battle of Franklin and has been at General Polk's with General Manigault. I administered the Holy Communion to the company assembled in the parlor and then carried the consecrated elements into the room occupied by General Manigault and Major Prince and using part of the service administered to them. General Manigault received with especial devotion, he is a most devout minded Christian.

Immediately after service Willie Huger drove me to town and I assisted Dr. Pise at the marriage of Miss Maria Naomi Hays to Major William E. Moore, Chief Commissary of the Army. I took the first part of the service and Pise the latter. The marriage was celebrated at the residence of the Bride's father, Dr. Hays, at 3 P.M.[21] Rode to Mr. Vaught's where I found

20. The eldest sister of President James K. Polk, Maria Polk Walker was the widow of James Walker (1792–1864), a former Presbyterian who became an Episcopalian when he was chastised for sending his son to a dancing school. Garrett, *Maury County Historical Sketches*, 89.

21. Maria Naomi Hays was the younger daughter of Dr. John B. Hays of North Carolina and his wife, Ophelia Clarissa, James K. Polk's younger sister. Garrett, *Maury County Historical Sketches*, 148, 241; Thurman, *Maury County, Tennessee, 1860 Census*, 89; Herbert Walker and Paul Bergeron, eds., *Correspondence of James K. Polk*, 4 vols. (Nashville: Vanderbilt University Press, 1969), 1:32. n.; Tom Price, Curator of Collections, James K. Polk Home, to editor, September 21, 2000.

General Hood and Staff. The General bears up with wonderful faith. He gave me the following letter which explains the disasters.

Headquarters, Strahl's Brigade
In the Field
December 18, 1864

Sir:

It is a duty I owe myself, brigade, division, the Commanding General, and to the country to state facts in regard to the panic of the Army on the afternoon of the 16th.

The lines were broken about 3 P.M. on a high hill west of the Granny White Pike about half a mile—which hill was occupied by Tyler's Brigade, Bate's Division, and given up to the enemy without a struggle. My command was on Tyler's left and the right of Cheatham's Division. This hill as occupied by the enemy overlooked the right of the Army, and the troops seeing it in the hands of the enemy, and seeing the left wing of the Army running without making a stand, fled also.

It was not fighting—nor the force of arms—nor even numbers which drove us from the field. As far as I can learn I did not lose more than thirty men, and about thirty-five small arms, already replaced.

For the first time in this war, we lost our cannon. Give us the first chance and we will retake them.

Respectfully, your obedient servant,
Andrew J. Kellar
Colonel Comd

To Colonel A. P. Mason
Army of Tennessee[22]

Bates is personally a most gallant man—but his Division is not handled well.[23] At Murfreesboro on the 7th the conduct of his Division was

22. This letter is reproduced at OR 45(2):707. Andrew Jackson Kellar had been lieutenant colonel of the 4th Tennessee Regiment, served on the Inspector General's staff in Richmond, and was then appointed colonel of the 5th Tennessee Regiment in the latter stages of the Atlanta campaign. He commanded Strahl's Brigade as its surviving ranking officer. Lindsley, *Military Annals*, 188, 193, 200; see OR 39(2):744; OR 45(1):667.

23. While Bate was not a superior officer, harsh criticism of his division's performance on December 16, 1864, is unjust. Exposed on the slopes of what is now known as Shy's Hill,

shameful. General Forrest wrote the following in a dispatch to the General Commanding from which I make the following extract:

I did not fall back for the purpose of drawing the enemy out but because he drove me back. The infantry (Bate's) sent me I do not think can be relied on to charge the enemy's works as his force numbers as many, if not more than my own. The enemy numbers at least six thousand at Murfreesboro. The affair today was most *disgraceful*, all of the men and most of the officers, with the exception of Smith's Brigade, having fled in confusion at the first approach of the enemy. The artillery was handled well. But the only thing that saved the Army was Armstrong's and Ross' getting in the enemy's rear and charging them, thereby checking their advance.

Very respectfully,
N. B. Forrest

Prayers at Headquarters at 8 P.M. Lieutenant Colonel Johnston and myself had a very long conversation with General Hood on the subject of his future movements. We both expressed the opinion that the General ought to hold the line of the Duck River if he could possibly do so. To fall back across the Tennessee will dispirit the men, cause desertion among the Tennessee troops, rouse the enthusiasm of the North, prolong the war—whereas if we can hold this line, put the machinery of our state government in operation, the campaign, even with our reverses, will be a splendid success. In the course of conversation, Colonel Johnston expressed the opinion that "while God is on our side, so manifestly that no man can question it, it is very apparent that our people have not yet passed through all their disappointments and sufferings." General Hood replied that the remark was a just one. He had been impressed with the fact at Spring Hill, where the enemy was completely in our grasp, and notwithstanding all his efforts to strike a blow, he had failed. Then at Nashville, after the day's fighting was well nigh over and the enemy made a last feeble effort to recover the fortunes of a day, when all had gone successfully until the evening, our troops broke in confusion and fled.

---

named for that Lt. Col. William M. Shy, who was killed in its defense, Bate's men had little chance of successfully resisting a determined Federal advance. See Sword, *Confederacy's Last Hurrah*, 372–74.

And it is true. From the beginning of the war neither side had ever had a *great* success. Neither side has reaped any great results from a victory won. But still my trust is in that God whose "right hand is full of righteousness."

The General is not decided as to his future movements.

DECEMBER 19TH, MONDAY

General Forrest reached Headquarters this morning before day. His opinion is that General Hood ought to withdraw without delay south of the Tennessee—that if we are unable to hold the state, we should at once evacuate it. At 9 A.M., cannonading began at Rutherford Hill—probably the advance of the enemy's cavalry. Cheatham sends word that he has repulsed them and the firing ceases in an hour or two. General Hood has decided to fall back south of the Tennessee. Governor Harris, in whose judgment I have great confidence, thinks it is the best we can do.

Received a letter from Kate dated "7th, Dec," the second since I left home. She encloses one from Mrs. Myers, the mother of Matt Myers of Florida, giving me an account of his death. I read the letter with a full heart and eyes filled with tears, thanking God that He permitted one in His good providence to be "instrumental in promoting the growth of grace in the heart of the dear boy." His mother says: "He loved you, believed you, trusted you and was not disappointed. You confirmed anew all his previous resolutions to serve his God, thus leading him, as I humbly trust, from grace to glory." She encloses the following lines which he sent her last June:

Calm

Calm me, O God, and keep me calm
Amid the storms that around me roll;
O let Thy goodness and Thy love
Fall like fresh dew upon my soul.
I need Thy peace, I need Thy strength,
I need love's blessed healing balm—
I need Thy calmness O my God,
Calm me, and keep me ever calm.

Calm when temptations press me sore,
When angry billows round me break,
When Satan enters like a flood,
O keep me calm for Thy dear sake.

Calm in afflictions' darkest hour,
Where'er I pass beneath Thy rod—
Calm while I feel the heavy strokes
That draw me closer to my God.

Aye, keep me calm when all life's joys
Have faded from my path away;
Calm when I see love's sweetest flowers
All falling sorely to decay;
Calm when the icy hand of death
Is hushing life's sweetest, solemn psalm
Calm in the shadows of the vale
Till I reach the eternal calm.

I thank God for such a life and example as dear Matt's.[24] His Mother relates the following touching incident. "A few minutes after we laid our beloved in his narrow bed a soldier boy apparently about sixteen came to me with suffused eyes and said, How do you do, Mrs. Myers. I replied, 'Who are you, my boy? I do not know you.' He answered, 'my name is Murphy: *you* do not know it, but *Orderly there* does, *he* has called it many a time. And O such an Orderly!' And bursting into tears, he sobbed, 'I would rather everyone of them would die than he—*he* taught us to pray and sing, and read the Bible.' He was quite overcome by his emotion."[25]

O Holy Ghost into my mind,
Send down Thy heavenly light,
Kindle my heart with fervent zeal,
To serve God day and night.

Prayers at Headquarters and the General begged me to have a hymn sung.

24. In the middle of the poem, CTQ pasted in the diary two newspaper clippings. The first related to a memorial resolution passed on December 7, 1864, by Gracie's Brigade, a former unit of the Army of Tennessee then at Petersburg, relative to the death of Brig. Gen. Archibald Gracie, Jr., who was killed in action on December 7, 1864. See Warner, *Generals in Gray*, 113–14. The second quotes Joseph E. Johnston's announcement to the Army of Tennessee of July 17, 1864, relative to his relief, and Hood's of July 18, 1864, relative to his assumption of command. See OR 38(5):887, 889.

25. At the time of Myers' death, Private S. T. Murphy was a member of Myers' Company A, 2nd Florida Cavalry. Hartman, *Biographical Rosters of Florida's Confederate and Union Soldiers*, 4:1416.

DECEMBER 20TH, TUESDAY

A day of darkness and thick gloominess to me. I feel in bidding farewell to Columbia that I am parting with my dearest and most cherished hopes. "Nor doth the general care—Take hold on me; for my particular grief—Is of so flood-gate and overbearing nature—that it engulfs and swallows other sorrows—and it is still itself." I remember our march into Tennessee—so full of delightful intercourse with Strahl and Marsh and other friends and I still remember them now silent in the tomb and I turn away from the place of their burial with a very bitter spirit. I am glad to have visited the graves of my friends on Sunday in the consecrated ground at St. John's Ashwood. Cleburne, when passing it, remarked that he should like to be buried there.

This morning I rode into town to say goodbye to Mrs. George Martin and family, then rode on to Pulaski (30 miles) passing the wagon trains and troops.[26] Reached Mrs. Ballentine's about 5 P.M. where I was warmly greeted by Lena and all the family. I was glad to find Colonel Rice and Captain Tom Henry in the house. It began raining about 3½ and the road was very muddy. Many of our men were marching over the pikes without shoes.

DECEMBER 21ST, WEDNESDAY

Occupied a bed with Colonel Rice. A wretchedly dark, rainy and cold night.

At 3 P.M. baptized:

Benjamin, born October, 1861
Frank   " " Feb 8, 1864
Children of Major Frank and Cynthia Carter—Sponsors: Mrs. Trotter
    and mother.[27]

26. Mrs. George Martin was possibly the wife of George W. Martin, a merchant originally from Pulaski who was connected by marriage to General Gideon J. Pillow. Garrett and Lightfoot, *Civil War in Maury County*, 217; Garrett, *Maury County Historical Sketches*, 239.

27. Benjamin Franklin Carter, Jr. (1828–1910), was the son of a prominent local physician and was then on the staff of Maj. Gen. John C. Brown. His wife, Cynthia Holland Rivers Carter (1833–1901), had vied with Federal occupation troops with varying success during his absence. Mrs. Myra Bell Trotter was Cynthia's mother and may have been the Mrs. Trotter referenced above. Mrs. Trotter's home a mile south of Columbia had been burned by Federal troops on November 26, 1864. She left Tennessee in January 1865 to visit her late husband's plantation in Mississippi, across the river from Helena, Arkansas,

At 5 P.M. baptized:
Mrs. Mildred Batt, wife of Dr. Wm. Batt
Edward Fields—adult
Julia Flournay—adult
Mildred, 6 months
Sponsor: Dr. Batt[28]

At 8 P.M. at the headquarters of General Hood (residence of Hon. Thomas Jones), I baptized:

Lucy Anne—8 years
Edward Spencer—10 years
Lee Walthall—6 years
Nicholas Tate—20 months
Children of Hon. Thomas M. and Marietta Jones
Sponsors: The parents[29]

After the baptism, Mrs. Jones' family joined us at prayers in the General's room. The General says he is afraid he has been more wicked since he began this retreat than for a long time past—that he had so set his heart upon success—had prayed so earnestly for it—had such a firm trust that he should succeed—that his heart has been very rebellious—but said he, "let us go out of Tennessee singing hymns of praise." This has been a terrible day, and exceedingly cold rain in the morning and snow in the evening. So many of our poor boys are bare footed that there is great suf-

but found that it, too, had been burned. She died in Helena on March 12, 1865. Her infant son, Frank, Jr., died shortly thereafter, on April 22, 1865, but Benjamin F. Carter III (1861–1929) survived to practice law in Washington, D.C. Margaret Butler, *Legacy: Early Families of Giles County* (Pulaski, Tenn.: Sain Publications, 1991), 96–97; Nathaniel C. Hughes, Jr., *Big Jim Holland* (Chattanooga: n.p., 2000), 59–85.

28. The 1860 federal census for Giles County, Tennessee, lists William Batte, then age thirty-seven; his wife, Mildred, then age thirty; Edward, then age eleven; and Julia, then age nine. Edward and baby Mildred lived to young adulthood; Julia married Tennessee historian W. R. Garrett. Mrs. Mildred Batte was the sister of Col. Hume R. Feild. Butler, *Legacy*, 108–9.

29. Marietta Perkins and Thomas M. Jones were married in 1838 and had three sons who served in the Confederate army, including Calvin E. Jones, one of the six young men who organized the original Ku Klux Klan. One of the children baptized, Edward Spencer Jones, became a newspaper editor. Butler, *Legacy*, 131–34.

fering and my heart bleeds for them. The citizens at Pulaski have done all they could to provide shoes.

I was delighted to see my friend, Lt. Col. Martin.[30] Dined with the Governor at Mr. Nathaniel Adams' and spent the night with Colonel Rice.

DECEMBER 22ND, THURSDAY
Have visited most of the Church people today. Dined with Major Jones, and for wonder as to time and place, had oyster soup.[31] General Hood and myself enjoyed the rarity. The General informs me that the enemy effected a crossing at Columbia at 12 o'clock today. They began shelling the town, but Forrest told them by flag that if the shelling was not stopped, he would put their wounded directly under the fire. They then ceased. Our forces all moved on towards Bainbridge and the General leaves in the morning. I join Governor Harris, as he will not be detained en route and I am extremely anxious to reach some place where there is a Church before Sunday, the blessed festival of the Nativity of our Lord and Saviour. Called at Mr. Adams' in the evening where I met Governor Harris, Colonel Whitthorne, Captain Gibson, and Major Murphy.[32]

DECEMBER 23RD, FRIDAY
Rode 30 miles to a little town called Lexington where Colonel Rice, Captain Andrew Ballentine and myself obtained rough accommodations from a family named Porter.[33] The family was thoroughly southern in feelings and had been ruined in worldly goods. They gave us cordial entertainment. Had Prayers with them.

DECEMBER 24TH, SATURDAY
Started for Lamb's Ferry thinking to find a boat there but on reaching Rogersville learned that Roddy had ordered it to Elk River to cross his

30. Lieutenant Colonel Martin cannot be identified.

31. "Major" Jones cannot be identified. Since army headquarters was then at the home of Thomas M. Jones in Pulaski, it is possible CTQ is referring to that Jones. See OR 45(1):673.

32. All persons mentioned in this entry have been identified previously except for Murphy. Major Murphy may have been J. J. Murphy, A. P. Stewart's chief commissary. Field Returns, September 20, 1864, Army of Tennessee Records, Joseph Jones Collection, Tulane University. See also OR 38(3):872.

33. The 1860 federal census for Lauderdale County, Alabama, lists five Porter families in Lexington.

command.[34] So we had ridden all morning and had the same distance to make to Bainbridge as we had at Lexington, 18 miles. In the afternoon, met my friend, the Hon. J. L. M. Curry with a body of cavalry and had a moment's chat with him. Found a young man named Tally who belonged to the cavalry, with whom I rode and chatted pleasantly for two or three hours.[35] Just at the close of the day I found my friend, Maj. General Clayton, camped on the roadside and not knowing General Hood's locality, I accepted his invitation to spend the night with him. We talked of the Blessed Christmas time and after supper he called up all his staff and couriers and we had prayers. Then I laid me down and the angels sang me the glorious song, "Glory to God in the highest, and on earth, peace, good will towards men."

DECEMBER 25TH, CHRISTMAS DAY
A sad and gloomy day, a day of clouds and rain. I rode down to the river and watched the work of putting down the pontoons. I have my Christmas gift—two five dollar gold pieces sent me by Mrs. Jones of Pulaski. Wigfall handed them to me early in the day. The enemy reached Huntsville on Thursday and today are in Florence. We heard their guns in the distance. General Pettus, in command of Stevenson's Division, was passed over the river in boats.[36] Had prayers at General Lowry's headquarters (Brown's Division). I spend the night with Dr. Rice.[37]

DECEMBER 26TH, MONDAY
Crossed the Tennessee River at 9 A.M.
God's Holy Will be done.

34. Brig. Gen. Philip D. Roddey (1826–1897) of Alabama at this time commanded the Confederate District of North Alabama, with a brigade-strength cavalry command. See OR 45(2):634.
35. Tally cannot be identified.
36. Brig. Gen. Edmund Winston Pettus (1821–1907) of Alabama normally commanded a brigade in Maj. Gen. Carter L. Stevenson's Division but was in command of the division at this time because Stevenson had assumed command of Lee's Corps during Stephen D. Lee's disability. OR 45(1):673; Warner, Generals in Gray, 238.
37. Brig. Gen. (and Baptist minister) Mark Perrin Lowry (1828–1885) of Tennessee and Mississippi had, prior to the disaster at Franklin, commanded a brigade in Cleburne's Division. The fact that Lowry was now in command of a different division is a stark reminder of the campaign's toll on the officers of the Army of Tennessee. See Losson, Tennessee's Forgotten Warriors, 236–37. Dr. Francis Rice was the division's chief surgeon. See OR 30(3):80; Crute, Confederate Staff Officers, 35.

DECEMBER 27TH, TUESDAY

Called to see the mother and sisters of Captain Johnston of Strahl's Staff. They were quite overcome at meeting me. I did all in my power to comfort them and had prayers with them before leaving. Dined with Colonel Harvie and General Bate at Mrs. Godley's.[38]

General Hood and Staff arrived at 2 P.M. The General says he has felt the disaster more since reaching Tuscumbia than at any time since the retreat began. Spent the night at Mrs. Dr. Newsom's.[39]

DECEMBER 28TH, WEDNESDAY

My toes being out of my boots I decided it was best for me to make to the rear to secure a pair of more substantial boots. I therefore decided to accompany Mrs. Major Moore and Mrs. Whitthorne to Okolona. Colonel Rice and Captain Ballentine go with us. Breakfasted at Mrs. Keller's where I read two of General Washington's letters, one dated 1779 and the other two or three years later. Rode fifteen miles to Frankfort, the county seat of Franklin County, Alabama which is very near the northern boundary line of the Chickasaw Indian tribe. It is the extreme northeastern corner of the nation. We arrived at Frankfort at 5 P.M. and found delightful accommodations at the house of Mr. Charles Womble who has two sons in Roddy's command.[40]

DECEMBER 29TH, THURSDAY

Started the wagon and ambulance at 6 A.M. Colonel Rice and myself waited for some time for Ballentine who at last concluded to return to Tuscumbia. Rode 27 miles and at nightfall after being turned away from one or two places, found miserable accommodations at the house of an old man named Wright.[41] The road today has been through a bushwhacking region. Great numbers of horse thieves are prowling round and an attempt was made at an early hour in the night on two of the horses of

38. The 1870 federal census for Colbert County, Alabama, lists Mrs. Sarah A. Godley, then age sixty, whose occupation was "keeping house."

39. Presumably the same Mrs. Dr. Newsom CTQ visited on November 21, 1864.

40. Although several Kellers are listed in the 1870 federal census for Colbert County, Mrs. Keller was probably Mary Keller, then age seventy-four, a native of Virginia. The 1860 census for Franklin County, Alabama, lists Charles Womble, then age forty-one, a merchant, with two sons of military age in 1864, William A. Womble and Isaac N. Womble.

41. The only male Wright listed in the 1860 federal census for Franklin County, Alabama, is William L. Wright, who in 1864 would have been fifty.

our party, but fortunately unsuccessful. We required the negroes to keep a strict watch all night.

DECEMBER 30TH, FRIDAY

A comfortable and quiet night. Had prayers at which none of the family were present except Mr. Wright. They are a miserable set.

On the road at 2 P.M. Passed from Franklin County, Alabama into Itawamba County, Miss. About 12 o'clock, reports of the Yankee raiders and their doings at Okolona reached us. It is said they have burned Okolona and passing down the road to Prairie Station have visited Aberdeen. They are reported to have crossed the river at Cotton-gin. If so they may be on our road though I do not credit it.

It was deemed advisable to wait for the baggage wagon, so I rode on ahead and here I am perched on a little knoll chewing cornbread and the end of reflection. I had hoped to reach Aberdeen in time for service on Sunday. O God, how I long for Thy house—how I long to bow at Thy Altar and offer once more the sacrifice of praise and thanksgiving.

"Calm me, O God, and keep me calm amid the storms that round me roll."

Rode 21 miles today and put up with Mr. Richey Elliott where we found comfortable accommodations. Had prayers with the family.[42]

DECEMBER 31ST, SATURDAY

A cold storm blew up during the night with snow. Rode 30 miles to Aberdeen, parting company with Colonel Rice, Mrs. Moore and Mrs. Whitthorne four miles from Cotton-gin.

Though an entire stranger in Aberdeen I received a most cordial welcome at the house of Mr. Needham Whitfield, a church family. My road this evening was intolerably heavy and my weary horse with difficulty made his way through the mud.

And so ends the year. God grant that whatsoever in me hath been decayed by the fraud and malice of the devil or by my own carnal will and frailness may indeed be renewed and I be so strengthened by the Holy Ghost in the inner man that I may work more earnestly for souls during the days that remain for me to serve at the Altar.

I have to thank my heavenly Father for His great goodness to me in

---

42. The 1860 federal census for Itawamba County, Mississippi, lists Richey Elliott, then age fifty-two, a farmer with a family of ten.

the preservation of my dear wife and children from sickness and the violence of the enemy. My heart goes out to them tonight.

The raiders on the Mobile and Ohio R. R. have torn up the track for 20 or 30 miles and appear to have gone west after burning Okolona. On my road today I met Charlie Vaught who informed me of the rumored death of President Davis.[43] Alas, for our poor bleeding land! Alas, for the friends I mourn—

"Darkest of all Decembers Ever my life has known." In the solemn stillness of the night, my heart clings to the *pleasant* and *mournful* past. I think upon my early home, my beloved parents from whom I have been so long separated, my brothers and sisters around whom the tendrils of my heart are twined, my own precious wife and darling children, the friends that are gone—Eastland, and Marsh and many other who has been a joy in this wilderness of sin.

How dear, yet oh, how painful too;
That joy how near to grief allied,
When thoughts of loved ones now no more;
Come rushing on me like a tide.

Departed ones of days gone by,
As slowly on, your visions roll,
My heart is softened and subdued;
Ye sooth and tranquilize my soul.

Like music wafted on the gale,
When midnight stillness wraps the land,
So sweet, the far-off strains ye breathe,
So sad, when waked by memory's hand.

43. Listed in the 1860 census for Maury County, Tennessee, Charles N. Vaught was the son of Nathan Vaught of Columbia, and a member of Company H, 1st Tennessee Infantry. CWCCT, *Tennesseans*, 1:412.

The Dark Days of the Revolution
January 1 to February 28, 1865

JANUARY 1ST, SUNDAY AFTER CHRISTMAS
There being no priest in the parish, the vestry opened the Church for me and I officiated both morning and evening—The evening congregation was large.

> Still keep us, Father, in Thy faith and fear,
> And grant Thy blessing on the coming year;
> Guard us at home, and guide in all our ways
> And fill our hearts with love, our lips with praise.

Lord as Thou increasest our gifts, increase also our gratitude—and if, in the desolations of the land, Thy rod should still and again be laid [on] me, grant me perfect resignation and abiding trust.

> My life's brief remnant all be Thine;
> And when Thy sure decree
> Bids me this fleeting breath resign
> O speed my soul to Thee.

JANUARY 2ND, MONDAY
In the house all day—sent my boots to be repaired.

JANUARY 3RD, TUESDAY
My boots brought by the servant. Paid $15.00 for half soling. Had service in the Church at 3 P.M. at the request of the Church people. Preached to them on earnestness in the Christian life. A good congregation was in attendance. Colonel Rice sent for me to spend the night with him at General Bradford's.[1] Had prayers with the family.

1. The 1860 federal census for Monroe County, Mississippi, lists B. M. Bradford, then age fifty-five, as a "manufacturer."

JANUARY 4TH, WEDNESDAY

Had morning prayers at 10½ and service and sermon at 3½ P.M.

Baptized a Negro child of Major Vasser's, named Beaulah Vinton.[2]

In the evening Mr. Whitfield spent an hour or so in my room. He told me many touching incidents of his little daughter, Sally, who died a few weeks ago, and requested me to write some verses on her death. Not being a poet and never fancying obituary verses, the request staggered me. However, I wrote the following and handed them to him. As they gratified him, I was pleased.

Sally Whitfield and the Violets

Just in the shadow of the Church
On consecrated ground,
A child of innocence and love,
Some bright blue violets found.

It was God's garden, and the child
Loved well the Holy spot
She longed to make the flowers her own
And yet she pluck'd them not.

With guileless words she said, "Mama
May I have one—just one?
Will God be angry if I take
That bright one in the sun?"

"No, darling, God will give you that
He made it grow for you,
It is his handiwork, and He
Hath pencil'd it with blue

To teach a lesson to your heart
Of truth and modesty.
Take it my child," the mother said
"God's blessing be on Thee!"

2. The 1860 federal census for Monroe County, Mississippi, lists a William H. Vassar, then age thirty-eight, a "gentleman."

God's Angel heard the darling child,
And gazed with loving eyes
On one so sweet in purity
To dwell in Paradise.

And when the Angel reapers came
To gather human love,
They took that little child away
To dwell with them above.

And now in Paradise, that child
Amid Elysium bowers
From every ill of earth removed
Gathers God's sweetest flowers.

The little one had asked her mother if God would be angry if she gathered the violets that grew in the Church yard.

Took tea with the family of Mr. Eckford. Mrs. E. is a very devoted daughter of the Church and she has a charming family of children.[3]

JANUARY 5TH, THURSDAY
Called upon several Church people and met a very pleasant party at the residence of Mr. John McNairy. Colonel Dowd of the 24th Mississippi—now belonging to Roddy's military court, I was very much pleased with.[4] Mr. McNairy had just returned from the neighborhood of Memphis, and so oysters were served for supper.[5]

JANUARY 7TH, SATURDAY
Last evening came out to the residence of Needham Whitfield. Saw an old gentleman of seventy-five years but who has a great deal of sunshine in his heart which glows all about him. I met here Colonel Jones of the

3. The 1860 Census for Monroe County, Mississippi, lists J. R. Eckford, then age sixty-two, a merchant, and his wife, M. S., then age forty.

4. McNairy is identified in the 1860 federal census for Monroe County as a single farmer, then age thirty-three, with property worth over $70,000. Col. William F. Dowd commanded the 24th Mississippi from 1861 until at least after the Confederate defeat at Chattanooga, where he appears to have been wounded. See OR 6:346; OR 31(2):698.

5. At this point in the diary CTQ copied a four-stanza poem entitled "Epiphany," by Croswell.

9th Texas Cavalry, and Mrs. Dr. Dalton.[6] Mrs. D. as Mrs. Matthew Lindsay, I had known in other days in Memphis. I had a long talk with them on all religious matters. Mrs. D. is an intelligent Church woman. Spent the day with Colonel Rice at General Bradford's. Captain Ballentine returning, I went to Mr. Whitfield's with him. Received letters from Mr. Richard Peters and my dear wife.

[JANUARY] 8TH, SUNDAY, 1ST SUNDAY AFTER EPIPHANY
Had a very large congregation in the morning and preached as earnestly as I could on the subject of *Repentance*. In the evening the congregation was still large. I preached from the text, "How shall ye escape if ye neglect so great salvation?"

Lieutenant Colonel Sykes of this place who with two other officers were killed by the falling of a tree—was brought to his residence yesterday and buried at 2½ this evening.[7] Rufus Polk and Captain Ballentine spent the night with me.

JANUARY 9TH, MONDAY
A cold, rainy day. Rufus Polk left in the morning for Columbus. I remained in the house reading. Sent an apology to Dr. Hatch with whom I was to take tea and omitted the service appointed for 3 o'clock. At night as the rain ceased, I mounted my horse and rode up to see Colonel Rice.[8]

Aberdeen is certainly very much isolated—no railway, no telegraph, and struck down in the midst of this prairie mud the citizens are a sway to the wildest rumors. It is said that Gen. Joseph E. Johnston has been restored to the command of the Army of Tennessee. It will undoubtedly have a beneficial effect on the Army, for never was a commander so be-

6. Dudley W. Jones was the colonel of the 9th Texas Cavalry, then part of Gen. Lawrence S. Ross' Texas cavalry brigade. Jones and his men helped cover Hood's retreat from Tennessee. See OR 45(1):767; OR 49(2):1134. Mrs. Dr. Dalton cannot be identified.

7. Lieutenant colonel of the 43rd Mississippi Regiment, Columbus Sykes had recently been home to bury his brother, W. E. Sykes, the regiment's adjutant, who was killed in skirmishing at Decatur, Alabama, in late October 1864. The story of Colonel Sykes' unfortunate death can be found in John L. Collins, "Sad Story of the War," CV 6 (March 1898): 116.

8. The 1860 federal census for Monroe County, Mississippi, lists B. L. Hatch, then age forty-eight, a farmer of substantial property, with no indication he was a physician. The 1870 census identifies him as Benjamin Hatch, with much less property. A number of newly freed black residents of the county also bear the name of Hatch in the 1870 census, indicating how Hatch sustained his losses.

loved or confided in, but I cannot but feel it will be an act of injustice to General Hood. But these are the dark days of the revolution and Hood is too thoroughly a patriot to stand in the way of the country's welfare. He would sacrifice himself in a moment for the good of the country.

Our lands are laid waste with fire and sword. Our slaves are carried off and withdrawn from the cultivation of our rich plantations. The enemy is victorious in almost every quarter except in glorious old Virginia. Our people are disheartened and talk of reconstruction—surely these are dark days. I have been struck in reading the "History of the French Revolution" by Theirs, with the similarity of the orders of the monster, Carrier, and of General Grant in reference to the destruction of property. "Carry off all the stock of all description," says Grant, "and negroes so as to prevent their further planting. If the war is to last another year, let the Shenandoah Valley remain a barren waste." "It is my plan to carry off from that accursed country, La Vendee," says Carrier in his letter to General Haxo, "all manner of subsistence or provision for man or beast. . . . In a word, leave nothing in that proscribed country; let the means of subsistence, provisions, forage everything positively—everything be removed to Nantes."[9]

Had a delightful conversation with Gabe Howard on the subject of Baptism. He is in the Ordnance Department of the Army.[10] In the evening Colonel Rice came in to spend the night with me. He is one of nature's noblemen with a well-cultivated mind. He unites gentle and dignified bearing with a large-heartedness. He possesses quick perception. Without affectation he is one of the most gallant of our officers.

> A king can mak' a better Knight
> A Marquis Duke and a' that;
> But an honest man's aboon his might
> Guid faith, he manna fa' that
> The pith of sense, and pride o' worth
> Are higher ranks than a' that.

9. Jean Baptiste Carrier, an agent of the Radicals at the height of the Terror during the French Revolution, was notorious for his drowning of children in the Loire and his boast that "We will make a cemetery of France." General Haxo became one of Napoleon Bonaparte's chief engineering officers. R. R. Palmer, *Twelve Who Ruled: The Committee of Public Safety during the Terror* (Princeton: Princeton University Press, 1941), 116, 220–24; John R. Elting, *Swords around a Throne: Napoleon's Grand Armée* (New York: Free Press, 1988), 35.

10. Howard cannot be identified.

And Rice possesses all those noble qualities, gentleness, cordialness, man-liness, which make the true man and endear him to my heart.

"In companions That do converse and waste the time together, whose souls do bear an equal yoke of love—Their needs must be a like propor-tion of lineaments and manners and of spirit."

"Men are not tied to one another" says [Edmund] Burke, "by papers and seals. They are led to associate, by resemblances, by conformity, by sympathies."

The motto of William of Wyckham, Bishop of Winchester, was "Man-ners makyth man." And we find in our intercourse with men that man-ners are what vex or soothe, comfort or purify, exalt or debase, barbarize or refine us by a constant, steady, uniform, insensible, operation; like that of the air we breathe in.

This morning Dr. Tindall, a graduate of the Memphis Medical Col-lege, called upon me. He was at the College while I occupied the Chair of Physiology and Pathological Anatomy. He recalled to my mind many pleasant incidents of my career as a Professor of Medicine.[11]

JANUARY 10TH, TUESDAY
Spent most of the day in my room. Ned Beasley came in and sat with me some time. He was with General Strahl in the fight at Franklin and was supporting the General in his arms when a third shot passed through the General's head and killed him instantly.[12]

On the death of Brig. General Strahl, and Lieutenant John H. Marsh, his Inspector.

Where the battle raged the fiercest;
Where the hardest blows fell fast;
Where the cannon thunders loudest,
In the hottest of the blast;

Where the stern and the true hearted
Marked each step with crimson gore,

11. The 1860 federal census for Monroe County, Mississippi, lists J. L. Tindall, Jr., then age forty-four, a physician, originally from Kentucky.
12. Pvt. James E. Beasley of the 4th Tennessee Regiment was Strahl's acting aide-de-camp at the time of the Battle of Franklin and was attempting to bear Strahl from the field when the general received his fatal wound. Lindsley, *Military Annals*, 190; Ridley, *Battles and Sketches*, 425.

Planting on the very breastworks
Freedom's banners that they bore;

Strahl, the true and noble hearted,
Marsh, whose soul mock'd every fear,
In their courage most celestial
Blazing wide and far and near;

While the banner'd cross waved o'er them
In the fiercest battle-tide,
Dealt with their blows for truth and freedom,
Heart in hand, and side by side.

They two noble Christ-confessors,
Cheer'd by hope and full of trust
Looked beyond the grave for glory
Looked beyond the "Dust to Dust."

With their garments blood-besprinkled,
With their souls so full of light,
They put off the sword and buckles,
They put on the robes of white.

On the gory field of battle,
On the cold and crimson sod,
Heard they words of cheer and welcome
To the Paradise of God.

Their heroic souls now ransomed —
Ours the cross which they laid down
Ours the sword, and ours the struggle,
Theirs the amaranthine crown.

Where the faithful go to worship,
Where God's anthems rise and swell,
(Mingling prayer and praise together)
They are sleeping as they fell.

By their sepulcher the angels
Ever watch with flaming sword,

While a requiem rolls above them
From the city of the Lord.

JANUARY 11TH, WEDNESDAY
Colonel Rice spent the evening with me at Mr. Whitfield's. No news
from the Army, a thousand wild rumors.

JANUARY 12TH, THURSDAY
A mail reached Aberdeen, the first in two weeks.

JANUARY 13TH, FRIDAY
Colonel Rice spent last night with me. Called at Mr. John C. McNairy's,
where I met most unexpectedly Major Frank McNairy, formerly of General Polk's Staff, now of General William Jackson's.[13] Spent some time in
speaking on religious subjects to Judge Davis and his two sisters, one of
whom is very ill. Before leaving the house, I had prayers with them. In
the afternoon I had service at the Church at which I baptized Miss Maria
Jane Davis. Her witnesses: Mrs. John C. McNairy, Miss Ellen Howard.[14]
    In the evening at 7½, Old Mr. Whitfield and myself went to the Fe-
male School to witness some tableaux vivant gotten up for the Ladies Soldiers Aid Society. The place was crowded but my heart was not in tune
with the exhibition and so after witnessing three or four beautiful group-
ings, I left.

JANUARY 14TH, SATURDAY
Left Aberdeen at 9 A.M. and reached Columbus at 5 P.M. Before leaving I
received a package from the ladies containing a pair of gloves in which
was a roll of bills to the amount of $50. I spent my last night in Aberdeen

13. Formerly on the staff of Maj. Gen. Benjamin F. Cheatham, Maj. Frank McNairy
was with General Polk when the bishop received his fatal shot at Pine Mountain, Georgia.
Polk, *Leonidas Polk*, 2:372. Brig. Gen. William Hicks "Red" Jackson (1835–1903) of Tennessee commanded the cavalry division Polk brought to the Army of Tennessee from Mississippi in May 1864, and at this time commanded a division under Forrest. Warner, *Generals
in Gray*, 152–53.
    14. Reuben Davis (1813–1890) of Mississippi was a former judge and Congressman who
resigned from the United States Congress in 1861 and became a major general of Mississippi state troops and served for a time in Kentucky. Later, he was elected to the Confederate Congress but was defeated in the 1863 election for governor of Mississippi. Bruce S.
Allardice, *More Generals in Gray* (Baton Rouge: Louisiana State University Press, 1995),
72–73. The 1860 federal census for Monroe County, Mississippi, lists Ellen Howard, then
age fourteen, in the household of B. R. Howard, a merchant.

at the house of Major Vasser. With Mrs. Winston, my travelling companion, was very kindly received at Columbus at the home of Mr. John C.
Ramsey, a vestryman of St. Paul's Church.[15]

On my way to Bishop Green's house in the evening I met Major Butler
who reached Columbus yesterday from my home where he had been
spending a week. He gave me a letter from my dear wife. Bishop Green
is absent on a visit to Macon, Mississippi but returns on Monday. Met the
Rev. Mr. Schwrar at the Bishop's residence.[16]

JANUARY 15TH, 2ND SUNDAY AFTER EPIPHANY
A large congregation. Schwrar read morning prayer, I, the Ante-Communion and preached a sermon on the position of the Church in the present
crisis. At night the Rev. Mr. Bakewell gave way to me, he taking the service, and I preached to a ――― congregation. Dined with Dr. Vaughan.
Met General J. C. Brown and lady, and General Lucius Polk at Mr.
Long's.[17]

JANUARY 16TH, MONDAY
Service at 4½ P.M. by Rev. Mr. Schwrar and myself.

JANUARY 17TH, TUESDAY
The people being anxious for services, I gave notice that daily evening
service might be expected during the week. After prayers by Mr. Schwrar,
I preached at 7½ P.M. Lt. Colonel Hoxton spent the night with me.

JANUARY 18TH, SATURDAY
Dined at Mr. Baskerville's with Mr. DeBow, Major Butler, and Captain
Hudson. Tea at the Bishop's. Schwrar read service and I preached. Britton
Hume called this morning and I engaged to see General Elzy on his be-

15. Mrs. Winston cannot be identified.
16. In light CTQ's encounters with other officers attached to Cheatham or his former
division during this time, Major Butler may have been Maj. B. J. Butler, who, at the time
of the Battle of Chickamauga, was Chief Commissary of Cheatham's Division. See OR
30(2):80.
17. The 1860 federal census for Lowndes County, Mississippi, lists B. A. Vaughan, then
age thirty-two, a physician. Mr. "Long" is the editor's best interpretation of CTQ's handwriting. B. S. Long is listed as a merchant in the same census, then age fifty, who apparently kept a boarding house in Columbus.

half to secure a furlough if possible.[18] It seems pretty certain that our Army is going to Georgia. Symptoms of a move are showing themselves.

JANUARY 19TH, THURSDAY

General Hood relieved of his command at his own request. Lt. General Taylor has gone to the front to take temporary command. In my room all day working on an ordination sermon preparatory for the ordination of The Rev. Mr. Schwrar to the office of priesthood Sunday next.

At night, full congregation. Prayers by Rev. A. G. Bakewell. I preached on the Confession of Christ.

JANUARY 20TH, FRIDAY

Received a telegraphic dispatch from General Hood stating that he would not leave Tupelo until Monday and would telegraph me again when he would start. In the afternoon Major General Elzy and Captain Swett called upon me.[19] At night I read service and the Rev. J. M. Schwrar preached.

I hear that both officers and privates are holding meetings in the Army asking for the return of General Johnston to the Command. And I am satisfied that no other man had he genius of Caesar or Napoleon could command the Army of Tennessee so well as General Johnston. General Hood has not fallen in the estimation of the officers of the Army. They still believe him gallant in action, judicious in counsel and competent in every way, but the troops long for Johnston and the country is crying out for him.

Sherman is in Savannah. Some ten days before our Army left Florence, Alabama he divided his Army sending four corps back in the direction of Atlanta and the balance to reinforce Thomas, the greater part of whose forces were massed at Pulaski, Tenn. We moved from Florence by the Waynesboro and Lawrenceburg roads, General Forrest in the advance, the enemy having a shorter line and a better road, reached Columbia before us. So soon as our infantry force reached Columbia, Forrest's cavalry and two corps of infantry were thrown across Duck River about four miles above Columbia with the hope of being able to strike the head

18. Although it would appear Hume served in the artillery, he cannot be identified.

19. Capt. Charles Swett commanded a battery of Mississippi artillery in many of the Army of Tennessee's battles earlier in the war. At this point, he appears to have been acting inspector general of the army's artillery, which would explain his presence with Elzey, the army's chief of artillery. See OR 38(3):683.

of the retreating column between Columbia and Franklin. Forrest struck the column at Spring Hill and fought them for several hours until the head of our infantry column arrived late in the evening, the infantry going into line of battle as it arrived. The first two divisions arriving attacked the enemy and drove him from his temporary line of works, but paused in consequence of the fact that the enemy's line extended to our right far beyond our own and the darkness of the night. General Hood took measures promptly to extend our right and if his orders had been strictly carried out, I have no doubt we would have captured or destroyed Schofield's command at that point. This was the great opportunity of the campaign and we lost it, Schofield escaping under cover of the darkness. The pursuit to Franklin was prompt and vigorous.

Who was to blame of the subordinate commanders, I cannot say exactly, but General Hood's orders were positive and specific, conveyed by two of his own staff officers and lastly by Governor Harris to General Cheatham. General Hood deserves well of the country for his bravery, his devotion, his energy and enterprise and he should be honored in all coming time for what he has done. Nor should one word of censure fall upon him for what he has failed to do.[20]

JANUARY 21ST, SATURDAY
The Rev. Father Miller of Mobile arrived in obedience to the summons of Bishop Green and we spent the evening until 10 o'clock in examining of The Rev. John Miller Schwrar (deacon) for Priest's orders.[21] We gave him a thorough examination and I was glad to find him well furnished.

JANUARY 22ND, 3RD SUNDAY AFTER EPIPHANY
After morning prayer was said by Father Miller I preached on the text, "What shall one then answer the messengers of the Nation? That the Lord

20. In the diary loose among the pages of this discussion of Spring Hill, there is a newspaper clipping entitled "Manual of Devotions" relative to CTQ's The Confederate Soldier's Manual of Devotions. The book is described as being " made up of more or less original, preaxial matter for the Government of Christian life, of prayers well adopted for the wants and circumstances of our soldiers, and of hymns suited to enkindle their devotion and piety, while enough is intermixed to guard the faith against the errors and mistaken liberality of the times by adding the Creed and a judicious selections [sic] from the collects and daily services."
21. Rev. Miller does not appear in Mobile city directories for either 1860 or 1866. The 1866 version lists six Episcopal churches in the city, but names the rectors for only two. Henry Farrow and W. B. Bennett, Directory of the City of Mobile for the Year 1866 (Mobile:

hath founded Zion and the poor of His people shall trust in it." Isaiah XIV. 32. After the service I presented the candidate to the Rt. Rev., the Bishop, after which the Bishop proceeded with the Litany. Father Miller and myself united with the Bishop in the imposition of hands.

The congregation was very large and attentive. It saddened me to think that Mr. S. was being ordained out of Tennessee to which diocese he is canonically attached. O Lord how long!

A heavy rain in the evening prevented service.

JANUARY 23RD, MONDAY
General Hood passed down the road this morning. He telegraphed me to join him but too late. Dined with the Bishop after which I went to Mr. Ramsey's to spend the balance of my time in Columbus. My visit at Dr. Vaughan's hospitable home has been very pleasant.

JANUARY 24TH, TUESDAY
At General Elzy's to-day. Met Colonel Baskerville, J. D. B. DeBow (of the Review), Captain Irwin, Captain Hudson, and others.[22] The policy of putting the surgeons in the Army as soldiers was discussed length, and all agreed to the policy. The rumors of foreign recognition on the basis of gradual emancipation was also discussed. Mr. DeBow stated that Governor Aiken of South Carolina, the owner of over a thousand slaves, had spoken to him over two years ago in favor of emancipation to secure recognition and had urged him to employ his pen to bring the subject before the people of the C.S.[23]

Colonel Horace Rice reached Mr. Ramsey's this evening, to my great delight.

JANUARY 26TH, THURSDAY
Colonel Rice and myself called on Bishop Green—thence to Dr. Vaughn's.

I spent an hour with George Williams and his wife (a daughter of Colonel Baskerville's) after that another hour with Mr. DeBow. Colonel, or

---

Farrow & Bennett, 1866), 106. Further, Miller is not named in an 1862 list of clergy in Alabama. Clebsch, *Journals*, III-214-15.

22. Like Hudson, Capt. Henry Irwin was an aide-de-camp to General Elzey. Henry Irwin CSR, Confederate General and Staff Officers, RG 109, M-331, NA.

23. William Aiken (1806–1887) of South Carolina had been governor of the state from 1844 to 1846.

rather Brig. General Stark and Mr. Matthews called upon me and we discussed some religious topics very agreeably—after which the question of emancipation came up and Mr. Matthews said that all his property was in slaves, but he was willing for either immediate or prospective emancipation if it would secure our independence.[24] Mr. Beverly Matthews is a lawyer of prominence in Columbus and well acquainted with the sentiments of the people of this section. His opinion is that there would be great unanimity on the question of emancipation provided it would adjust in the settlement of the War.

From the Army, I get no news of interest. Lee's Corps has already moved to Georgia and Cheatham's is on its way. Stewart is still at Tupelo. I learn that Generals Beauregard, Hood and Taylor united in a request to President Davis for General Johnston's restoration to command.

Spent the evening at Mrs. Perkins'.[25] Bishop and Miss Green with Mr. Schwrar rode out with me. A select party of some fifty persons was present.

JANUARY 27TH, FRIDAY
No train yet and therefore the Bishop and myself did not get off as we expected for Macon, Mississippi. The Bishop handed me an envelope containing $200, an offering from the vestry of the parish. Though in no particular need of money, I appreciated the gift very highly and was glad it was made through the Bishop. Surely I have abundant cause for thankfulness for the manner in which I have been supplied with means. Tea at Dr. Brownrigg's with Father Miller where I had much pleasant conversation with the family on Christ and the Church.[26]

JANUARY 28TH, SATURDAY
At home all day reading. The telegraph reports that Mr. Blair is making a second visit to Richmond and that Vice-President Stephens, Judge

24. Peter Burwell Starke (1815–1888) was a Mississippi politician who commanded a regiment of cavalry through much of the war. At this point, Starke was stationed near Columbus awaiting the organization of a brigade he was to command. Warner, *Generals in Gray*, 288; OR 49(1):992.

25. Of the various Perkinses listed in the 1860 federal census for Lowndes County, Mississippi, the most likely to host a party for a "select . . . fifty persons" was Loueza Perkins, then age forty-three, wife of Calvin Perkins, then age fifty-four, a planter with property valued at $180,000.

26. The 1860 federal census for Lowndes County, Mississippi, lists John Brownrigg, then age thirty, a physician.

Campbell, Assistant Secretary of War, and the Hon. R. M. T. Hunter have gone to Washington on a peace mission. The thought of peace makes me almost hold my breath, but I fear the time is not yet. Great good will, I am sure, grows out of their efforts. If it does not result in peace, it will at least unite our country and stimulate our army.

JANUARY 29TH, 4TH SUNDAY AFTER EPIPHANY
After Morning Prayer by the Rev. Mr. Schwrar, and Ante-Communion by Bishop Green, I preached to a crowded congregation, "Repentance." The people gave me their undivided attention for a very long sermon.

In the evening at 3½ I read prayers and Schwrar preached a very good sermon on the text "Rejoice Evermore." He is going to be a useful man in the Church.

JANUARY 30TH, MONDAY
Tea at Mr. Evans with Captain Course.[27] No locomotive on the branch road to this place and so I do no know how long I may be detained. I have been wonderfully interested in reading the diary of John Wesley. Surely he was abundant in labors, a very apostle in faithfulness up to the utmost limit of human life. One thing is very evident—he had no idea of setting up a Church. He says under the date of 25th of July, 1786—"Our Conference began. About eighty preachers attended. On Thursday in the afternoon we permitted any of the Society to be present and weighed what was said about separating from the Church. But we all determined to continue therein without one dissenting voice. And I doubt not but this determination will stand, at least till I am removed into a better world."

In all notices on this subject his language is emphatic. Under date, July 3, 1789—"Our little Conference began in Dublin. I never saw such a company of preachers before, so unanimous in all points, particularly as to leaving the Church which none of them had the least thought of."

"July 28, 1789. The Conference began, about one hundred preachers present. The case of separation from the Church was largely considered,

27. Mr. Evans cannot be identified with certainty. Two possible candidates are listed in the 1860 federal census for Lowndes County, Joel Evans, then age forty-one, a merchant who apparently resided in a boarding house, and Richard, then age fifty-four, a lawyer of some means. The only means of identifying "Course" is a note on the endpaper of the first volume of the diary, bearing the signature of "R. M. Cource, Corps of Engineers, Meridian, Miss."

and we were all unanimous against it." (See *A Charge to the Clergy of Norwich* by Bishop Horne given at his primary visitation.)[28]

JANUARY 31ST, TUESDAY

Reading most of the day in my room. Telegraph reports Ex-President Pierce is on his way to Washington to meet our Commissioners. May the Lord show His loving kindness and our land give once more her increase.[29]

At this point the first volume of the surviving diary ends. Quintard made notations on the flyleaf and endpapers relative to the deaths of Beckham, Strahl, Marsh, Young, Granbury, and Cleburne. He also pasted a newspaper clipping of Albert Sidney Johnston's address to his troops before Shiloh and other miscellaneous items.

The next volume starts with another miscellany. Included are several postwar newspaper articles; an article criticizing the proposition that Jefferson Davis was not a Christian; an Order of Service prescribed by Bishop Elliott of Georgia; a prayer for the president and government of the Confederate States offered at St. Paul's Church on February 22, 1862; a newspaper clipping with Stephen D. Lee's address to his troops dated December 18, 1864 (see OR 45[2]:706–7); a letter from L. H. Whittle of Macon, Georgia, dated May 14, 1878, relative to the affairs of the University of the South; a newspaper clipping of a published letter from Henry S. Foote of Tennessee relative to his efforts to secure a peace, dated December 24, 1864; a proclamation by Jefferson Davis of a day of fasting and prayer dated March 10, 1865; newspaper accounts of a resolution of the Confederate Congress inviting John Bell Hood to visit the Congress and of the two marriages (Clare-Hadley and Moore-Hays) celebrated in December near Nashville; and a newspaper printing of Quintard's poem on Strahl and Marsh.

FEBRUARY 1ST, WEDNESDAY

The telegrams report the commissioners at Petersburg on Monday—so that it will be some days before we can hear any news from Washington.

28. This parenthetical note was CTQ's.
29. At this point in the diary appear a romantic poem attributed to Capt. Thomas Henry, a postwar newspaper clipping with a poem entitled "My Wife," and an undated letter from Lt. Gen. Stephen D. Lee that states: "Will send for your horse and will send him with mine."

I am still detained in Columbus, as the locomotive has not yet returned to the branch road, but is still employed in transporting troops south.

This evening I spent very pleasantly at Mrs. Baskerville's with Mr. DeBow and Mr. Gallagher.[30] Mr. DeB. is of the opinion that we shall have peace by 1st of May. I think the decline in Gold in Richmond, in the face of our recent disasters is his principal reason for believing that England, France and Spain have given some ultimatum to the U. S. Government.

FEBRUARY 2ND, THURSDAY

Genl Elzy is still disappointed in the arrival of the steamer "Admiral," on which we expect to embark for Demopolis.

Read with great pleasure the sermon on "The Origin of Civil Government" by Dr. George Home—Lord Bishop of Norwich. He argues that even a state of nature is a state of subordination since a parent must have had supreme authority over the child—as mankind multiplied, they were compelled to separate and disperse, which they did under their natural rulers the chiefs of families. By these means the earth became gradually filled with *little* governments. When between these disputes were ———, terminating in war, victory at last declared for one of the parties, and the other was obliged to submit. Thus, the *larger* governments arose by conquest, first swallowed up the lesser into themselves and ——— did with and overthrew each other. See X Genesis for an account of lesser governments with which the earth was overspread by the progeny of the sons of Noah. And in the same Chapter we read it very soon after. Nimrod—a mighty hunter—or conqueror—reared the government of Babel, which in process of time, under different names became universal, till grown too great to support its own weight, it was subverted by the Persian, as a Persian was by the Grecian and the Grecian by a Roman; out of which last were formed the empires, kingdoms and states, at this day subsisting.

He says, "If we consider it"—the utmost energy of the nervous style of Thucydides, and the great copiousness and expression of the Greek language, seem to sink under the historian when he attempts to describe the disorders which arose from faction, throughout all the Grecian commonwealths, "that Appian's history of the Roman civil wars contains the most

30. The only two Gallaghers listed in the 1860 federal census for Lowndes County, Mississippi, are William Gallagher, then age sixty-four, and Amzie Gallagher, then forty-five, both farmers.

frightful picture of massacres, proscriptions, forfeitures, that ever was presented to the world;" (Hume) if at the same time we recollect the confusion and desolation once occasioned in our own country, by the project of creating a government upon the plan of those famous democracies, we shall find no temptation to exchange a regular and well constituted monarchy for a *Republic*—especially as we must be first thrown into that imaginary political chaos, falsely called a state of nature, before the fair creature can emerge. Like the Israelites of old we must first break off all that is precious and valuable, and cast it into a fire, and from thence may come out this idol, at the feet of which kings and kingdoms are to fall down and worship.

I have read also with great interest Sir William Temple's "Essay upon the Origin & Nature of Government" written in 1678. He has the following definitions: "Now the Father of a Family or Nation, that uses his *servants* like *children* in point of justice and care; and advises with his children in what concerns the commonwealth, and thereby is willingly followed or obeyed by them all, is what I suppose the schools mean by a *Monarch*. And he that by harshness of nature, willfulness of humor, intemperance of ———, and arbitrariousness of commands, uses his *children* like servants, is what they mean by a Tyrant."

Wishing to extend the circulation of the "Church Intelligencer" I asked Mrs. Waddell and Miss Ramsey to call upon some of the Church families and ask for subscriptions.[31] They brought me fifteen names—and $150 for the papers and $157 to be expended in Church Tracts.

Lt. Col. Llewelyn Hoxton spent a night with me. He is a man for whom I feel a very cordial friendship. Of an old Virginia family—from Alexandria—he was carefully nurtured in the Church and had instilled into his mind and heart the principles of virtue and religion by the quiet and silent, but steady influences of a Christian home. He graduated at the West Point Military Academy in 1861 and after reaching Washington resigned his commission in the U.S. Army. His resignation was not accepted but his name was stricken from the roll. He crossed over to Virginia, and was ordered on duty by the Secretary of War with General Polk. He has been a most faithful soldier and on many a battlefield has dis-

31. The 1860 federal census for Lowndes County, Mississippi, lists Elizabeth Waddell, then age thirty-two, residing in Dr. Brownrigg's household. The census also lists John C. Ramsey, a merchant, with two daughters who were possibly CTQ's "Miss Ramsey": Felicia, then age sixteen, and Mary, then age twelve.

played a most conspicuous gallantry. While our Army was at Shelbyville in 1863, I presented him, with others, for Confirmation though he had previously received the Holy Sacrament at the hands of the Rev. Dr. French, Chaplain at West Point.[32] He adorns the Christian profession by an earnest and humble walk. I have strong hopes that he will ultimately take orders in the Church.

FEBRUARY 3RD, FRIDAY

The telegraph reports the appointment of General Lee as Commander in Chief of the Armies of the Confederate States. It will give profound satisfaction to the people. I called this morning on the Rev. Dr. C. now under sentence of suspicion. It is a sad and most lamentable case. He has been a most useful minister of the church for years. At one time was the Editor of the *Banner of the Cross*. A man of fine intellect and extensive reading—but he fell grievously—through strong drink.[33]

Mr. J. D. B. DeBow handed me $50 for the Church Tracts—making a total of $207.

Lt. Charles Martin of Columbia Tenn. spent the night with me. Heavy rain all night.[34]

The moral, or practical part of the apostolical sermons and epistles, is generally the last and the shortest, and comes after the apostles have enlightened the understanding with a knowledge of Christ, and warmed the heart with some great doctrine of salvation; as they knew, that one stroke, when the iron was hot, did more execution than twenty when it was cold. See I Cor. XV. Where after 57 verses upon a doctrine, the apostle closes with one only, by way of practical inference.

32. John W. French became a chaplain and a professor at West Point in 1856. Francis B. Heitman, *Historical Register and Dictionary of the United States Army, from Its Organization, September 29, 1789, to March 2, 1903*, 2 vols. (Washington: U.S. Government Printing Office, 1903), 1:437.

33. The *Banner of the Cross* was "a well known and influential church weekly" published in Philadelphia. It is probable "Rev. Dr. C." was Rev. Dr. John Coleman (1804–1872), one time rector of Trinity Church in Philadelphia and for many years the editor of the *Banner. National Cyclopedia of American Biography*, s.v. "Coleman, Leighton." Another source states that Coleman was born in 1803 and died in St. Louis in 1869. Thomas William Herringshaw, *Herringshaw's Encyclopedia of American Biography of the Nineteenth Century* (Chicago: American Publisher's Association, 1902), 235.

34. The 1860 federal census for Maury County, Tennessee lists a Charles F. Martin, then age seventeen. There is no listing for a Lt. Charles F. Martin among Tennessee Confederate soldiers.

"Take up your cross and follow me" may be a hard saying, but "Depart ye cursed into everlasting fire," is a much harder.[35]

Absolute Supremacy of Christ
I. Tim. VI.15—Rev. XVII.14 Rev. XIX.16

Here, if in the first text absolute supremacy is proved to belong to God so by the latter the expression being the same it proves it to belong to Christ who therefore is a Supreme God.—The same might be said of the other titles of God, which in one part or other of the scriptures are all given to Christ.

"Morality without religion"—says Bishop Home, "is the scheme of the deists; who yet that they may not seem destitute of a system, affect a religion which they call natural. But their natural religion hath no affinity to Christianity, it is inconsistent with it, and opposite to it. It hath no Saviour, no Sanctification, no fall of man, no atonements, no sacrifice, no sacraments, no Sabbath, no temples, no Church, no priesthood, no resurrection, no life everlasting. It hath no creed for it hath nothing to form a creed upon; and so is a religion without that principle, which alone gives value and signification to every moral action. The heathens never depended for acceptance on any such plan of religion; they had recourse to rites of worship, sacrifices, supplications, and other acts of what we call devotion, for obtaining the pardon of sin, and the averting of divine vengeance." (Charge to Clergy of Norwich 8.3).

At night—read a quaint little book entitled "A Letter from a Blacksmith to the Ministers & Elders of the Church of Scotland in which the manner of public worship in that Church is considered—its inconveniences and defects pointed out and etc." It bears date "Inverary May 8, 1758" and is quite a remarkable production. Its argument against extemporary prayers and in favor of prescript forms is full and very complete. The author's account of the sacramental *"occasions"* as they are called exhibits a fearful degree of irreverence as prevailing at the period in which he wrote in the Kirk of Scotland. "As it is managed at present," he says, "it is liken anything than the administration of the Supper of our Lord." The field preachings which preceded the administration is described as "an odd mixture of religion, sleep, drinking, courtship, and a confusion of sexes, ages and characters."

35. Here CTQ inserts a footnote: "Titles applied to Christ: Jer. XXIII.6 Isa. VIII.13 1 Cor X.9, — — — XXXIII.17 18 Isa IX.6 Jude. ult. Rom IX 5. Rev XXII 6—16 Rev. I.8.11."

In the Kirks in Scotland the communion is administered at tables long enough to seat about an hundred persons at which the communicants sit. This practice is very well handled by the "Blacksmith" but in no part of his subject is he so *full and unanswerable* as that of Public Prayer.

FEBRUARY 4TH, SATURDAY

A disagreeable day—but I found sufficient entertainment in the first Volume of the "[The Literature and the] Literary Men of Great Britain & Ireland, by A. Mills." In his XX Lecture I find a very fair notice of Chillingsworth—the author of "The Religion of the Protestants a Safe Way to Salvation." This great work placed its admirable author in the very first rank of religious controversialists, and is one of the ablest defenses of Protestantism ever produced.

While a student at Oxford the Jesuit John Perse—or as he is commonly called, Fisher, took every opportunity of coming into contact with Chillingsworth and other university students and the Jesuit ultimately succeeded in arguing him into a belief in the doctrines of popery by main argument, and led to this result, was that which maintains the necessity of an infallible living guide in matters of faith, to which character the Romish Church appeared to him to be best entitled. Chillingsworth left Oxford and repaired to the Jesuits College at Dornay, in France. Archbishop Land, his godfather, then Bishop of London, induced him to return to England and he re-entered the University of Oxford where, after additional study of the points of difference he declared in favor of the Protestant faith. The controversies growing out of his change of views gave rise to his great and unanswerable work, which was published A.D. 1637.

John Yanden did great service to the cause of the royalists by various publications, but his great service to that party consisted in writing the famous "Ikou basilike, or the Portraiture of his most sacred Majesty in his solitude and his Sufferings." The sensation which it produced in favor of the unfortunate Charles was extraordinary. Many have not scrupled to ascribe to that book the subsequent restoration of the royal family. Milton compares its effects to those which were wrought on the tumultuous Romans by Antony's reading to them of the will of Caesar. In 1662, after the Restoration, Yanden was made Bishop of Worcester, but he died on the 20th of September of the same year.

Genl Elzy sent me a note this evening informing me of the arrival of the "Admiral," but I have determined to remain over Sunday, as Bishop

Green promises to give me the Offertory, for the purchase of church tracts for the Army.

FEBRUARY 5TH, FIFTH SUNDAY AFTER EPIPHANY
A rainy and disagreeable day. A small congregation. Schwrar read Morning Prayer—the Bishop the Ante-Communion and I preached. After the sermon the Bishop confirmed Mr. Samuels of Memphis, who I hope will not only witness a good confession before men, but glorify God in the ministry.[36] No service in the evening in consequence of the inclemency of the weather. The offertory amounted to $157.75. Lt. Colonel Hoxton and myself dined at Major Beckwith's. Bishop Jeremy Taylor has a following beautiful passage on

Useful Studies
"Spend not your time in that which profits not, for your labor and your health, your time and your studies are very valuable; and it is a thousand pities to see a diligent and hopeful person spend himself in gathering cockle-shells, and little pebbles, in tilling sands upon the shores, and making garlands of useless daisies. Study that which is profitable, that which will make you useful to Churches and commonwealths, that which will make you desirable and wise. Only I shall add this to you, that in learning there are variety of things as in religion, there is mint and cumin, and there are the weightier matters of the law; so there are studies more and less useful, and everything that is useful will be required in its time; and I may in this also use the words of our blessed Saviour 'These things ought you to look after, and not to leave the others unregarded.' But your great care is to be in the things of God and of religion, in holiness and true wisdom, remembering the saying of Origen "That the knowledge that arises from worship, is something that is more certain and more divine than all demonstrations, than all other learnings of the world."

Yesterday I had a very earnest conversation with Col. Samuel C. Williams, of the Artillery, on the subject of his duty to confess Christ. I presented him a Prayer Book. Both Hoxton and himself remain in Columbus, as attendants of General Lee, at his marriage which takes place on Thursday next.[37]

36. Mr. Samuels cannot be identified. There are no Samuels listed in the 1860 federal census for Shelby County, Tennessee.

37. Lt. Col. Samuel C. Williams of Knoxville, Tennessee, commanded the artillery of Stewart's Corps during the Battle of Nashville, where he sustained a wound. OR 45(1): 668; James A. Turpin, "Darden's Battery," CV 9 (November 1901): 514.

FEBRUARY 6TH, MONDAY
A rainy and disagreeable day. In the evening called to say goodbye to Mr. Sherman, Captain Course, Mrs. Waddell and Mrs. Ward. Mrs. Ward's only son Charles died in Macon, Georgia of a wound received in the Georgia Campaign.[38] He was attended in his last hours by the Rev. Telfair Hodgson and received the Holy Communion just previous to his death.[39]

Later I called on Lt. General Lee who gave me a letter published in the Columbus (Geo.) Times of February 1st comparing the relative merits of Generals J. E. Johnston and Hood, in which are some remarkable statements. It is signed "Texas." I must get a copy when I reach home. The General urged me to remain over Thursday—but I felt compelled to decline—which I greatly regret as I would have the pleasure of meeting Gen. Randall Gibson who I specially desired to see. Bishop Green and the Rev. Mr. Miller came up to take tea with me and after supper Colonel Williams and Major C.[40]

Obtained transportation to Columbus, Georgia from Major Anderson, Post Quartermaster, by order of Lt. General Taylor.

FEBRUARY 7TH, TUESDAY
Left Columbus in a car very much crowded but had some pleasant travelling companions among whom were Colonel Duckworth and Major Allen, at present under sentence of arrest for refusing to report in obedience to orders to Colonel Rucker. They are gallant soldiers who proved their steel on many a well-fought field. They go to Enterprise to spend the time that yet remains until the expiration of their sentence.[41]

38. Mr. Sherman was probably G. W. Sherman, who appears in the 1860 federal census for Lowndes County, Mississippi, as a merchant, then age forty. The 1860 federal census for Lowndes County lists E. B. Ward, then age forty-six, his wife Harriet, then age thirty-eight, and their son, Cocke, then age sixteen. Pvt. Charles Cocke Ward served in Company K, 14th Mississippi Regiment, which was engaged around Atlanta. Howell, *I'll Take My Stand*, 3:3067.

39. Telfair Hodgson (1840–1893) of Virginia enlisted as a private in the 44th Virginia Infantry and later a major on the staff of Maj. Gen. Joseph Wheeler. Ordained as a priest during the war by Bishop Elliott on the same day as CTQ's Columbus friend Frank Starr, Hodgson was later associated with CTQ at the University of the South as dean of the School of Theology and as vice chancellor. Donald Smith Armentrout, *The Quest for the Informed Priest: A History of the School of Theology* (Sewanee: School of Theology, University of the South, 1979) 55–56; Elliott diary, May 8, 1864, GDAH.

40. Major C cannot be identified.

41. William Lafayette Duckworth was colonel of the 7th Tennessee Cavalry and Philip T. Allin the major of the 26th Tennessee Cavalry Battalion, also known as "Forrest's Regiment." Duckworth and Allin, both veterans of the fighting in the west, disagreed with an order dated August 30, 1864, appointing Col. Edward Winchester Rucker commander of

232 / DOCTOR QUINTARD, CHAPLAIN C.S.A.

As I expected, the down train was packed so full that the only place we could find was on the platform of one of the cars. Finding it extremely disagreeable I got off determining to wait another day, but as I was passing by the ladies car General Sharpe called out to me begging me to come in, he would make standing room. I acted upon the —————— and on entering the car found several friends among them Brig. Gen. Lyon just out from Kentucky. He crossed the Tennessee at Gunter's Landing.[42]

Captain Stepleton, General Strahl's Quartermaster, was on board. He had been in West Tennessee and had seen the mother of my dear friend John Marsh. So my trip to Meridian was a very pleasant one. I made the acquaintance of Capt. A. A. Frierson of Tennessee, now A.I.G. of Strahl's Brigade. He is an exceedingly intelligent and agreeable man. Met Dr. Foster, Post Surgeon at the depot at Meridian, and I accepted his invitation to sojourn with him during my detention at this place. At his quarters, I found a squad of Nashville friends—General Maney, Capt. Alex Porter, Captain Rice, Major Vaulx, Captain Kelly and etc.

Had a very agreeable evening. I presented Major Tom Foster cloth for a suit of clothes and he gave me a pair of boots of which I am greatly in need.[43]

As I was leaving Columbus Mr. DeBow sent me a copy of the morning paper with his compliments, from which I clipped the following:

---

their brigade, deeming the senior officer of the brigade more appropriate. J. P. Young, *The Seventh Tennessee Cavalry* (1890; reprint Dayton, Ohio: Morningside Bookshop, 1976) 100–101; *OR* 39(2):831–32. At the time CTQ encountered these officers, Rucker was a Federal prisoner, having been wounded and captured in the retreat from Nashville. *OR* 45(1):766.

42. Here, the MS is difficult, reading "Brig. Gen. Ly——." In light of the reference to Kentucky and the crossing at Gunter's Landing, it is highly probable the officer in question was Brig. Gen. Hylan Benton Lyon of Kentucky (1836–1907), commander of the Confederate Department of Western Kentucky, who led a raid toward Clarksville, Tennessee, in conjunction with Hood's Tennessee campaign and ended up crossing the Tennessee River in canoes with the survivors of his command. See *OR* 45(1):803; Warner, *Generals in Gray*, 197; Jerry Keenan, *Wilson's Cavalry Corps: Union Campaigns in the Western Theatre, October 1864 through Spring 1865* (Jefferson, N.C.: McFarland & Co., 1998), 126–37. General Sharpe was probably Brig. Gen. Jacob Hunter Sharp (1833–1907) of Alabama and Mississippi, who commanded a Mississippi brigade of Lee's Corps that had been furloughed after escaping from Middle Tennessee. See *OR* 47(2):1285.

43. Maj. Thomas Foster was quartermaster of Maney's Brigade, although he spent several months in 1864 on sick leave with rheumatism. At this time, he was seeking to be relieved from field service in favor of a position at a hospital on account of his disability. T. Foster CSR, Confederate General and Staff Officers, RG 109, M-331, NA.

The Daily Southern Republic
Columbus, Mississippi, Tues., 2/7/65
Dr. Quintard

This eminent divine, who blends in harmonious proportion all the dignity and elevated graces of the Christian philosopher with the kindly and tender offices of the philanthropist, "going about doing good," after a visit of a few weeks, is about to leave us. The prayers of the devout and the heart's well wishes of the undevout go with him; for, while his matchless presentation of Christian truth has taken captive the soul of the one, it has charmed the understanding of the other. In developing food for serious thought it has developed the germ, in time will come the fruit of Christian life.

Amid all the vicissitudes of the fierce war that is raging, this "Soldier of the Cross" has found fitting post in the field—enduring its privations and its toils, ministering alike with glorious words of consolation and hope at the dying couch of great captains and humble followers of the camp. Beloved alike by soldier and general, his triumphs are those of Love and Peace and Truth, and his march has been onward through deeds nobler than those of helmeted knight to the highest recognition and, we trust in time, appointments of his church; for it may be truly said of this man:

> "There is a daily beauty in his life
> That makes *us* ugly."

It is pleasant enough to have agreeable things said of one but my friend's partiality has led him too far in the present instance if I know myself. God give me grace to value popularity only as an instrument of promoting the salvation of men. If He gives me favor in the sight of the people He will reckon with me for the use I will make of the talent committed. At the best it is a dangerous gift and favor is deceitful. "After ye have done all, say ye are unprofitable servants." May He give me the grace of humility that so I may walk surely amid all the changes and chances of life, whether fortune smiles or frowns on me.

FEBRUARY 8TH, WEDNESDAY
Visited Colonel Hurt commanding Maney's Brigade a mile out from Meridian. It is smaller than my old Regiment at the beginning of the war and

of all the thousand and more who came out in the 1st Tenn. Regt. in May, 1861—with the addition of the 27th Regt. and Captain Fulcher's Battalion— I found but fifty men remaining. Many have been killed—others have sickened and died, some are "in the house of bondage," and some have deserted their colors. It was a sad visit to me, but it rejoiced me very much to find them all well clothed, and there still remain one half of the clothes presented to me by Mr. Brown. Captains Rice and Porter accompanied me.[44]

FEBRUARY 9TH THURSDAY
Started at 6 A.M. for Demopolis in a miserable box car in which there were a number of soldiers returning to their commands. Their "filthy conversation" vexed me exceedingly. However, after a ride of two miles we reached the point at which the road was interrupted and after a walk of a quarter of a mile we found some passenger coaches and were comfortably enough seated. We reached Demopolis at 3 P.M. and shortly after Mr. Beckwith came in. We had a most cordial meeting. I went out with him to his home, the delightful residence of Mrs. Walter Winn—three miles from town.[45] The roads in this section of the county abound in mud during the winter season.

FEBRUARY 10TH, FRIDAY
Rode in town with Beckwith and spent the morning with Mrs. Wirt Adams. Here I had the pleasure of meeting my friend Dr. David Gordon and his accomplished sister Miss Mattie G. of Mississippi.[46] Dined at the Hon. Frank Lyons where a pleasant company was assembled—Dr. Sam'l Choppin of New Orleans, Lt. W. M. Polk, Mrs. General Deas and the

44. The 1st Tennessee Regiment had been consolidated with the 27th Tennessee Regiment in late 1862, prior to the battle of Murfreesboro. Apparently as an afterthought to the reorganization of April 1862, a battalion of three companies from Nashville previously known as Hawkins' Battalion was added to the 1st Tennessee, and designated as Company L, under Capt. Joseph W. Fulcher. Lindsley, *Military Annals*, 159, 160, 426.

45. The 1850 federal census for Marengo County, Alabama, lists Walter E. Winn, then age sixteen, as a student. The 1860 census lists W. E. Winn, then age twenty-five, as a lawyer, and his wife, Willie, then age twenty-three.

46. Mrs. Adams was the wife of Confederate cavalry general William Wirt Adams, who at that time commanded a brigade under Forrest. Warner, *Generals in Gray*, 2–3. Neither David Gordon nor his sister Mattie can be positively identified.

Misses Gale of Nashville.[47] Litany service at the Church at 4 P.M. which was well attended. Received a telegraphic dispatch from J. Rhodes Brown informing me that my family is all well.[48]

FEBRUARY 11TH, SATURDAY

Beckwith and myself sat up until 3 o'clock this morning comparing notes on diverse and sundry subjects. Having learned of the bad news of the death of young Cicero Hawks, son of my friend the Rev. William N. Hawks, I visited his grave this morning and for his poor mother's sake placed an evergreen cross upon it. He was mortally wounded by an accident on the railway—both legs being fractured and serious injuries internally rendering him insensible. The accident occurred on Sunday—and he died the following Tuesday. Mr. Beckwith was not informed [of] the matter until a very short time before his death. He officiated at his burial.

I made arrangements to have a substantial wooden cross placed at the head of his grave.

FEBRUARY 12TH, SEPTUAGESIMA SUNDAY

This morning the Church was packed full—the aisle, vestry room and all being crowded. I had been very much at a loss as to the character of sermon which would be most profitable. I was decided by meeting at Mrs. Wirt Adams with a Miss Farmer (her governess) who had just two days ago received intelligence of the death of her father who was accidentally killed at Canton, Mississippi.[49] The poor girl was in great distress and in

47. Francis Strother Lyon (1800–1882) was a lawyer, state legislator, and member of first the United States and then the Confederate Congresses. Samuel Choppin was the medical inspector on Beauregard's staff. See OR 39(2):824–25. Mrs. Deas was the wife of Brig. Gen. Zachariah Cantey Deas (1819–1882), who commanded a brigade in Maj. Gen. Edward "Allegheny" Johnson's division until Johnson was captured at Nashville, when he temporarily assumed command of the division. Warner, *Generals in Gray*, 70–71; CMH, 8:401–3. The Misses Gale are identified below as Anna and Mary Gale. In light of their presence with "Meck" Polk, it is likely they were sisters of Polk's brother-in-law, Captain William D. Gale, previously identified as A. P. Stewart's assistant adjutant general. See OR 47(3):750.

48. At this point is pasted a newspaper clipping from the *Telegraph*, entitled "Official Report of the Peace Commissioners." CTQ noted underneath: "So dies another hope."

49. If Miss Farmer and her family actually lived in Canton, Mississippi, it is likely that she was America Farmer, listed in the 1860 federal census for Madison County, Mississippi, as then age sixteen, in the household of W. H. Farmer, then age forty-two, an iron molder from Virginia.

religious matters entirely at sea—having been raised among the sects and not feeling good enough to come to Christ. I therefore preached on Repentance—its sacrificial character and etc. and she thanked me most hearty for it after the service. I never preached to a more attentive congregation. Many seemed deeply affected and Dr. Hinkley, the Post Surgeon, came to me with a full heart, and cheeks wet with tears, to tell me how thankful he was that all his doubts were satisfied.[50]

I rode out in the carriage with Mrs. Winn, Mrs. Beckwith and Mrs. Griffin and after dinner accompanied Mrs. Beckwith to the residence of Dr. Reese to attend a service for the negroes.[51] The service was held in a large back hall very comfortably seating from seventy five to a hundred. Mrs. Winn played the melodeon and the chanting was very good. The negroes repeated the 6th Selection of Psalms. After service by Mr. Beckwith I preached to them of the love of God. We took tea with the family and then went to my room at Mrs. Winn's where we spent some three hours very pleasantly before I retired. These people abound in wealth and ought to have a chapel for the negroes.

FEBRUARY 13TH, MONDAY
Another one of "Job's comforters" is giving me a good deal of annoyance, and I did not venture out of the house until evening when I rode to town to see Anna and Mary Gale, who were to leave for Jackson, Miss.

I went with them to the ferry-boat and returned with Meck Polk to Mr. Lyons' to dinner.

Dr. Gordon rode out to Mrs. Winn's to spend the night with me.

I ordered a substantial wooden cross made for the grave of Cicero Hawks.

FEBRUARY 14TH, TUESDAY
Though suffering a good deal from my boil, I rode to town in the buggy to dine at Mrs. General Adams'. The company consisted of the family,

50. Hargrove Hinkley of Tennessee was the surgeon in change of Demopolis' Way Hospital. Cunningham, *Doctors in Gray*, 289; H. Hinkley CSR, Confederate General and Staff Officers, RG 109, M-331, NA.
51. The 1850 federal census for Marengo County, Alabama, lists Henry W. Reese, then age thirty-seven, as a physician, and the 1870 census lists Dr. H. W. Reese then age fifty-eight, as a farmer. H. W. Reese also shows up as a planter in the 1860 census, but oddly is listed as age forty-four. While the census records do not list a likely Mrs. Griffin for this time period, in 1860, Goodman G. Griffin, with two teenaged sons and no wife, lived in the same locality with the Winns and Dr. Reese. It is possible CTQ's Mrs. Griffin was wed in the interval between the census and CTQ's visit.

Beckwith and myself. The dinner was very excellent, including oysters among its good things. Miss Mattie Gordon was in her happiest mood and it was a very pleasant visit. Mrs. Adams read to us a letter from her husband in which he speaks very despondingly of our prospects. Says the scouts report Thomas' army moving down to New Orleans, where are already gathered 20,000 troops, to attack Mobile. General Adams is a man of very hopeful disposition but he is "let down" a little in this letter.

FEBRUARY 15TH, WEDNESDAY
After riding in town to attend to a little business, Beckwith and myself started on horseback, for Greensboro, to visit Bishop Wilmer. Dr. Reese accompanied us to General Bocock's (eight miles) where we spent the night. General B. is an old Virginian, has everything of this world's goods to minister to his happiness, has a finely cultivated mind, and is a most agreeable gentleman.[52]
We spent the evening in discussing the life and times of John Randolph and his contemporaries. Genl B. was perfectly familiar with Mr. R.'s private life as well as his public career, and related many striking anecdotes of the eccentric statesman. Among others the following: At one time Mr. R, was threatened by a clique with personal indignity should he attempt to keep an appointment which he had made for a public discussion of the state of the country. It was immediately after his return from Russia. He began by saying: "My friends, I was early taught by the best of mothers, that the fear of the Lord is the beginning of wisdom, and I have learned by my own experience, that the fear of man is the consummation of folly."

FEBRUARY 16TH, THURSDAY
Dr. Reese returned home and after lunch at 11 o'clock we left the elegant mansion of Genl B. for a ride of 18 miles over wretched roads. We arrived at Greensboro at 4 P.M. and had a most cordial welcome from the Bishop and his family.

FEBRUARY 17TH, FRIDAY
A delightful day! The Bishop drove us out in the morning and the evening was passed in most agreeable conversation. Mrs. and Miss Avery met us

52. The 1870 federal census for Hale County, Alabama, lists W. B. Bocock from Virginia, age sixty-five, as a farmer with real and personal property valued at $26,000.

238 / DOCTOR QUINTARD, CHAPLAIN C.S.A.

at dinner.[53] The Bishop, while he is a most Godly man, in fact one of the most earnest minded and tenderest hearted of Christians that I have ever met,—has in full play a wit at once keen and searching. He was called on by Beckwith to relate his encounter with Dr. Nott (Nott & Glidden) celebrated for his free thinking and his antiscriptural writings.[54]

On an occasion of a visit to Mobile, Dr. Nott was introduced to the Bishop at an evening party. For some time the conversation ran on in the usual strain of the day, on the war, Dr. Nott evidently anxious to enter on a discussion with the Bishop, in which he could develop his peculiar views, finally said, "Bishop, there is one point on which we should not agree!" "What is that?" inquired the Bishop, all attention. "The human race is a failure," said the Dr. "Speak for yourself, Dr.," replied the Bishop. But it closed his mouth.

On another occasion the Bishop [was] visiting the sick wife of a notorious infidel who persistently urged his absurd notions without receiving any attention from the Bishop, and being provoked thereby, finally said, "Mr. Wilmer, you don't seem inclined to discuss religious topics." "I never do except in the most serious manner," replied the minister. "Well, why did Michael contend with the Devil for the body of Moses?" "Ah my friend, that is a question in which you at least are not interested." "And why not?" "Because the devil will never have any discussion concerning your body, that point is settled." During the evening the Bishop gave me the following lines, which I think very beautiful, the author is unknown.[55]

FEBRUARY 18TH, SATURDAY
Spent the morning with the Bishop, in his study. Colonel Allen Jones and Captain Weymiss called. We dined at the parsonage with the Rev. R. H. Cobbs.[56] His wife was Miss Fanny Avery and I was very much pleased to

53. No Averys are listed in the 1860 federal census for Hale County, Alabama. Twenty-one are listed in the 1870 census, making the identification of Mrs. and Miss Avery impossible.

54. Dr. Josiah Clarke Nott (1804–1873) started the medical school of the state university at Mobile in 1858 and served as a surgeon in the Confederate army. As CTQ indicates, he wrote several works on natural history that challenged biblical authority, two of which with Englishman George R. Glidden. Owen, History of Alabama, 4:1288–91.

55. At this point CTQ copies a four-stanza poem of a religious nature entitled "Nothing But Leaves."

56. Allen C. Jones held an Alabama state commission and was charged with the superintendence of the construction of certain river defenses in late 1862. OR 52(2):400. Captain Weymiss is the editor's best interpretation of a difficult portion of the diary and cannot be

meet her again. After dinner we rode several miles and on our return called on Gen. Lucius Polk at Colonel Jones'. In the evening Profs Wills and Lupton of the Methodist College called in.[57] They are pleasant men and men of sense. The one occupies the Chair of Mathematics, the other, that of Chemistry. What a remarkable development Methodism has had since the date of Mr. Wesley's letter to the Rev. Francis Asbury—dated London, 20th Sept. 1788, in which he says: "I study to be little; you study to be great. I creep; you strut along. I found a school; you a *college*; nay and call it after your own names! O beware!" With all its driftings Methodism has lost its individuality and must ultimately be absorbed by the Church. God hasten the day when in all the earth there shall be but one Lord, one Faith and one Baptism as there is but one God and Father of us all.

FEBRUARY 19TH, SEXAGESIMA SUNDAY
As there was to be a Confirmation Bishop Wilmer requested me to preach on the subject of the "Laying on of Hands." Morning Prayer was said by the Rev. Mr. Beckwith—the Bishop reading the Ante-Communion Service. I preached for more than an hour, and the congregation listened attentively apparently without waning—and I trust with much profit. Five candidates were presented by Mr. Cobbs. Three of them soldiers— one came up leaning on his crutch. How true it is that those men who do their duty to their community are most likely to do there duty to their God.

After the service a collection was taken up for Army Missions amounting to $530. In the afternoon I read service and Beckwith gave us one of his admirable sermons—on the life and character of St. Paul. I am more and more impressed with his power both in the desk and in the pulpit and feel confident that the day is not distant when he will be called to do some great work for Christ and the Church. After evening service Colonel Allen Jones took me one side and stated that several gentlemen of the congregation desired him to present me a small token of their kind regard

---

identified. Rev. Richard H. Cobbs was rector of St. Paul's Church in Greensboro. Clebsch, *Journals*, III-214.

57. The Methodist college was Southern University, which began operation in Greensboro under the sponsorship of the Methodist Episcopal Church in 1859. The school survives as the present-day Birmingham Southern University. J. C. Wills was professor of mathematics from 1859 to 1871, and N. Thomas Lupton was professor of chemistry for the same period. Owen, *History of Alabama*, 2:1259–62.

and handed me $700. It took me greatly by surprise. Surely the Lord has given me favor in the sight of the people.

We said farewell to the Bishop and family and rode out a couple of miles to the residence of Mrs. Avery to spend the night. Mr. and Mrs. Cobbs spent the evening with us. This day has been a most agreeable one and I trust the word preached may be blessed to all who heard it.

Greensboro is one of the pleasantest towns I have visited in Alabama. Being off from the main line of travel, with no railroad, it is very quiet and shows few marks of war. The people know very little of its horrors.

FEBRUARY 20TH, MONDAY
Up early and rolled in a bowling alley before breakfast. It is a capital exercise. Miss Mary Avery beat me badly so I set myself down as a poor player. We started for Demopolis at 10 o'clock and reached Mr. Henry Taylor's at 3 P.M. where we dined. Arrived at Mrs. Winn's at 5 and found the Rev. Mr. Hanson who had called to see us.[58]

In the evening Major Gibson from the Transmississippi Department came in.[59] He is here to get a wife and is to be married on Wednesday evening. He is an intelligent gentleman and gave me a great deal of information in regard to the condition of our army in his Department. He says that all of the reports we hear of the ———culation by General Kirby Smith's army are greatly exaggerated and most of them false. That our army there is in really good condition and ready for active operations.[60]

58. The 1870 federal census for Hale County, Alabama, lists Henry C. Taylor, age thirty, as a stage agent. The 1860 federal census for Marengo County, Alabama, lists T. J. Hanson of Maryland, then fifty-three, a minister. Also, pasted here is a newspaper clipping entitled "One Year's Work of Forrest's Command," wherein Forrest recounts the work done under his command by the Confederate cavalry in the District of Mississippi and East Louisiana in 1864. The address from whence the excerpt was printed can be found at OR 45(1):759–60.

59. Major Gibson may have been Maj. Albert C. Gibson, who originally served as chief of ordnance in Maj. Gen. Simon Boliver Buckner's division when it was stationed in East Tennessee in 1863. In 1864, he applied for duty in the Trans-Mississippi Department with Buckner. There is no record of Gibson past October 27, 1864, when he applied, with the recommendation of Trans-Mississippi commander Gen. Edmund Kirby Smith, for the position of aide-de-camp. He was paroled at Meridian, Mississippi, on May 12, 1865, which suggests that he never made it back across the river. A. C. Gibson CSR, Confederate General and Staff Officers, RG 109, M-331, NA.

60. At this point in the diary is a newspaper clipping entitled "Their Resting Place," relative to CTQ's burial of Cleburne, Strahl, Granbury, and Marsh near the black and white Federal soldiers at Columbia. According to the article, CTQ "remembered that General Cleburne, as he rode by a certain country church and cemetery, near Columbia,

Thomas has gone down the Mississippi with his forces—his destination not known. Sherman is moving toward Columbia, S.C., but the papers contain nothing of interest.

FEBRUARY 21ST, TUESDAY
Breakfasted with Rev. Mr. Hanson, and Mr. Taylor (of Virginia) at Dr. Reese's, thence to town and called on the Lyons; and Mrs. Major Ross, thence back to dinner at Dr. Reese's.[61] Meck Polk is ordered to Mobile, which I regret. Colonel Williams of the artillery and Hoxton are also there, so that he will have pleasant companions. I learned at the office of the Railroad that orders have been received to have everything in readiness to remove the rolling stock from the railway from this place to Meridian—10,000 cavalry reported to have crossed Big Black.[62]

FEBRUARY 22ND, WEDNESDAY
Left Demopolis about 3 P.M. for Selma where I arrived about 10½ O'clock. Had for traveling companion my excellent friend Frank Dunnington, Esq. of Columbia, Tenn. We put up for the night at the Gee House and in the morning I paid for lodging and breakfast $13.00. I declined breakfast.

FEBRUARY 23RD, THURSDAY
Had the great pleasure of meeting Harry Yeatman and Major Thomas Peters.[63] During the morning I visited the Naval works and spent some time

a few days before, had remarked that if he had choice of his burial spot, that would be the place. The next day the Doctor had the bodies of those veteran heroes disinterred and removed to their resting place, in Ashwood, one of the most charming spots that they could rest in."

61. The 1860 federal census for Marengo County, Alabama, lists three Virginians of substance who might have been Mr. Taylor. The same census lists three planters of substance who might have been "Major Ross," two of whom with what appears to be a wife of a suitable age to be "Mrs. Major Ross." Neither candidate appears on Confederate soldier rosters.

62. At this point in the diary there are several miscellaneous items, the first being a newspaper clipping with a story credited to the February 7, 1865, *Richmond Examiner*, describing a rally of "ten thousand people" addressing the failure of the peace conference at Hampton Roads. Next appears a poem relative to a sculptor boy attributed to Bishop Donne, and, finally, another newspaper clipping entitled "The Pope's Manifesto—The Most Important Document of the Century," relative to an encyclical letter against "isms" and "revolution," issued on December 8, 1864.

63. Like Yeatman, Peters had once been on Bishop Polk's staff, in this case as quartermaster. At this time Peters was probably serving as chief of steamboat and railroad transportation of the Department of Alabama, Mississippi, and East Louisiana. See OR 39(2):837.

with Catesby Jones. We had much pleasant chat about our Virginia friends. He has done a vast amount of work at this place. He has some 400 workmen employed only 90 of whom are whites. He has up to this time turned out 190 guns besides doing much other work for the government. He went through the works with me and showed the different steps from the melting of the ore to the drilling of the guns. He is casting the Brooks gun almost exclusively and says that it combines more good points than any other. While in the office Mr. Phillips of North Carolina called in to see the works. He is just from Richmond having traveled with Vice President Stephens to Georgia. He says that Mr. Hunter during the four hour interview with Mr. Lincoln and Mr. Seward suggested many instances in which governments had treated with insurgents and mentioned an instance in the time of Charles I. Mr Lincoln said: "Seward may know about the history of that, all I know is that Charles I lost his head." Dined with Yeatman and about 5 P.M. we went to Major Peters' for tea. Heavy rain all afternoon.

FEBRUARY 24TH, FRIDAY
Rain all night and all the morning. On Sunday the 19th the enemy is reported to have confronted a portion of Cheatham's Corps two miles from Newberne Court House which is in a northwesterly direction from Columbia, S.C. It is said to have been only a feint to cover operations on Columbia. They retired rapidly on Sunday night and burned the bridges over the Congaree and Saluda at Alston and Saluda pressing on to join their main army toward Charleston. On Saturday another body of the enemy on . . .[64]

Took Steamer "Cherokee" at 5 P.M. for Montgomery. Had excellent accommodations, but the night was dark and tempestuous. The continual lightning—it may have helped us along.

FEBRUARY 25TH, SATURDAY
Reached Montgomery at 10 o'clock A.M., too late by a couple of hours for the Columbus train and so I am compelled to spend Sunday in this city of Montgomery. My expenses on the steamer were $25, to wit—three cups of genuine coffee, furnished by one the servants—$15 and gratuity, to the boy for waiting on me and caring for my "traps" $10.

I drove immediately to the Rectory and was most cordially welcomed

64. At this point the diary is illegibly faded for a space of about twenty lines.

by my friend Mitchell whose excellent wife is just now recovering from a severe illness she was visited with as I passed through here in November. Several persons called upon me during the day, and at night Mitchell and I attend[ed] the meeting of the citizens called to consider the present condition of our public affairs. The theater was crowded to excess, we could scarcely get standing room. When we reached the place Governor Watts was addressing the assembled multitude. He spoke for more than an hour—made many good points—defended President Davis, and altogether his speech was an able one, practical and thoroughly patriotic, he referred to the difference in spirit exhibited by the people at home and the soldiers in the Army and said a tribute to the soldiers of Georgia, Louisiana, Mississippi and Tennessee for the noble resolutions they had passed; he condemned the recent message of Governor Joseph E. Brown of Georgia in immeasured terms and said that it contained more false statements than he had ever known in a public document. He did not mean to accuse Governor Brown of lying but Governor B. owed it to himself as a public man to have verified the rumors and reports on which his statements were based. Governor Watts was followed by the Hon. W. P. Chilton, Lt. Colonel Gaines, 53d Alabama Regiment, Col. Mike L. Woods, 45th Alabama and others.[65] Hon. B. S. Bibb presided—the following resolutions were adopted.

The committee, through Mr. Samuel G. Jones, reported the following resolutions, which were adopted unanimously by a rising vote:

WHEREAS, The United States are, by their own confession, waging a war for the subjugation or extermination of the people of the Confederate States, and have unequivocally refused to consider any proposition of peace, which does not involve our unconditional submission to the Government of the United States, the emancipation of our slaves and the general confiscation of our property, with

65. William Parish Chilton (1810–1871) was an Alabama legislator and judge who served in the Confederate Congress, and Benajah Smith Bibb (1796–1884) was an Alabama legislator and judge, at this time the judge of the criminal court in Montgomery. Owen, *History of Alabama*, 3:142, 324. Lt. Col. John F. Gaines of the 53rd Alabama Cavalry was wounded at Waynesboro, Georgia, in November 1864. Michael Leonard Woods, colonel of the 46th Alabama Infantry, was captured with his regiment at Champion's Hill in the Vicksburg campaign. There is no record of any subsequent service, although he appears to have been a prisoner as of the end of 1864. *CMH*, 8:200, 283–84; *OR* 24(2):102; *OR*, Series 2, 7:1227, 1278.

our only leasehold upon life itself dependent upon the assurances of Abraham Lincoln, that he will make a liberal use of the pardoning power for the benefit of repentant rebels—Therefore

Resolved, That, with undiminished faith in the right and justice of our cause, and in humble dependence on Almighty God, we will maintain the struggle, until our independence is established; and to this end we pledge our lives, our fortunes and our sacred honor.

Resolved, That we regard the gallant achievements of our brave defenders, both officers and privates, with patriotic pride; that we cannot be too grateful for their self-sacrificing services; and we tender them assurances of our heartfelt thanks, and our deepest sympathies in their toils and sufferings.

Resolved, That the crime of desertion, confessedly deserving, and always punishable, with death, in the army, is more excusable in a soldier in the field, than in persons at home, who, shielded by the army from the hardships of the war, in the hour of their country's need, desert her cause, and seek to curry favor with a foe, whom they have not the manliness to oppose.

Resolved, That the surest remedy for desertion in the army, is a zealous and uncompromising support of our cause, by the people at home.

Resolved, That, as a practical manifestation of our appreciation of the services of our armies, we solemnly pledge ourselves to each other and to the soldiers in the field to renewed exertions to relieve the necessities of their families, and thus lift from their hearts the only burden calculated to unnerve the arm of a freeman in a contest like this.

Resolved, In the language of the eminent senator from Virginia, that we recommend to the people of our whole Confederacy, "faith in our cause, faith in our Government, faith in ourselves, faith in each other, and faith in God."

FEBRUARY 26TH, QUINQUAGESIMA SUNDAY
Morning prayer was said by the Rev. Mr. Mitchell and myself, the Rev. J. Avery Shepherd, reading the Ante-Communion service. I preached on Repentance. At 5 P.M. after dinner at Dr. Thomas Taylor's, I baptized in the adjoining house
Albert
Son of Lt. Col. Albert J. and Lou H. Smith

Age 3 weeks
Sponsors
   Larkin Smith
   Eva J. Smith

At night Mitchell read the service and I preached.[66]

FEBRUARY 27TH, MONDAY
Left Montgomery at 8 A.M. and arrived in Columbus, Georgia at 5 P.M., having had a pleasant trip—the ladies car in which I secured a seat not being crowded. I am devoutly thankful to Almighty God for bringing me in safety to my home and family once more.

FEBRUARY 28TH, TUESDAY
Everything indicates an early attack on Mobile. Twenty two steamers and six Mississippi river transports are reported in the lower bay and a large number of troops are on Dauphin Island and at Pensacola.[67] No reliable news from either army in the Carolinas.[68]

66. No "Dr." Thomas Taylor appears in either the 1860 or the 1870 federal census for Montgomery County, Alabama. The 1860 census lists a Thomas B. Taylor, a planter then age forty-six, with assets in excess of $400,000. The 1860 census for Tuscaloosa County, Alabama, lists the only Larkin Smith in the state, but his wife was not named Eva.

67. Through much of February 1865, Federal Maj. Gen. E. R. S. Canby assembled a force at Dauphin Island, at the entrance of Mobile Bay, for an assault on Mobile. See OR 49(1):92, 594, 780.

68. At this point in the diary is inserted a newspaper clipping that prints the substance of Robert E. Lee's first three general orders as General in Chief of the Confederate Armies. See OR 46(2):1226–27, 1229–31. A second clipping prints resolutions by "Johnson's Old Tennessee Brigade," a portion of what was then part of Brig. Gen. William McComb's brigade, which was a combination of Bushrod R. Johnson's old brigade, which came to Virginia from the Army of Tennessee in 1864, and the Army of Northern Virginia's old Tennessee brigade. See OR 46(1):1272. The resolutions reaffirmed the brigade's devotion to the Confederate cause. Similar resolutions were passed in other units of the Army of Northern Virginia after the failure of the Hampton Roads peace conference. J. Tracy Power, *Lee's Miserables: Life in the Army of Northern Virginia from the Wilderness to Appomattox* (Chapel Hill: University of North Carolina Press, 1998), 245–50. Finally, CTQ pasted a proclamation by Bishop Elliott to the Clergy of the Diocese of Georgia proscribing an order of service for the day of Fasting, Humiliation, and Prayer proclaimed by President Davis on January 25, 1865, to be celebrated on March 10, 1865. See OR, Series 4, 3:1037.

The Affairs of the Confederacy Have Come to Naught
March 1 to May 26, 1865

MARCH 1ST, ASH WEDNESDAY

Incessant rain all day. I read the full service for the day. Congregation small. Rev. Hawks was able to attend service, but is looking bad and I fear his labors are almost at an end.

General S. D. Lee passed through the city, en route to his command. Maj. Gen. John C. Brown is in the city, the guest of William Meigs.[1] No army news on telegraph.

MARCH 3RD, FRIDAY

Baptized William Thomas and John Henry, children of David and Frances McFarland.[2]

MARCH 8TH, WEDNESDAY

Baptized Capt. Eugene Rodolph Morerod, Co. G, 33rd Tenn. Regt., Strahl's Brigade. Capt. M. is of Swiss parentage [and] a native of Indiana. Was a practicing physician before the war. Has been a Methodist. While in hospital in Macon from a severe wound, I visited him and gave him a Prayer Book—and I trust he will grow in grace and Churchmanship.

On Sunday, the 5th Brother Hawks was able to read the Ante-Communion. I preached both morning and afternoon.

MARCH 10TH, FRIDAY

The day appointed by the President for fasting, humiliation and prayer. The church was crowded. I preached from Isaiah LX. 12. In the afternoon I delivered the second of a series of lectures preparatory to Confirmation which will be continued D.V. throughout Lenten tide. I hope and think this day has been observed by our people in acts of penitence and devo-

---

1. Pasted near the end of the 1865 portion of the diary is a newspaper article referring to Brown's visit, noting that while he had not recovered fully from the serious wound he had sustained at Franklin, he had, "with characteristic determination, started forward to the front." William Meigs cannot be positively identified.

2. The McFarland family cannot be identified.

tion. God have mercy upon [us] in our great extremity. I believe He has brought us down to the very depth to make us know and feel that He is our only hope.

MARCH 12TH, SUNDAY, 2ND IN LENT
Full congregations morning and afternoon. After morning service officiated at a funeral of a very poor old woman, a refugee from Marietta. A hasty dinner at Rhodes Brown's and thence to the Church—where the Congregation had been kept waiting some time. After Evening service baptized four poor children belonging to the parish school presented by Miss Shorter and Mrs. Counsel. Brig. Gen. Felix H. Robertson went with me to Mr. Meigs' to take tea with General John Brown who leaves in the morning for his command in Carolina. He made a full statement to me of his movements at Spring Hill which satisfied me fully that his skirts are all clear of even a shadow of blame. I always believed it for he is at once one of the noblest of men and most accomplished of soldiers but I was glad to have a full and frank statement from his mouth of the movements of his division at Spring Hill. During the last week we have had as guests Lt. Colonel Dawson, 154th Tenn. Regiment, who is now nearly recovered from his severe wounds and Brig. General Robertson, who is also nearly recovered.

The reports from the army are a little more favorable. General Johnston has been restored to the command of the Army of Tennessee—which is of itself equal to a great victory to our cause. Charleston, the glorious "city by the sea"—after a more gallant defence than the records of history,—either ancient or modern furnish, has fallen. Grand and glorious will be her record. Columbia, S.C. has suffered severely from the brief visit of the enemy.

I received a letter today from Mrs. Andrew Erwin, a refugee from Wartrace, Tennessee, now residing in Lafayette, Alabama, giving me an account of the death of her nephew Capt. Henry Webster of the 1st Tennessee Regiment. He died of consumption contracted in a prison up north. He died with full faith and trust in Christ expressing a great desire to see me and to be received into the communion of the Episcopal Church.[3]

3. Andrew Erwin of Bedford County, Tennessee, brother-in-law of both 1860 presidential candidate John Bell and Henry Clay, was the third colonel who married Mary Jossey Webster (1807–1881). John Trotwood Moore and Austin P. Foster, *Tennessee: The Volunteer State, 1769–1923*, 4 vols. (Chicago: S. J. Clarke Publishing, 1923), 2:559. Henry J. Webster

Mr. Brown sent me a present of a dozen pounds of coffee which is now selling at $75 per lb.

I gave notice today in Church that on Easter Sunday the collection would be taken up for the purpose of establishing a church home in this parish. We shall see the result. During the past week Miss Shorter and myself have collected funds to pay off all of Brother Hawks' debt—some three or four thousand dollars.

MARCH 18TH, SATURDAY

Hard at work all the past week. Daily service at 10½ A.M. and service and lecture on Wednesday and Friday. The lectures this week have been on the history of the Church of England as independent of Rome in its establishment, government and teaching. The Church of England, apostolic in origin and the Roman usurpation continually protested against one way or another—from the period of St. Augustine's visit in 596 to the Reformation. The congregations have been large and very attentive.

Among others baptized this week was Mrs. Marshall Ellis—on Wednesday evening—her three children, today. She was raised a Unitarian and traces her conversion to my sermons preached here last fall. Major Warner, chief engineer of the Naval Works and Sgt. Vincent were baptized this morning. I was one of Major W.'s witnesses.[4]

On Tuesday last I received a letter from the Rev. W. P. Harrison, a Methodist preacher of this city, calling me to account for my statement in reference to Dr. Adam Clarke's confirmation. He has written me two letters to both of which I have replied.[5]

The most disturbing news of the death of Mr. J. K. Sass, President of the Bank of Charleston, greeted me yesterday in receiving the daily

was captain of Sam Watkins' "Co. Aytch" for a short period of time after the reorganization of the Army of Tennessee in late April 1862. Webster obtained a furlough shortly after his promotion and was captured by the Federals at that time. Lindsley, *Military Annals,* 159; Watkins, "Co. Aytch," 53.

4. Neither Mrs. Ellis nor Sgt. Vincent can be identified.

5. William Pope Harrison (1830–1895) was minister of St. Luke's Methodist Church in Columbus in 1864 and 1865. He was a cleric of some note after the war, editing the *Methodist Quarterly Review* and authoring several articles and books. John H. Martin, ed., *Columbus, Geo., From its Selection as a "Trading Town" in 1827, to its Partial Destruction by Wilson's Raid, in 1865* (Columbus, Ga.: T. Gilbert, 1874), 165, 176; Harold Lawrence, ed., *Methodist Preachers in Georgia* (Tignall, Ga.: Boyd Publishing, 1984), 234. Dr. Adam Clarke cannot be identified.

papers. It is stated that he died at Unionville, S.C. after having escaped from Columbia. He will be a great loss to us. He was one of the noblest laymen in the Church. Of large heart and mind, full of love for Christ and the Church, abundant in labors, earnest minded and pure hearted. I do not know who can fill his place.

The news of the horrible atrocities of Sherman's army is enough to make the blood boil. The citizens of Georgia are sending money and provisions to the suffering. General Bragg has had a victory at Kinston, capturing 1600 prisoners, and today the news is all of an encouraging character. It seems impossible for the Governments of Europe to much longer keep out of our affairs—recognition must come shortly.[6]

Rhodes Brown—bless his great big heart—handed me a note today—brief and pointed to the following effect.

"To Dr. Q for his private use from a few friends."

It contained $2500. Given me I have no doubt for the purchase of theological works. I think he did it all.

Wrote General Johnston, Bishop Elliott, Richard Peters, Esq. and Captain Shorter by Lt. Colonel Shepherd.

Kate purchased two calico drapes today—paying $30 per yard—$300 a drape.

MARCH 19TH, SUNDAY
Frank Starr read the first part of the service which was of great assistance to me. I preached from the first verse of the Epistle of the day in the morning and in the afternoon from the words: "Whosoever shall confess me before men & etc." which were the words of my text on Sunday evening last. The church was crowded in the morning and [a] full congregation in the afternoon. I dined at Captain Graybill's with Dr. Stout.[7]

MARCH 21ST, TUESDAY
Dr. Stanford operated on poor brother Hawks this morning—removing a cancer with the knife. Several surgeons were present. Bro. H. was placed

6. At Kinston, North Carolina, a hastily assembled force under Braxton Bragg engaged troops commanded by Jacob D. Cox. Although there was an initial Confederate success on March 8, by March 10 Bragg was forced to retreat. Nathaniel C. Hughes, Jr., *Bentonville: The Final Battle of Sherman and Johnston* (Chapel Hill: University of North Carolina Press, 1996), 27. CTQ betrays a lack of realism with his remark concerning European intervention. The prospects of European intervention had been effectively dead since late 1862. Hubbard, *The Burden of Confederate Diplomacy*, 102–24, 177–81.

7. Capt. J. Henry Graybill was assistant post commissary at Columbus and apparently had some responsibility for supplying the military hospitals there. See OR, Series 4, 3:718–

under the influence of chloroform and bore the operation well. Had prayers with his wife and himself before the operation.[8]

MARCH 22ND, WEDNESDAY
Yesterday, I received a third letter from the Rev. W. P. Harrison. I sent my reply this morning and shall notice him no further.

MARCH 24TH, FRIDAY
Today, received a long letter from Mr. Harrison full of ———— and abuse which will go home to roost and hurt me not one whit.

The Lenten services are fully attended. The lectures prepare [the] way to confirmation—delivered on Wednesday and Friday afternoon [they] attract large congregations.

As the clouds grow darker in the outer world it is a blessed thing to enjoy and rest [in] the peace of the City of God.

APRIL 5TH, WEDNESDAY
This evening at 5½ o'clock I united in the holy bonds of wedlock Capt. John S. Smith, C.S.A., aide de camp to General Hood, and Sallie C. Hawks, daughter of the Rev. Wm. N. Hawks, Rector of Trinity Church, Columbus. The ceremony was performed at the rectory in consequence of the illness of Bro. H. who was, however able to sit up in his chair and after the twain had been made one, gave them his priestly and parental benediction as they knelt before him. The bridal party were to have left for Montgomery, but in consequence of the advance of the enemy on that city their plans were changed and thus they went off to the plantation of a friend some twenty miles distant.

Affairs are growing more and more gloomy but it is the part of the true patriot to hold fast his hope. I trust in the righteousness and success of the great cause. Governor Watts of Alabama has issued the following proclamation:

Proclomation by Governor Watts
Executive Department, Ala.
Montgomery, Ala., April 4, '65

---

19. Dr. Samuel Hollingsworth Stout, medical director of the Army of Tennessee's hospitals, moved them to Columbus on October 1, 1864. Standard, *Columbus, Georgia, in the Confederacy*, 52; see Cumming, *Journal*, 63, n. 3.

8. At this point in the diary appear newspaper clippings relative to the passage of Federal transports into Mobile Bay on March 9, and the death of Col. Thomas L. Bransford of Nashville on February 26.

To the People of Alabama:

On the 3rd of March I warned you that our enemies were making efforts to invade the State from several directions. I then ordered the State militia to report, and called up all patriotic citizens to rally to the defense of the State.

Our enemies have now come. They have come from North Alabama and have penetrated to the interior to Selma. They have taken Selma, and have burned the largest part of it. This force does not exceed nine thousand and may be less. They have, in large numbers, attacked Spanish Fort, on the eastern shore of the Mobile Bay. At last advises those several attacks on this fort had been repulsed with great loss to them. They may attempt to occupy Montgomery. The military authorities here are determined to defend the city.

With my consent the seat of government will not be surrendered as long as there is a reasonable hope of defending it. I have just seen Gen. Adams' address. I trust our people will promptly and heartily respond to it. If you will at once come, we can save our State. The only safety to property, firesides, families and liberties, is to rally to the support of the Confederate authorities. Let no idle fears deter you from responding at once. The stern resolve of men determined to remain free will nerve your arms and trace your hearts for the perils of the contest. The base and cowardly tears but invite the enemy to destroy you all.

Without delay the commandants of the several counties East and South of the Alabama river will send their men to this place to report here to the Ajutant [sic] General of the State. All who will volunteer will do the same. Bring all the arms and ammunition you have or can get.

Gen. D. W. Adams, a tried soldier and an able commander, is in command of this district. Brig. Gen. A. Buford, who has fought with honor on many fields of glory, will have charge of the defenses of the city.

T. R. Watts
Governor of Alabama[9]

General Howell Cobb writes to the Mayor of Columbus (Mr. Wilkins) urging him to do all in his power to raise up the citizens to a sense of

9. Watts' proclamation is pasted in the diary as a newspaper clipping.

duty, opposing the arming of the negroes and promising from the military authorities all the co-operation and assistance that can be rendered.[10] General Johnston's Hdq'rs are now at Smithfield, yet our line remains at the Neuse.

The papers speak with confidence. The fall of Selma is a great blow to us. The immense naval machine shop, foundries, rolling mills and etc. which I visited with my friend Catesby Jones—are all lost except a number of car loads of machinery and tools sent to this place. Montgomery will go next. The fight at Selma is reported to have been anything but creditable to our forces. The Episcopal Church was burned. I very much fear that Mr. Sam Noble who left my house on Friday reached Selma just in time to find himself in the hands of the enemy. Rumors of the evacuation of Richmond, and of a great battle between Generals Lee and Grant are very plentiful.

APRIL 7TH, FRIDAY
The papers of today give accounts of the fall of Richmond. It has been gallantly defended by the wisest and most sagacious of generals, by the bravest and most determined body of troops. History will delight to linger over the record of noble deeds done by our noble army, and tell the mournful tale of the fall of our capital with sorrow. The days grow dark but still my trust is in a God who is ordering these events for the good of his people.[11]

It does very well for the puritans and such like sectaries who brought on all this bloodshed to dedicate their verses to the "War Clergy of the U. S. Bps, Pr & Deacons," and thus to involve the Episcopal Church in their horrible crime, but I thank God that the pure white robes of the Church are spotless and that the Bishops, Priests and Deacons of the Church were not instrumental in bringing about this fratricidal war.

APRIL 9TH, SUNDAY BEFORE EASTER
This morning I preached a Sermon on the subject of the Church Home to be established in connection with Trinity Church. The house was full.

10. On April 3, 1865, Colonel Von Zinken had telegraphed Secretary of War John C. Breckinridge asking for authority to arm a brigade of "negroes." OR 49(2):1193.

11. At this point, a newspaper clipping datelined Danville, Virginia, April 5, 1865, is pasted in the diary, describing a defiant address made by Jefferson Davis on the fall of Richmond. Also pasted is an "Extract" of Colonel Von Zinken's General Orders No. 15, dated April 4, 1865, relative to preparations of the garrison at Columbus in case of an alarm. Finally, the satiric poem "Respectfully Dedicated to the War Clergy of the United States, Bishops, Priests and Deacons" appears, to which CTQ refers in the next passage.

I made a strong appeal — in behalf of fatherless children and widows. The collection to be taken up on Sunday next is to be invested in some way for the Home.

APRIL 14TH, FRIDAY
It was with great delight that I this day received into the Church by Holy Baptism my old friend General Washington Barrow of Nashville, Tennessee. He was one of my earliest friends in Tennessee and he has always commanded my highest respect. At the time Tennessee seceded, Genl B was one of the Commissioners on the part of the State to enter into union with the Confederate States. On the fall of Nashville he was imprisoned in the state penitentiary and removed thence with General Harding to Johnson's Island.[12] Thence he was sent South and has been in Columbus some ten months. With him I baptized two other adults.

The enemy is in Montgomery. The city was surrendered by the Mayor without an effort at defence. Everything in Columbus is in commotion. Preparations are being made to defend the place, but it is absurd — the force that can be gathered here is too insignificant. The enemy is rapidly advancing.

APRIL 16TH, EASTER DAY
   Christ the Lord is risen today,
   Sons of men and angels say;
   Raise your joys and triumphs high,
   Sing ye heavens and earth reply.

Mrs. Quintard and myself spent the night at Mrs. Shorter's in order to be in time for early service at 5½ o'clock A.M. "The first day of the week cometh Mary Magdalen *early*, when it was yet *dark*, unto the sepulchre, and seeth the stone taken away from the sepulchre." St. John XX.I

There was a full attendance at this service — but all hearts were filled with forebodings of what was to come. The enemy is close at hand and the struggle is upon us. At 10½ the service began with Litany, and consisted of that and the Communion office. Not more than six or eight gentlemen were in Church. All had gone to the trenches. I did not preach feeling that it was a time of prayer and supplication only. Brig. General Finley of Florida came in just in time to communion, so also Lieutenant Green, son of Bishop Green. I was much affected by seeing an officer,

12. William G. Harding of Tennessee, who, in 1862, was imprisoned with Barrow at Ft. Mackinac, Michigan.

who was very devout, kneel at the chancel and hasten away equipped for the battle, clasping his wife by her hand, as he tore himself away—God protect him. I also took up an offertory as previously announced and to my great surprise it amounted to $33,000.

Mr. Sam Noble arrived this morning from Selma—having been released by the enemy and then taken up as a spy by our soldiers. He was accompanied to this place by a lieutenant who instantly released him—on his being recognized by Mr. Rhodes Brown. He went out with my wife and myself to my house. At noon the guns opened.

APRIL 22ND, SATURDAY

It is difficult to tell the story of the last few days. The fight for the defense of Columbus was quite a brisk affair. Maj. Gen. Howell Cobb was chief in command, his second being Colonel Von Zinken, commander of the Post. I remained at my house—two miles out in a state of great anxiety and suspense.

Our whole force was less than four thousand while that of the enemy amounted to some twelve or fifteen thousand under Maj. General Wilson. The enemy was twice repulsed, but our troops had to give way before superior numbers. The enemy not only greatly outnumbered our force, but was splendidly equipped with sabre, pistols and the Spencer rifle, which fires seven or eight shots—without trouble of reloading. About 10½ o'clock our troops fell back across the river into the city and beat a hasty retreat out our road to Macon, numbers of them passing by my house. At this time I had made no preparation for the coming of the enemy. I had at my house the money collected at the offertory in the morning. This Mr. Noble put in the top of a tall pine tree in the stable yard. The silver was rapidly gathered up and put into a sack and lowered into the well. Some battlefield trophies were thrown down in another well. A sword, from the field of Murfreesboro given me by Captain Carnes of the artillery. It was presented to Lieut. Porter of an Iowa Regiment by the members of his Company.[13] About 12 o'clock we all retired thinking we might be disturbed by the enemy before morning. But it was not until 8 o'clock that they made their appearance. The first man who rode into the front yard was a Sergeant Myers of the 10th Missouri Cavalry Regiment. His first question was—"Have you seen any Confederates about here?" "Not

13. As stated in the diary, Lieutenant Porter was of "an Ia. Regt." Presumably, CTQ's reference is to an Iowa regiment, which is odd, insofar as there were no Iowa regiments engaged at the Battle of Murfreesboro.

since last night." "Which way were they going?" "Towards Macon." "Can we get something to eat?" "Yes, breakfast will soon be ready. Will you walk in?" He rode off and called "Lieutenant!" A lieutenant rode up who hitched his horse in the yard—taking the precaution to open the front gates. As he went up the steps I asked his name. He gave the name of Jones, but after breakfast told me his name was Freece. He seemed a gentlemanly fellow enough and gave Mr. Noble the following paper for my protection:

> I have paid a visit to the house of the Rev. C. T. Quintard, where Saml Noble of Penna. is a guest. For the protection of his person & property, all soldiers will leave everything unmolested until Genl Wilson can send out a guard as applied for. This property must remain unmolested.
>
> Columbus, Ga. Apl. 17/65
> Henry H. Freece
> 1st Lieut Co. "D," 10th Mo. Cav.
> Volunteers U.S.A.

Armed with this document my good friend Noble determined to keep out all intruders. I can never be sufficiently be grateful to him for his efforts in my behalf. I feel that he was sent to me by Divine Providence. Our friends Mrs. Daniel Griffin and children, Mrs. Frank Sevier, wife of Lt. Col. S. and Miss Annie Leonard took shelter at my house and all added to my anxiety, especially when I learned that some infamous scoundrel had been at Mrs. Leonard's, my nearest neighbor and outraged one of the negro women in the presence of the ladies.[14] Mr. Noble went down and succeeded in protecting Mrs. Leonard, although the wretches twice put their pistols to his head threatening to shoot him.

After this I determined to go to town and endeavor to secure a guard. Mr. Woodruff my neighbor decided to accompany me and a little dutch soldier named Happy agreed to see us safely to the city.[15] Another soldier

14. The 1860 federal census for Muscogee County, Georgia, lists Daniel Griffin, a civil engineer, then age fifty-three, and his wife, Mary, then age thirty-one. Identified above, T. Frank Sevier was at this point serving on the staff of A. P. Stewart in North Carolina. See OR 47(2):1437, 1456. The 1860 federal census for Muskogee County identifies Anna Leonard, then age fourteen, as the daughter of Col. Van Leonard, then age seventy-two, a farmer.

15. Mr. Woodruff was probably George Woodruff, listed in the 1860 federal census for Muscogee County, Georgia, as a merchant, age thirty-six.

named Howard agreed to protect my premises until my return. I called first on General Winslow with a note from Noble addressed to both Genl. W. and Captain A. Hodge, his A.A.G. He had made their acquaintance in Selma and Capt. H. expressed a great desire to see Mr. N as he (N) was authorized by the U.S. authorities to secure cotton from burning and had come into the Confederacy for that purpose.

Captain Hodge treated me with great courtesy, but went with me to Colonel Noble's Quarters at the Percy House, Col. N. being Provost Marshall.[16] He was not in, and so I determined to call on General Wilson. I wrote a statement of the outrage at Mrs. Leonard's and sent in my card. After waiting some time the General came out to the front door and said, "Where is the reverend gentleman desiring to see me?" "I am the man, sir," I said. He shook hands and invited me into the front room, where was General McCook. I said, "General will you please read that statement?" He read it carefully—got up from the sofa, paced the floor and said "Dr., can you recognize these men?" "No sir." He then said with a good degree of indignation, "Dr., I would hang such a man in a moment if I could put my hands on him." He immediately gave orders to his A.A.G. who in turn gave orders to Colonel Noble. So round to the Percy House once more, where I met Colonel Noble who gave orders on the Lt. Colonel of his regiment, whose quarters were at the house of Mr. Curtis. He gave me two men—one to guard Mrs. Leonard's and one for my own house. The young man Howard I sent to Mrs. Woodruff's—on a paper furnished me by Captain Hodge, and a fourth guard I secured for Mr. Robert Carter at the camp near the cemetery.[17]

I reached home about 5 P.M. to the great relief of my family who feared from my long delay that some mishap had occurred. And so we had a quiet night.

I had the good fortune to save both my horses. On leaving the breakfast table I walked out to the front porch, Lieut. Freece and Mr. Noble going into the parlor. While standing on the porch, I saw two soldiers putting

16. John W. Noble, colonel of the 3rd Iowa Veteran Volunteer Cavalry, was provost marshal of Columbus. Noble seems to have deemed his greatest accomplishment in that post the seizure of the bulk of the type, forms, paper and ink, and a part of the press of that "defiant rebel sheet," the *Memphis Appeal*. OR 49(1):489–95.

17. The 1860 federal census for Muscogee County, Georgia, lists Robert Carter, a druggist, then age forty-two, and his wife, then age thirty-eight. See the entry for October 20, 1864. The same census lists two men named Curtis. CTQ's Mr. Curtis is probably Lawrence Curtis, a merchant, age thirty-four in 1860, a native of Connecticut.

their saddles on my horses. I called out to the Lieutenant to know if I must give them both up. He immediately came out, buckled on his sword, went to the men and ordered them to unsaddle and give up the horses. They immediately obeyed.

About an hour or so after my negro boy Henry, who had been sent to town early in the morning with a letter, came dashing up with three Yankee soldiers and rode up to the stable at full speed. They did not find the horses, which had been put in the basement of the house. Mr. Noble went out to them and soon put them off the lot. Henry did not return, but went off with his new friends. Not at all to my regret. I purchased him in Atlanta in March, 1864 for $5,000. I had done my utmost to give him a comfortable and a happy home. Later in the day he rode up to the house of Captain Cothran with a soldier and while there, a federal officer came up and ordered them both out of the yard and gave Henry a sound beating with his sword and cursed him. Such was his first taste of freedom.[18]

On Tuesday morning the 18th the guards were all called in, the troops pressed forward to move on the road to Macon. A number of stragglers came to the house, and made efforts to enter the house, but Mr. Noble kept all out. The last ones were not gone till about 11 o'clock.

Last night the torch was applied to the government property—factories and etc. and the heavens were lighted up most brilliantly. At intervals there were tremendous explosions, but the loudest one was at 1 o'clock on the 18th when the magazine was fired. It shattered the glass in Mrs. Leonard's house. All along the river the enemy left a scene of ruin and desolation. The railroad and carriage bridges were destroyed, the factories, the naval works, nitre works, cotton warehouses, were all destroyed. The stores in town were all pillaged, chiefly by the poor of the town and the scenes were indescribably disgusting. The poor people of this section are the *meanest* of the poor and their outrages show very clearly that we have not as a people reached a very high degree of civilization.

MAY 25, THURSDAY
ATLANTA, GEORGIA.
The affairs of the Confederacy—its armies, its political organization, have all come to naught. The overwhelming forces of Grant and Sherman

18. Henry was obviously the result of CTQ's search for a slave boy "suitable for a gentleman's servant." William C. Williams to CTQ, January 25, 1864, Quintard Papers, U of S. Cothran was either Samuel, listed in the 1860 federal census as a rock mason, age thirty-nine, or Thomas, age thirty-seven, a fisherman.

compelled the capitulation of General Lee on Sunday the 9th of April at Appomattox Court House, Virginia. The army commanded by Gen. Joseph E. Johnston could have held out longer, but feeling it would only lead to a useless effusion of blood and that sooner or later he would be compelled to surrender General Johnston held a convention with General Sherman which led to the capitulation.[19]

Our admirable President, Mr. Davis, was escorted by certain cavalry brigades as far as Washington, Georgia. From that point accompanied by his family, Mr. Reagan of the Post Office Department,[20] and the members of his military staff he attempted to make his way to the Gulf Coast by taking a direct southerly route. At Irwinton, Georgia the party was surprised in its encampment by a body of federal cavalry and brought back to Macon. Vice President Stephens and several others being added to the party, they were sent to Atlanta and thence by special train to Augusta and Hilton Head, where they took steamer for Washington.[21]

The President of the United States offered a reward of $100,000 for the capture of the President, a like sum for Senator C. C. Clay of Alabama, for Beverly Tucker of Virginia and lesser sums for George N. Sanders and others.[22] Senator Clay on learning of the reward offered for his apprehen-

19. At this point CTQ pasted a newspaper clipping from the Columbus newspaper with an extract from papers in South Carolina that reported the surrender of the Army of Northern Virginia, including a copy of General Lee's famous General Order No. 9 and other documents relating to the release of Confederate soldiers on parole. Of particular interest is the fanciful passage that describes General Grant's declining to accept General Lee's sword: "That officer, however, with a courtesy for which we must accord him due respect, declined to receive it, or receiving, declined to retain it, and accompanied its return with substantially the following remarks: 'General Lee, keep that sword. You have won it by your gallantry. You have not been whipped, but overpowered, and I cannot receive it as a token of surrender from so brave a man.'"

20. John Henninger Reagan (1818–1905) of Tennessee and Texas was the Confederacy's postmaster general and the only member of the Jefferson Davis' cabinet with the president at the time of his capture.

21. Here CTQ inserted two newspaper clippings, one entitled "The Real Feeling of the Savannah People," relating to residual anti-Union feeling in that city even after Sherman's occupation, and the second, probably from the Columbus newspaper, reporting the observation of the March 10, 1865, day of fasting and prayer proclaimed by Jefferson Davis and visits by Army of Tennessee veterans Maj. Gen. John C. Brown and Brig. Gen. Robert Charles Tyler, the latter of whom was killed in action on April 16, 1865, in an action at West Point, Georgia, defending a small earthwork against a federal brigade of James H. Wilson's cavalry corps. Warner, *Generals in Gray*, 312–13.

22. Sought with Davis were Clement Claiborne Clay (1816–1882), Confederate Senator from Alabama; Beverly D. Tucker (1820–1890) of Virginia, a Confederate diplomat; and George Nicholas Sanders (1812–1873) of Kentucky, a political ally of deceased Illinois poli-

sion instantly determined to surrender himself to Major General Wilson at Macon. He was at the time at LaGrange, Georgia and remarked to a friend: "I will give myself up and if executed, I will vindicate myself and Mr. Davis." The President of the United States most absurdly charges them with complicity in the murder of Mr. Lincoln.

The charge is absurd in the extreme. The murder of Mr. Lincoln was a most atrocious act and no possible amount of testimony will ever convince me of the truth of the charges. They have been trumped up for hanging purposes, for no one can for a moment imagine that the officers of the Confederate government could be found guilty of treason by a fair and impartial trial and other charges had to be made out. Secretary Mallory and Hon. Ben Hill of Georgia were brought to Atlanta three days ago. Mr. Hill has been an intimate friend of President Davis. He is a man of fine intellect and bears himself nobly in his present depressing condition. I had a long and most interesting conversation with him yesterday. Mr. Mallory said to me that his saddest regret was that he had spent four years of his life working for a people utterly unfit for independence.

Last night Maj. Gen. Howell Cobb, although a *paroled* prisoner, was brought under guard from Macon last night and will accompany Mr. Hill and Mr. Mallory to Washington. I had a half hours conversation with him this morning. He told me that he had no regrets for the past so far as his own conduct was concerned, that he was willing to let his record stand without the dotting of an I or the crossing of a T, that he felt the future had nothing in store for him, that he was willing to submit to the United States' laws and obey them, that he had no desire to escape from the U.S. officers, indeed, were "there two paths before him, one leading to the woods and the other to the gallows, he would rather take the latter than compromise his self respect by attempting to escape."

I left Columbus with my family on the 17th for Atlanta via LaGrange and reached this city on Saturday evening at 4 P.M. Our excellent friends Mr. and Mrs. Richard Peters received us to their hospitable mansion. I desire here to record my ——— of the kindness of our friends in Columbus. The stay of my family in that city has been marked by every kind attention that can be thought of on the part of our Church people in par-

tician and Lincoln rival Stephen A. Douglas. Sanders, like Tucker, served as a Confederate agent in foreign service. Oddly, Tucker's son, also named Beverly, served in the Confederate artillery, and was later ordained a priest in the Episcopal Church and married the daughter of that John Augustine Washington, whose death CTQ had mourned in 1861. *CMH*, 4:1216–17; *CMH*, 8:524; *Dictionary of American Biography*, s.v. "Sanders, George Nicholas."

ticular. To the Shorters I am under many obligations and to Daniel Griffin, Esq and his accomplished wife I feel that I can never requite them for their kind offices. The Church people made me up a purse of over two hundred dollars in gold, silver, and bank bills to defray all my expenses back to Tennessee. I find Col. B. B. Eggleston of the 1st Ohio Volunteers in command of the Post here. He is very highly spoken of by the citizens.[23]

On Sunday (the 21st) I officiated in the Central Presbyterian house of worship. The congregation was very full in the morning. I did not deem it advisable to use the Prayer for the President of the United States in absence of any authority from the Bishop of the Diocese. I therefore modified the service and omitted the Prayer. I think the Prayer ought to be used and feel that every rule of political ethics requires its restoration.

Last evening I rode out with Lt. Colonel Ruyter (1st Ohio) to the cemetery and visited the grave of poor Samuel Smith who, although he commanded an Arkansas regiment, was buried in the yard of the 20th Army Corps of the United States Army, all the graves of which were carefully tended.[24] Some vandal had broken the marble head stone and I noticed that two of the colonel's friends had put their initials to the following written on the back of the stone: "I will avenge this dishonor done your memory my dear old friend."[25]

MAY 26, FRIDAY

Major E. B. Beaumont, A.A.G. on Brevet Major General Wilson's staff called to see Mr. Peters and took tea with us this evening. He is from

23. Colonel Beroth B. Eggleston (1818–1890) commanded the 1st Ohio Cavalry and was assigned to receive the surrender of the Confederate troops that had reoccupied Atlanta after Sherman abandoned the city. He commanded the Federal post of Atlanta from May 5, 1865, to June 18, 1865. He doubtlessly gained the appreciation of its citizens by restoring order to the city upon his arrival, where "mob rule had prevailed." OR 49(2):586–87, 618–19, 622, 1011; W. L. Curry, *Four Years in the Saddle: History of the First Regiment Ohio Volunteer Cavalry* (1898; reprint, Jonesboro, Ga.: Freedom Hill Press, 1984), 374.

24. Stephen C. Writer was the 1st Ohio Cavalry's lieutenant colonel at this time. Curry, appendix to *Four Years in the Saddle*, 3. Col. Samuel Granville Smith (ca. 1837–1864) commanded the consolidated 6th/7th Arkansas, Govan's Brigade, Cleburne's Division. He was wounded during the Battle of Atlanta, July 22, 1864, and captured along with the bulk of Govan's Brigade at the Battle of Jonesboro on September 1, 1864. OR 38(1):812; OR 38(3):655, 739, 743. Smith died before the exchange of Govan's Brigade on September 19, 1864. CMH, 14:372.

25. At this point CTQ inserted a newspaper clipping relating to the Confederate surrender of Mobile, Alabama, to the Federals.

THE DIARY: THE AFFAIRS OF THE CONFEDERACY HAVE COME TO NAUGHT / 261

Wilkesbarre, Pennsylvania and an intimate friend of Mr. Peters' relatives in Pennsylvania. So soon as he had reached Macon, he had written Mr. Peters requesting him to call upon him for any assistance he might require. He is now on his way home on a 30 days leave. He is a graduate of West Point, and like all with whom I have ever been brought in contact from that institution, a gentleman.

We had a pleasant evening and from him I heard the Federal side of the history of the fight at Columbus. How utterly absurd was our attempt to defend the place, we with a handful of untrained militia and a squad of veterans from the hospital, against 13,000 of the best disciplined and best equipped troops of the federal army. Our men using muskets neither new in pattern nor effective in execution and the federals armed with the Spencer rifle which discharges seven loads in as many seconds.[26]

26. At this point the 1865 portion of the diary ends, and CTQ attached a copy of President Andrew Johnson's proclamation of May 2, 1865 (referred to in the entry of the previous day), as issued by Major General Wilson's headquarters. See *OR* 49(2):566, 665.

BIBLIOGRAPHY

Primary Sources

MANUSCRIPTS AND GOVERNMENT RECORDS

Army of Tennessee Records. Joseph Jones Collection. Tulane University, New Orleans, La.

Compiled Service Records of Confederate Generals and Staff Officers and Non-regimental Enlisted Men. War Department Collection of Confederate Records. RG 109, M-331. National Archives, Washington, D.C.

Compiled Service Records of Confederate Soldiers from Organizations from the State of Tennessee. War Department Collection of Confederate Records. RG 109, M-268. National Archives, Washington, D.C.

Elliott, Stephen. Diary. Georgia Department of Archives and History. Atlanta.

Quintard, Charles T. Diary. Charles T. Quintard Collection. Du Pont Library. University of the South, Sewanee, Tenn.

———. Papers. Charles T. Quintard Collection. Du Pont Library. University of the South, Sewanee, Tenn.

———. Papers. Special Collections. William R. Perkins Library. Duke University, Durham, N.C.

Quintard Genealogy File. Charles T. Quintard Collection. Du Pont Library. University of the South, Sewanee, Tenn.

Walter, Harvey Washington. Papers. Southern Historical Collection. Wilson Library. University of North Carolina, Chapel Hill.

PUBLISHED PRIMARY WORKS, LETTERS, DIARIES, MEMOIRS, AND REMINISCENCES

Buck, Irving A. *Cleburne and His Command*. 1908. Reprint, Wilmington, N.C.: Broadfoot Publishing, 1987.

Cheatham, Benjamin F. "The Lost Opportunity at Spring Hill, Tenn.—General Cheatham's Reply to General Hood." *Southern Historical Society Papers* 9 (October, November, and December 1881): 525.

Clebsch, William A., ed. *Journals of the Protestant Episcopal Church in the Confederate States of America*. Austin: Church Historical Society, 1962.

"Concerning Re-Enlistment at Dalton." *Confederate Veteran* 9 (January 1901): 13.

Cumming, Kate. *Kate: The Journal of a Confederate Nurse.* Edited by Richard Harwell. 1957. Reprint, Baton Rouge: Louisiana State University Press, 1998.

Curry, W. L. *Four Years in the Saddle: History of the First Regiment Ohio Volunteer Cavalry.* 1898. Reprint, Jonesboro, Ga.: Freedom Hill Press, 1984

Davis, Robert S., Jr., ed. *Requiem for a Lost City: Sallie Clayton's Memoirs of Civil War Atlanta.* Macon, Ga.: Mercer University Press, 1999.

Dowdy, Clifford, and Louis H. Manerin, eds. *The Wartime Papers of R. E. Lee.* New York: Bramhall House, 1961.

Eggleston, J. R. "Captain Eggleston's Narrative of the Battle of the *Merrimac.*" *Southern Historical Society Papers* 41 (1916): 166.

Evans, Clement A., ed. *Confederate Military History: A Library of Confederate States History in Seventeen Volumes, Written by Distinguished Men of the South, and Edited by Gen. Clement A. Evans of Georgia.* Extended ed. 17 vols. 1899. Reprint, Wilmington, N.C.: Broadfoot Publishing, 1987–1989.

Freeman, Douglas S. ed. *Lee's Dispatches: Unpublished Letters of General Robert E. Lee, C.S.A., to Jefferson Davis and the War Department of the Confederate States of America, 1862–65.* New ed., with additional dispatches and foreword by Grady McWhiney. New York: Putnam, 1957.

Freemantle, Arthur J. L. *Three Months in the Southern States.* New York: John Bradburn, 1864.

Gailor, Thomas Frank. *Some Memories.* Kingsport, Tenn.: Southern Publishers, 1937.

Head, Thomas A. *Campaigns and Battles of the Sixteenth Regiment, Tennessee Volunteers.* 1885. Reprint, McMinnville, Tenn.: Womack Printing, 1961.

Hill, Daniel Harvey. "Chickamauga—The Great Battle in the West." In vol. 3 of *Battles and Leaders of the Civil War,* 4 vols., edited by Robert Underwood Johnson and Clarence Clough Buel. 1887–1888. Reprint, New York: Youseloff, 1956.

Hood, John Bell. *Advance and Retreat.* New Orleans: Beauregard, 1879.

Johnston, Joseph E. *Narrative of Military Operations Directed During the Late War Between the States.* New York: D. Appleton & Co., 1874.

Jones, Catesby ap Roger. "Services of the *Virginia (Merrimac).*" *Southern Historical Society Papers* 11 (February–March 1883): 65.

Jones, J. William. *Christ in the Camp; or, Religion in Lee's Army. . . .* Richmond: B. F. Johnson & Co., 1888.

Liddell, St. John R. *Liddell's Record.* Edited by Nathaniel C. Hughes, Jr. 1985. Reprint, Baton Rouge: Louisiana State University Press, 1997.

Lindsley, John Berrian, ed. *Military Annals of Tennessee: Confederate.* 1886. Reprint, Wilmington, N.C.: Broadfoot Publishing, 1995.

Manigault, Arthur Middleton. *A Carolinian Goes to War: The Civil War Narrative of Arthur Middleton Manigault.* Edited by R. Lockwood Tower. Columbia: University of South Carolina Press, 1983.

McGuire, Judith W. *Diary of a Southern Refugee During the War.* 3rd ed. Richmond: J. W. Randolph and English, 1889.

Quintard, Charles Todd. *Balm for the Weary and Wounded.* Columbia: Evans & Cogswell, 1864.

———. "B. F. Cheatham, Major General, C.S.A.: A Tribute to His Memory by Bishop C. T. Quintard," *Southern Historical Society Papers* 16 (1888): 349.

———. *The Confederate Soldier's Pocket Manual of Devotions.* Charleston: Evans & Cogswell, 1863.

———. *Doctor Quintard, Chaplain C.S.A. and Second Bishop of Tennessee, Being His Story of the War (1861–1865).* Edited and extended by Rev. Arthur Howard Noll. Sewanee, Tenn.: University Press, 1905.

Ratchford, James. *Memoirs of a Confederate Staff Officer from Bethel to Bentonville.* Edited by Evelyn Sieburg and James E. Hansen II. Shippensburg, Pa.: White Mane Books, 1998.

Ridley, Bromfield. *Battles and Sketches of the Army of Tennessee.* 1906. Reprint, Dayton, Ohio: Press of the Morningside Bookshop, 1995.

Stephens, Alexander H. *A Constitutional View of the Late War Between the States.* 2 vols. Philadelphia: National Publishing, 1870.

Toney, Marcus B. *The Privations of a Private.* Nashville: M. E. Church, South Publishing House, 1907.

Watkins, Sam R. *Co. Aytch: A Sideshow of the Big Show. With a New Introduction by Roy P. Basler.* New York: Collier Books, 1962.

Weaver, Herbert, and Paul Bergeron, eds. *Correspondence of James K. Polk.* 9 vols. to date. Nashville: Vanderbilt University Press; Knoxville: University of Tennessee Press (vol. 9); 1969–.

Young, J. P. "Hood's Failure at Spring Hill." *Confederate Veteran* 17 (January 1908): 26.

———. *The Seventh Tennessee Cavalry (Confederate): A History.* 1890. Reprint, Dayton, Ohio: Press of the Morningside Bookshop, 1976.

NEWSPAPERS

Atlanta Southern Confederacy
Chattanooga Daily Rebel
Franklin (Tenn.) Review
Memphis Commercial Appeal
Memphis Daily Appeal
Nashville Daily Gazette

GOVERNMENT PUBLICATIONS AND DOCUMENTS

Civil War Centennial Commission of Tennessee. *Tennesseans in the Civil War: A Military History of Confederate and Union Units with Available Rosters of Personnel.* 2 vols. Nashville: Civil War Centennial Commission, 1964–1965.

Naval War Records Office. *Register of Officers of the Confederate States Navy,*
1861–1865. 1931. Reprint, Mattituck, N.Y.: J. M. Carroll & Co., 1983.
United States Census Bureau. Records by county or parish for Alabama, Florida,
Georgia, Louisiana, Mississippi, Tennessee, and Virginia. 1850, 1860, 1870.
United States Navy Department. *Official Records of the Union and Confederate*
Navies in the War of the Rebellion. 31 vols. Washington, D.C.: U.S. Govern-
ment Printing Office, 1895–1929.
United States War Department. *War of the Rebellion: A Compilation of the Offi-*
cial Records of the Union and Confederate Armies. 128 vols. Washington, D.C.:
U.S. Government Printing Office, 1880–1901.

Secondary Sources

BOOKS

Allardice, Bruce S. *More Generals in Gray.* Baton Rouge: Louisiana State Uni-
versity Press, 1995.
Armentrout, Donald Smith. *The Quest for the Informed Priest: A History of the*
School of Theology. Sewanee, Tenn.: School of Theology, University of the
South, 1979.
Aycock, Roger. *All Roads to Rome.* Roswell, Ga.: Wolfe Associates, 1981.
Bergeron, Arthur W., Jr. *Guide to Louisiana Military Units.* Baton Rouge: Louisi-
ana State University Press, 1989.
Bowman, Virginia McDaniel. *Historical Williamson County: Old Homes and*
Sites. Nashville: Blue & Gray Press, 1971.
Butler, Margaret. *Legacy: Early Families of Giles County.* Pulaski, Tenn.: Sain
Publications, 1991.
Caldwell, Joshua W. *Sketches of the Bench and Bar of Tennessee.* Knoxville:
Ogden Brothers & Co., 1898.
Carter, Hodding, and Betty W. Carter. *So Great a Good: A History of the Episco-*
pal Church in Louisiana and of Christ Church Cathedral, 1805–1955. Se-
wanee, Tenn.: University Press, 1955.
Century Review, 1805–1905, Maury County, Tennessee. 1905. Reprint, Columbia,
Tenn.: Maury County Historical Society, 1971.
Cheshire, Joseph Blount. *The Church in the Confederate States: A History of the*
Protestant Episcopal Church in the Confederate States. New York: Longmans,
Green & Co., 1912.
Chitty, Arthur Ben, Jr. *Reconstruction at Sewanee: The Founding of the University*
of the South and Its First Administration, 1857–1872. 1954. Reprint, Sewanee,
Tenn.: Proctor's Hall Press, 1993.
Coat of Arms Certification Concerning the Family Name of King/Barrington. N.p.,
n.d.

Colt, Margaret Barton. *Defend the Valley: A Shenandoah Family in the Civil War.* New York: Orion Books, 1994.

Committee on the History of the Diocese. *Historical Sketches of the Parishes and Missions in the Diocese of Washington.* Washington, D.C.: n.p., 1928.

Connelly, Thomas L. *Army of the Heartland: The Army of Tennessee, 1861–1862.* Baton Rouge: Louisiana State University Press, 1967.

———. *Autumn of Glory: The Army of Tennessee, 1862–1865.* Baton Rouge: Louisiana State University Press, 1971.

Crutchfield, James A., and Robert Holliday. *Franklin: Tennessee's Handsomest Town.* Franklin, Tenn.: Hillsboro Press, 1999.

Crute, Joseph H., Jr. *Confederate Staff Officers, 1861–1865.* Powhatan, Va.: Derwent Books, 1982.

Cunningham, H. H. *Doctors in Gray: The Confederate Medical Service.* 1958. Reprint, Baton Rouge: Louisiana State Press, 1993.

Daniel, Larry J. *Soldiering in the Army of Tennessee.* Chapel Hill: University of North Carolina Press, 1991.

Davis, John H. *St. Mary's Cathedral, 1858–1958.* Memphis: Chapter of St. Mary's Cathedral, 1958.

Davis, William C. *Duel between the First Ironclads.* Garden City, N.Y.: Doubleday, 1975.

Elting, John R. *Swords around a Throne: Napoleon's Grand Armée.* New York: Free Press, 1988.

Freeman, Douglas S. *R. E. Lee: A Biography.* 4 vols. New York: Charles Scribner's Sons, 1974.

Garrett, Jill K. *Maury County, Tennessee, Historical Sketches.* Columbia, Tenn.: n.p., 1967.

Garrett, Jill K., and Marise P. Lightfoot. *The Civil War in Maury County, Tennessee.* Columbia, Tenn.: n.p., 1966.

Green, William Mercer. *Memoir of Rt. Rev. James Hervey Otey, D.D., LL.D., the First Bishop of Tennessee.* New York: J. Pott & Co., 1885.

Hoehling, A. A. *Thunder at Hampton Roads.* Englewood Cliffs, N.J.: Prentice-Hall, 1976.

Horn, Stanley F. *The Army of Tennessee: A Military History.* 1941. Reprint, Wilmington, N.C.: Broadfoot Publishing, 1987.

Hubbard, Charles M. *The Burden of Confederate Diplomacy.* Knoxville: University of Tennessee Press, 1998.

Hughes, Nathaniel C., Jr. *General William J. Hardee: Old Reliable.* Baton Rouge: Louisiana State University Press, 1965.

———. *Bentonville: The Final Battle of Sherman and Johnston.* Chapel Hill: University of North Carolina Press, 1996.

———. *Big Jim Holland.* Chattanooga: n.p., 2000.

———. *The Pride of the Confederate Artillery: The Washington Artillery in the Army of Tennessee.* Baton Rouge: Louisiana State University Press, 1997.

Jones, Charles C., Jr., and Salem Dutcher. *Memorial History of Augusta, Georgia.* Syracuse, N.Y.: D. Mason, 1890.

Jones, James Pickett. *Yankee Blitzkrieg: Wilson's Raid through Alabama and Georgia.* Athens: University of Georgia Press, 1976.

Keenan, Jerry. *Wilson's Cavalry Corps: Union Campaigns in the Western Theatre, October 1864 through Spring 1865.* Jefferson, N.C.: McFarland & Co., 1998.

Losson, Christopher. *Tennessee's Forgotten Warriors: Frank Cheatham and His Confederate Division.* Knoxville: University of Tennessee Press, 1989.

Martin, John H., ed. *Columbus, Geo., From its Selection as a "Trading Town" in 1827, to its Partial Destruction by Wilson's Raid, in 1865.* Columbus, Ga.: T. Gilbert, 1874.

McMurry, Richard M. *John Bell Hood and the War for Southern Independence.* Lexington: University Press of Kentucky, 1982.

Moore, John Trotwood, and Austin P. Foster. *Tennessee: The Volunteer State, 1769–1923.* 4 vols. Chicago: S. J. Clarke, 1923.

Palmer, R. R. *Twelve Who Ruled: The Committee of Public Safety during the Terror.* Princeton: Princeton University Press, 1941.

Parks, Joseph H. *General Leonidas Polk, C.S.A.: The Fighting Bishop.* Baton Rouge: Louisiana State University Press, 1962.

Polk, William M. *Leonidas Polk: Bishop and General.* 2d. ed. 2 vols. New York: Longmans, Green & Co., 1915.

Power, J. Tracy. *Lee's Miserables: Life in the Army of Northern Virginia from the Wilderness to Appomattox.* Chapel Hill: University of North Carolina Press, 1998.

Purdue, Howell, and Elizabeth Purdue. *Pat Cleburne, Confederate General: A Definitive Biography.* Hillsboro, Tex: Hill Junior College Press, 1973.

Raab, James W. *W. W. Loring, Florida's Forgotten General.* Manhattan, Kans.: Sunflower University Press, 1996.

Rankin, Anne, ed. *Christ Church Nashville, 1829–1929.* Nashville: Marshall & Bruce, 1929.

Robertson, James I., Jr. *Stonewall Jackson: The Man, the Soldier, the Legend.* New York: Macmillan, 1997.

Rowland, Dunbar. *Military History of Mississippi, 1843–1898.* 1898. Reprint, Spartanburg, S.C.: Reprint Co., 1978.

Schroeder-Lein, Glenna R. *Confederate Hospitals on the Move: Samuel H. Stout and the Army of Tennessee.* Columbia: University of South Carolina Press, 1994.

Smith, Frank H. *Frank H. Smith's History of Maury County, Tennessee.* Columbia, Tenn.: Maury County Historical Society, 1969.

Smith, Reid. *Majestic Middle Tennessee.* Prattville, Ala.: Paddle Wheel Publications, 1975.

Spence, John C. *Annals of Rutherford County.* 2 vols. Nashville: Williams Printing, 1991.

St. Thomas Church. New York: n.p., 1965.

Standard, Diffee William. *Columbus, Georgia, in the Confederacy: The Social and Industrial Life of the Chattahoochee River Port.* New York: William-Frederick Press, 1954.

Sword, Wiley. *The Confederacy's Last Hurrah: Spring Hill, Franklin, and Nashville.* Lawrence: University Press of Kansas, 1992.

Telfair, Nancy. *A History of Columbus, Georgia, 1828–1928.* Columbus, Ga.: Historical Publishing, 1929.

Thomas, Albert Sidney. *A Historical Account of the Protestant Episcopal Church in South Carolina, 1820–1957.* Columbia: R. L. Bryan, 1957.

Thomas, Emory M. *Bold Dragoon: The Life of J. E. B. Stuart.* New York: Harper & Row, 1986.

Turner, William Bruce. *History of Maury County, Tennessee.* Nashville: Parthenon Press, 1955.

Warner, Ezra. *Generals in Gray.* Baton Rouge: Louisiana State University Press, 1957.

———. *Generals in Blue.* Baton Rouge: Louisiana State University Press, 1964.

Wellman, Manly Wade. *Giant in Gray: A Biography of Wade Hampton of South Carolina.* New York: Charles Scribner's Sons, 1949.

Woodworth, Steven E. *Six Armies in Tennessee: The Chickamauga and Chattanooga Campaigns.* Lincoln: University of Nebraska Press, 1998.

Woolridge, John. *History of Nashville, Tenn.* 1890. Reprint, Nashville: Charles Elder Bookseller, 1970.

ARTICLES

Burroughs, Bryant. "The Life and Death of Lieutenant Colonel Robert Beckham, C.S.A." *Southern Partisan* 17 (First Quarter 1998): 24.

"Captain W. W. Carnes—A Worker." *Confederate Veteran* 31 (June 1923): 205.

Collins, John C. "Sad Story of the War." *Confederate Veteran* 6 (March 1898): 116.

Crawford, W. T. "The Mystery of Spring Hill." *Civil War History* 1 (June 1955): 101.

Cummings, Charles M. "Otho French Strahl: Choicest Spirit to Embrace the South." *Tennessee Historical Quarterly* 24 (Winter 1965): 341.

Davis, John Henry. "Two Martyrs of the Yellow Fever Epidemic of 1878." *West Tennessee Historical Society Papers* 26 (1972): 20.

Frank, John G. "Adolphus Heiman: Architect and Soldier." *Tennessee Historical Quarterly* 5 (March 1946): 38.

Grinnen, Daniel. "David Crockett Richardson." *Virginia Historical Magazine* 38 (1930): 64.

Howell, Isabel. "John Armfield of Beersheba Springs." *Tennessee Historical Quarterly* 3 (March 1944): 60.

"The Last Roll: Captain R. K. Polk." *Confederate Veteran* 10 (December 1902): 561.

Lee, Fitzhugh. "Speech of General Fitz. Lee, at A.N.V. Banquet, October 28, 1875." *Southern Historical Society Papers* 1 (February 1876): 99.

"List of Virginia Chaplains, Army of Northern Virginia." *Southern Historical Society Papers* 34 (1906): 313.

McNeilly, James H. "Col. John Overton." *Confederate Veteran* 7 (January 1899): 34.

Morrow, Sara Sprout. "The Church of the Holy Trinity: English Countryside Tranquility in Downtown Nashville." *Tennessee Historical Quarterly* 34 (1975): 333.

Pratt, Isabel. "Captain Thomas E. King." *Southern Bivouac* 2 (July 1884): 511–14.

Scott, Emma Cook. "Major Clare and Mary Hadley." *Confederate Veteran* 16 (August 1908): 399.

"Some South Carolina Marriages in Georgia." *South Carolina Magazine of Ancestral Research* 20 (Winter 1992): 9.

Summerville, James. "Albert Roberts, Journalist of the New South, Part I." *Tennessee Historical Quarterly* 42 (Spring 1983): 18.

Swint, Henry Lee. "Traveller's Rest: Home of Judge John Overton." *Tennessee Historical Quarterly* 26 (Summer 1967): 119.

"Tribute to Lieut. John Marsh." *Confederate Veteran* 5 (December 1897): 599.

Turpin, James A. "Darden's Battery." *Confederate Veteran* 9 (November 1901): 514.

White, Levi S. "Confederate Ordnance: The Good Work Done by General Gorgas in His Department." *Southern Historical Society Papers* 29 (1901): 319.

BIOGRAPHICAL DIRECTORIES AND ENCYCLOPEDIAS

Berry, Mary Kent, comp. *Records of Marriage, Baptism, and Burial from the First Register of Trinity Parish (1836–1903)*. N.p., 1985.

Booth, Andrew B., comp. *Records of Louisiana Confederate Soldiers and Louisiana Confederate Commands*. 3 vols. 1920. Reprint, Spartanburg, S.C.: Reprint Co., 1984.

Coleman, Kenneth, and Charles Steven Gurr, eds. *Dictionary of Georgia Biography*. 2 vols. Athens: University of Georgia Press, 1983.

Farrow, Henry, and W. B. Bennett. *Directory of the City of Mobile for the Year 1866*. Mobile: Farrow & Bennett, 1866.

Hartman, David, and David Coles, comps. *Biographical Rosters of Florida's Confederate and Union Soldiers*. 6 vols. Wilmington, N.C.: Broadfoot Publishing, 1995.

Hays, L. F., comp. *Georgia Service Records*. N.p., 1936.

Henderson, Lillian, ed. *Roster of the Confederate Soldiers of Georgia, 1861–1865*. 6 vols. Hapeville, Ga.: Longins and Porter, 1960.

Heitman, Francis B. *Historical Register and Dictionary of the United States Army, from Its Organization, September 29, 1789, to March 2, 1903*. 2 vols. Washington: U.S. Government Printing Office, 1903.

Hempstead, Fay. *Historical Review of Arkansas: Its Commerce, Industry, and Modern Affairs*. 3 vols. 1911. Reprint, Easley, S.C.: Southern Historical Press, 1978.

Herringshaw, Thomas William. *Herringshaw's Encyclopedia of American Biography of the Nineteenth Century*. Chicago: American Publisher's Association, 1902.

Howell, H. Grady, Jr., comp. *For Dixie Land I'll Take My Stand!: A Muster Listing of All Known Mississippi Confederate Soldiers, Sailors, and Marines*. 3 vols. Madison, Miss.: Chickasaw Bayou Press, 1998.

Joint Committee on Printing. *Biographical Directory of the United States Congress, 1774–1989*. Washington, D.C.: U.S. Government Printing Office, 1989.

Kirk, John Foster. *A Supplement to Allibone's Critical Dictionary of English Literature and British and American Authors*. Philadelphia: J. D. Lippencott, 1891.

Lawrence, Harold, ed. *Methodist Preachers in Georgia*. Tignall, Ga.: Boyd Publishing, 1984.

Mainiero, Lina, ed. *American Women Writers: A Critical Reference Guide from Colonial Times to the Present*. 5 vols. New York: Frederick Ungar, 1979–1994.

McBride, Robert M., and Dan M. Robison. *Biographical Directory of the Tennessee General Assembly*. 6 vols. Nashville: Tennessee State Library and Archives and Tennessee Historical Commission, 1979–1991.

Owen, Thomas McAdory. *History of Alabama and Dictionary of Alabama Biography*. 4 vols. Chicago: S. J. Clarke, 1921.

Powell, William S., ed. *Dictionary of North Carolina Biography*. Chapel Hill: University of North Carolina Press, 1994.

Scott, E. C. *Ministerial Directory of the Presbyterian Church, U.S., 1861–1941*. Austin: Von Boeckman-Jones, 1942.

Thurman, Sandra Wilson, comp. *Maury County, Tennessee, 1860 Census*. Columbia, Tenn.: P-Vine Press, 1981.

Treece, Joel D. *Biographical Directory of the American Congress, 1774–1996*. Alexandria, Va.: CQ Staff Directories, 1997.

Wright, Buster W., comp. *Burials and Deaths Reported in the Columbus (Georgia) Enquirer, 1832–1872*. N.p., 1984.

Index

Hume, Britton, 218
Hunter, Robert M. T., 112n, 223, 242
Huntersville, Va., 20, 21, 33
Hurt, Charles Stuart, 114, 114n, 233–34

Irwin, Henry, 221, 221n
Irwinville, Ga. (misnamed "Irwintown"),
258

Jack, Thomas M., 74, 74n, 75
Jackson, Andrew, 105n
Jackson, Henry Rootes, 22, 22n, 25
Jackson, James Streshly, 54, 54n
Jackson, Miss., 46
Jackson, Thomas Jonathan, 7, 35, 35n, 36;
brigade of, 37; dispute with Loring,
36–38, 38n
Jackson, William Hicks ("Red"), 217, 217n
Johnson, Andrew, 71, 71n, 108n, 261n
Johnson, Bushrod Rust, 54, 54n; brigade of,
245n
Johnson, Edward, 94n, 183, 194
Johnson, J. P., 107n; misnamed "Johnston,"
107, 200
Johnson, Mrs., 191
Johnston, Albert Sidney, 38, 49, 91, 116n,
224
Johnson, Capt.(brother of James W.), 188
Johnston, James W., 74, 74n, 187, 188, 189,
207
Johnston, Mrs. James, 193, 193–94n
Johnston, Joseph Eggelston, xii, 38, 63, 63n,
64, 83, 83n, 84, 84n, 85, 86n, 87n, 89,
89n, 111, 116n, 117, 202n, 213, 219, 231,
247, 249, 252
Johnstone, Mrs., 47, 47n
Jones, Allen C., 238, 238n, 239
Jones, Calvin E., 204n
Jones, Capt., 93, 178
Jones, Catesby ap Roger, 44, 44n, 115, 242,
252
Jones, Dudley W., 212, 213n
Jones, Edward Spencer, 204, 204n
Jones, Jesse S., 105, 105n, 191, 193
Jones, Lee Walthall, 204
Jones, Lucy Anne, 204

Jones, Marietta, 109n, 204, 204n, 206
Jones, Nicholas Tate, 204
Jones, Samuel G., 243
Jones, Thomas McKissick, 108, 108n, 204,
204n, 205, 205n
Jonesboro, Ga., 161

Kellar, Andrew J., 199, 199n
Keller, Mrs., 207, 207n
Kelly, W. D., 106, 106n, 113, 114n, 196–97,
232
King (Hand), Eliza Barrington, 9n
King, Roswell, xi, 9n
King, Thomas E., 17, 17n, 78, 79n, 85n;
family of, 79n
Kingston, Ga., 127
Kirby Smith, Edmund, 52, 52n, 58; army of,
240; background, 56–57, 146
Knight, F. L., 142
Knoxville, Tenn., 17, 38

Latane, James A., 20, 20n, 33
Lawton, Georgia, 167
Lay, Henry Champlin, xii, 87, 87n, 88
Lay, John F., 46, 46n
Lee, Mary Custis, 32, 86n
Lee, Robert Edward, xii, 7, 21, 22, 22n, 28n,
29–30, 32, 49n, 95, 125, 147–48, 184,
227, 245n, 258, 258n
Lee, Stephen Dill, 96, 96n, 183, 185, 224,
230, 231, 246; corps of, 222
Lee, William Henry Fitzhugh ("Rooney"),
29, 29n
Lee and Gordon's Mill, 77
Leonard, Annie, 255, 255n
Letcher, John, 38
LeVert, Octavia Walton, 46, 47n
Lexington, Ala., 205
Liddell, St. John Richardson, 69n, 81, 97;
brigade of, 69
Lincoln, Abraham, 14, 15, 112n, 115, 115n,
120, 125, 242, 259
Lincoln, Mary Todd, 79n
Long, B. S., 218, 218n
Long, Capt., 189
Longstreet, James, 77, 77n, 78, 78n, 87n

Winchester, Tenn., 76, 140, 141, 142
Winchester, Va., 35, 36, 37, 39
Winder, John Henry, 19, 19n
Wingfield, John Henry Ducachet, 42, 42n, 44
Winn, Mrs. Walter, 234, 234n, 236, 240
Winslow, Edward F., 122, 122n, 124n, 256
Winston, Mrs., 218
Wintter, D., 93, 93n, 175
Woldridge, John H., 55n; misnamed "Woolridge," 55
Womble, Charles, 207, 207n
Wood, James R., 9
Wood, Sterling Alexander Martin, 68n, 69; brigade of, 68
Wood, Susy, 181
Woodruff, George, 255, 255n
Woods, Michael Leonard, 243, 243n

Wool, John Ellis, 41n; misnamed "Wood," 41
Wooldridge, Dr., 191–92, 192n
Woolfolk, Manah B., 162, 163
Wright (old man), 207, 207n, 208
Wright, Marcus Joseph, 86, 86n
Writer, Stephen C., 260n; misnamed "Ruyter," 260

Yates, Mrs. A. E., 174, 175, 175n
Yates, Robert Elliot Valentine, 93, 93n, 174, 174n
Yeatman, Henry C., 50, 50n, 65, 66, 68, 115, 127, 241, 242
Yerger, Sally M., 47, 47n
Young, Robert B., 187, 189, 190, 224
Young, William F., 93, 94n, 178

Zollicoffer, Felix K., 196n